Surviving Sexual Violence

Surviving Sexual Violence

LIZ KELLY

University of Minnesota Press,
Minneapolis

Library of Congress Cataloging Number 88–22033

Published by the University of Minnesota Press
2037 University Avenue Southeast, Minneapolis MN 55414.
Printed in Great Britain.

The University of Minnesota
is an equal opportunity
educator and employer.

Contents

Acknowledgements

Whilst 'breaking the silence' has become a feminist cliché in the past few years, it encapsulates an important fact. Feminism has provided a context in which many women, throughout the world, have been enabled to name their experiences of violence and abuse and to speak openly about them. This book was made possible by 60 women who chose to be part of this process. It is dedicated to them and all survivors of sexual violence.

As with any book and/or research project, there are many others to whom I am in debt for their support, advice and critical comments. I thank all of the following for their particular contributions: Catriona Blake, Louise Dunne, Annabel Farraday, Sophie Laws, Su Kappeler, Emma Kelly, Mick Kelly, Mary MacIntosh, George Okey, Kathy Parker, Jill Radford, Isobel Ros-Lopez, Penny Snelling, Betsy Stanko, Michelle Stanworth, Marga Suvaal, my local refuge support group, the British Sociological Association working group for women doing research on sexual violence, the Incest Survivors Campaign, the Rape in Marriage Campaign, and the Trouble and Strife Collective.

Guide to transcription of interviews

Whilst transcribing the taped interviews on which this book is based I became aware of problems involved in transposing the spoken to the written word. Meaning in the spoken word is often conveyed through gesture, tone of voice and emotional expression. Surprisingly little attention has been paid to this issue in the research literature; the methods used in linguistics and conversational analysis are far too detailed for a number of in-depth interviews (in this case over 160 hours of tape). In order to retain some of the meaning that is lost in transcription, I developed a method for coding tone of voice and emotional expression. This guide explains aspects of this transcription coding which appear in the quotations from interviews:

A dash (—) indicates a jump; the spoken word is seldom as coherent as the written.
Three dots (. . .) indicate a passage of speech has been deleted.
Six dots (. . . . . .) indicate a long pause.
Italics indicate that the word or words were stressed.
Emotional expression is recorded in brackets after the passage of speech it refers to: for example (angry), (ironic), (upset).

Introduction

As I was thinking about the introduction to this book, two statements on the radio drew my attention. A woman speaker at the 1986 British Trade Union Congress urged trade unionists to take the 'epidemic' of cervical cancer seriously. In a commentary on international terrorism a male reporter stated that something must be done 'about the plague of violence that threatens our basic human rights'. When the incidence of cervical cancer is defined as an 'epidemic', what word could adequately reflect the vastly greater incidence of sexual violence in the lives of British women? When the impact of international terrorism is represented as a threat to basic human rights, what words could illuminate the fact that it is domestic terrorism which more directly threatens countless women's lives across the globe?

These examples do not simply illustrate the power of rhetorical speech. They highlight a deeper, more fundamental point: that it is only in relation to certain issues that such forms of argument are considered to be justified. When radical feminists point to the appalling incidence of sexual violence we are seen by many as hysterical and, even by other feminists, as placing too much emphasis on women's victimization. Most men and many women do not want to acknowledge the extent of sexual violence in, and its impact on, women's lives. It is still illegitimate for us to refer to it as being of 'epidemic' proportions, threatening women's 'basic human rights'. Yet a cursory reading of the UN Declaration on Human Rights in the light of recent feminist studies of the prevalence and impact of sexual violence highlights how many of these 'basic human rights' are still to be secured for women.

Surviving Sexual Violence is part of a growing body of feminist scholarship, primarily undertaken in but not restricted to first world liberal democracies, which documents the extent to which women's and girls' rights to life and liberty are threatened daily. That such a fundamental assumption of liberal democracy is tenuous for the majority of the population yet not a major source of concern, suggests that there are vested interests at stake here – men's interests.

During the six months I was writing this book, a number of instances, or consequences of, sexual violence occurred to women in my social network: for example, an incest survivor attempted suicide twice in a week after a BBC Television Childwatch programme triggered her memories; a woman's life was temporarily devastated when her ex-husband raped her; two women were attacked near to their homes; a student's sense of safety was so undermined by a peeping tom that she left college; an incest survivor discovered her son's girlfriend was being abused; during 'rag' week, a woman teacher was pinned to the ground by several young men in masks and then photographed; three women were beaten up by their husbands/male lovers and, in just one week, in the refuge for battered women I work in one woman had a miscarriage and another her leg amputated as direct consequences of the violence they had experienced.

Despite feminist campaigns and actions in many countries which have, to a greater or lesser extent, made sexual violence a public issue, the prevalence and impact of sexual violence in women's lives is still not publicly acknowledged. In this context it is vital that the extent and range of sexual violence continues to be documented. Limiting our work to this, however, can result in women being seen as 'inevitable victims'. This book also records the other side of women's experiences: our resistance and strength in coping with and surviving abuse. Any woman who has gone through this process (and any woman who has supported another woman through the pain and despairing moments) will recognize the connection between victimization and survival. This book attempts to validate that knowledge and make some of it accessible to those without it.

Surviving Sexual Violence is based on a feminist sociological research project and has two basic aims: to present the 'findings' of the study; and to validate and give voice to women's experience and understanding.

There are points at which these two aims sit uneasily with each other, where to present the 'data' I have chosen to use figures and tables. I hope that overall the book can serve several purposes for different audiences. It is a record of doing feminist social research; it presents detailed findings about the prevalence of sexual violence in the lives of 60 women; and it makes the voices of these women central to chapters 4 to 9.

Chapter 1 documents the process of conducting the research in the context of a broader discussion of what constitutes feminist research. Chapter 2 explores feminist theory which attempts to account for the link between men's interests and the abuse of women and offers some reflections on how to define sexual violence and on several contemporary debates. Chapter 3 presents a critical overview of the recent dramatic increase in social science research on rape, incest and sexual abuse and domestic violence. Chapters 4 and 5 build on some of the insights in feminist theory and suggest looking at sexual violence as a continuum, both in relation to extent of sexual violence and the range of men's behaviour that women experience as abusive. Chapter 6 highlights how it is in men's interest to deny this range and limit definitions of sexual violence, thus making defining one's own abuse a difficult and complex process for women. Chapters 7 and 8 document the side of women's and girls' experiences of sexual violence that is usually ignored – the extent of resistance during assault(s) and the variety of coping strategies used in coming to terms with the consequences of sexual violence. Chapter 9 reflects on how individual survival might be transformed into collective resistance in order to end sexual violence in the lives of women and girls.

Which parts of the book an individual reader reads, and the order in which they read them, will depend on their own needs and concerns.

1

'Sharing a particular pain': researching sexual violence

'It's only since getting a bit closer that I found out that one way and another it's happened to most women. Something similar, be it with their lovers, their husbands or whoever, has happened to them.'

'Because this society sanctions it, so long as it's alright to slag off women, to joke about women, there's always going to be the other end of the spectrum, where actual violence starts . . . . . . and ends.'

'I felt more resentment about sex roles and the day in day out, as I see it, degradation of women. That's affected me more than the violence. But the violence has been part of it too. It has erupted through my rebellion against all the suppositions about women.'

These three quotations from the interviews on which this book is based encapsulate the three core themes that run through it: that most women have experienced sexual violence in their lives; that there is a range of male behaviour that women experience as abusive; and that sexual violence occurs in the context of men's power and women's resistance.

The issue of violence against women has been an important focus for feminist theory and action in the current wave of feminism. The first rape crisis line was established in the USA in 1971 and the first refuge for battered women opened in England in 1972. Thousands of projects and groups now exist world-wide, offering safety, support and advice to women who have been abused. Campaigning and supportive work has also been undertaken around the issues of incest, child sexual abuse, pornography, prostitution and sexual harassment. Women in or from particular countries have also focused on forms of sexual violence specific to their culture.[1] Globally, the amount of work, often unpaid, undertaken by feminists around this issue is incalculable.

Getting and staying involved

In 1973, after five months in a Women's Liberation Group, I joined a group which aimed to set up a refuge for battered women. I did not consciously choose to work on the issue of violence. I simply wanted to 'do something'. I became one of the founder members of the refuge group in my home town and, to the amazement of some (though not me), I am still an active member. Whilst in the subsequent fourteen years the group and I have changed enormously, it was there that I gained self-confidence, skills and an understanding of sexual violence and it is still the base for my feminist work and politics.

It was through supporting women in crisis, discussing theory and practice with other activists and comparing what I knew with what I read that the ideas informing the study on which this book is based arose. I noticed how many women had experienced more than one form of sexual violence yet these forms were separated from one another in feminist service provision, campaigning and research. This separation in practice contrasted sharply with the theoretical discussions of 'violence against women'. During the 1980s, a number of other studies have been published which address one or more of these issues,[2] but, at the time I began, most published work focused either on a specific form of sexual violence or on theoretical issues which assumed, rather than discussed, the links between forms of sexual violence. Experiences were seldom placed in the context of women's lives and, at that time, there was very little information or discussion about either incest and child sexual abuse or the long-term impact of sexual violence. I started the research project, therefore, with three main aims: to talk to a wide range of women about all the forms of sexual violence they had experienced; to explore how the various forms of violence were connected; and to investigate the long-term impact of sexual violence on women.

Throughout the research and the writing of this book I have

remained involved in both my local refuge group and several national campaigning groups. I was not involved in these groups because I was doing research and I did not 'use' them as sources of data. Involvement did, however, contribute in very direct ways as there was a continual exchange of information, ideas and support. Within the literature on research methods there is no term which covers this form of contribution, perhaps best described as 'active participation'. There is equally no term to cover the fact that I have talked to at least as many women again informally about their experiences of sexual violence as the 60 I interviewed. Whilst I kept no records of these conversations, I made mental notes if new insights emerged. As most women were interested in the research, I was able to discuss my current ideas and receive valuable comment and feedback.

But what is feminist research?

Feminists have, since the early 1970s, criticized a range of academic disciplines for being gender blind.[3] As more feminists undertook research, increasing attention was paid to how research was done and the term 'feminist methodology' appeared within sociology. Being a feminist sociologist means that my discussion of research practice refers directly to my own discipline but many of the points I want to make apply across disciplinary boundaries. Part of my criticism of the discussion within sociology is that it ignores feminist research in other areas.

For a considerable period of time, I accepted, almost without question, that there was a feminist methodology, which drew on the practice of consciousness raising in stressing the importance of women's experience. Sophie Laws notes that within much of the sociological literature feminist research has been defined in terms of interviewing women. She suggests that this is in part due to a simplification of the original intention of consciousness raising.

The original purpose of consciousness raising, where women speak about their own experiences to other women, was to discover what women have in common, in order to produce theory about women's oppression. Now this last stage seems to have been forgotten and women speaking, whatever it is about and whatever they say, is seen as A Good Thing.[4]

She argues that much of the recent discussion of feminist methodology is linked to this interpretation and that, in a wider context, the focus on individual emotional release has become the most important function of consciousness-raising (perhaps accounting for the recent growth of self-help groups and feminist therapy).

This challenging interpretation led me to reconsider my perspective on feminist research and to see how limited the discussion of method had become. Rather then define certain methods as feminist, Laws asserts that what distinguishes feminist research is the theoretical framework underlying it. She suggests a minimal definition of feminism as 'a belief that women are oppressed and a commitment to end that oppression'.[5] For research to be feminist it must be predicated on both the theoretical premise and the practical commitment: its purpose being to understand women's oppression in order to change it. Feminism is, therefore, both a mode of understanding and a call to action.

Research is not feminist simply because it is about women and, equally, feminist research need not have individual women as its subjects. This definition allows for the fact that there is more than one theory explaining women's oppression and that a variety of research methods and sources of data can be, and are, used in feminist research. A major point of Laws' analysis is to reassert the importance of theory, partly in response to the prioritizing of experience by writers such as Liz Stanley and Sue Wise.[6]

A further limitation of the prioritization of experience is raised by Hester Eisenstein.[7] If women are to use only their own experience, or that of women similar to them, as the basis of their feminist politics and research practice, how are we to understand and take account of the differences between women? Prioritizing experience at the expense of reflection and theory can lead to a 'politics of identity'. In her attempt to make feminist theory inclusive of Black women's experience, bell hooks suggests that the ability to see and describe one's own reality 'is a significant step, but only a beginning'.[8]

Whilst accepting these critiques of the 'politics of experience' there is still a sense in which one's experience is fundamental to feminist research. Feminist researchers are themselves women and they are, therefore, located within the group whose oppression they seek to document, understand and change. This locating of oneself within the group one is studying is not the same as Howard Becker's suggestion that sociologists take the side of the 'underdog'.[9] Feminist researchers do not have the privilege of choice; they are themselves within the underdog category. Angela McRobbie draws out one of the implications of this: 'Feminism forces us to locate our own autobiographies and our experience inside the questions we might ask'.[10] Feminists doing research both draw on, and are constantly reminded of, their own experience of 'the concrete practical and everyday experience of being, and being treated as, a woman'.[11] This does not mean, however, that it is only our experience, or the experiences of other women, which will be reflected in research; at least one feminist has suggested that we should study men.[12] Moreover, it is crucial that we explore the specific nature of our own experience, and that of the women who might be part of our study, in order to understand how it might differ from other women's.

Helen Roberts uses the sociological concept of 'reflexivity' to describe the process through which feminist researchers locate themselves within their work. Unlike non-feminists, we do not choose reflexivity as one research practice amongst many; it is integral to a feminist approach to research. Roberts notes that in being honest about this we

expose [ourselves] to challenges of lack of objectivity from those of [our] male colleagues whose ideological insight does not enable them to see that their own work is effected in similar ways by their experience of the world as men.[13]

The debate within sociology as to the discipline's status as a science, and the role of objectivity and values within this, has a long and complex history. The feminist critique of the construction of knowledge within a patriarchal framework has raised yet further questions.[14] To question the usefulness and, indeed, possibility of objectivity does not mean that feminist researchers reject any principles for ensuring that their work contains honest and accurate accounts. Barbara Du Bois, for example, maintains that feminist research should be: 'passionate scholarship . . . [which] demands rigour, precision and responsibility to the highest degree'.[15]

This discussion suggests that, whilst there are grounds for defining research as feminist, there is not, as yet, a distinctive 'feminist methodology'. Many of the methods used by feminist researchers are not original. What is new are the questions we have asked, the way we locate ourselves within our questions, and the purpose of our work. Given the short history of feminist research, perhaps we should shift our attention from discussions of 'feminist methods' to what I now call 'feminist research practice'.

One of the crucial distinctions between feminism and other theoretical perspectives is that its theory and practice are not specific to academia or designed with research in mind. Feminist researchers hold beliefs and principles of practice in common with many more outside the research community than within it.

One of the basic principles of feminist practice has been to challenge relationships based on power and control. An important aspect of this has been a commitment to the conscious sharing of knowledge and skills. This clearly has implications for research where power, knowledge and skills are not shared equally between researcher and researched. Liz Stanley and Sue Wise in chapter 6 of *Breaking Out* argue that research inevitably involves power relationships, if only because the end result is filtered through the consciousness of the researcher. More importantly for them, it is impossible to truly understand another's experience.[16] The contradictions that this raises for feminist research leads them to suggest that, not only must feminist researchers locate themselves within the research question, but that the only research practice that truly reflects feminist principles is a form of ethnomethodology which draws primarily on the researcher's own experience. Unfortunately, this leads us back to the problems associated with the prioritizing of personal experience noted earlier. It also invalidates much of the feminist research published to date! In fact, Stanley and Wise's shift in their analysis of their own experience of obscene phone calls does not rely solely on the experience itself but directly reflects shifts in feminist analysis of sexual violence: from stressing victimization to including women's resistance.[17]

They are, however, correct in highlighting the fact that issues of power and control are problematic for feminist researchers. One group of feminist researchers has published a detailed and honest account of the complexity of power sharing in research.[18] They contrast the ease of changing interview practice with the difficulties of opening out analysis and writing. Whilst they tried to find ways of sharing these later stages of the project, many of the women who participated did not share the researchers' politics.

Whether or not to confront groups or individuals with interpretations of their lives which are radically different from their own is an ethical question faced by anyone attempting critical social research. This is particularly true when the researcher's interpretation is not only different but potentially threatening and disruptive to the subject's world view.[19]

Furthermore, their decision to reflect the range and complexity of women's experiences, by including life-histories and extended quotes, was questioned by many of the participants who urged them to include more analysis: 'They were hesitant about being negative, but were clearly critical. What they wanted, they said, was more of our sociological analysis. They wanted us, the researchers, to interpret their experience to them.'[20]

Other honest accounts of the problems encountered by feminists in attempting to democratize research practice have been published recently.[21] Hilary Barker, in her discussion of feminist community work, suggests that we are in danger of creating a 'false-equality trap' whereby feminists deny their own possession of knowledge and skills in order to minimize differences between women. Rather than a sharing of power this is, in fact, a denial of its existence.

The majority of feminist discussions of method, to date, have been limited to discussions of how to change interviewing techniques. We have yet to explore in as much depth other research methods and the possibility of changing how we analyse and document our research findings. Drawing on the traditions of action research, particularly the practice of researchers in the Third World, might provide some new insights.[22]

The issues are, however, even more complicated than this. The position of, and options available to, feminist researchers vary according to their choice of research topic and methods and, perhaps most importantly, research subjects. The issues of power and control are different in a study of women in a local community compared to one focusing on male professionals. There are further, and different, sets of questions where research is based on analysis of texts or statistical data sets.

Feminist research is relatively new. Rather than foreclosing development through limited definitions of 'feminist methodology', we should be exploring a range of approaches and encouraging honest accounts of the problems of translating feminist group practice into feminist research practice.

How the research was conducted – feminist research practice

To record truthfully and fully the history of a research project would require a book in itself! Most accounts appear in appendices and are reconstructed and sanitized descriptions of the research methodology; the problems, doubts, changes of direction that beset all research are censored out. This has been referred to as 'hygienic' research or 'the chronological lie'.[23] Nevertheless, some honest accounts have appeared in volumes which deal with the 'reality' of sociological research practice.[24] The discussion of the methodology of this project will be presented in the context of a description of my feminist research practice.

The first stage of this project involved the construction of an interview guide and four pilot interviews. Two decisions I made at this point had major impacts on the project methodology. First, I decided to do the pilot interviews with friends and meet a second time to discuss the interview style and content. Second, I decided to discuss the redrafted interview guide, revised following the pilot interviews, with both academic colleagues and friends. The women who did the pilot interviews felt that hearing their own tape gave them time to reflect on and add to what they had said and this resulted in the decision to return a transcript of the interview to each woman and to do follow-up interviews with them. The discussions on the revised interview guide resulted in the inclusion of a final section which focused on the future rather than the past. This meant that potentially distressing interviews could end on a positive, forward-looking note. It was the co-operative framework in which the pilot interviews and discussions took place which resulted in these crucial methodological developments.

The final draft of the interview guide began with reflections on childhood and moved through adolescence to adulthood. Questions about a range of possible experiences of sexual violence were thus placed in context of women's lives. The wording and placement of questions about sexual violence was carefully chosen in order not to presume shared definitions. For example, a question on whether women had ever felt pressured to have sex came much earlier in the interview than the question about ever having been raped. This both encouraged disclosure of incidents that women found difficult to define and made possible the analysis of definitions in chapter 6. More detailed questions, cross-referenced as far as possible, covered experiences of rape, incest and domestic violence.

The majority of research on sexual violence has used convenience samples of women drawn mainly from medical or social service caseloads or crisis centres. In some way, therefore, the abuse has been made public. Given that one of the research aims was to reach women whose experiences had not been made public, and that to study the long-term impact of sexual violence required at least a one-year gap between the assault and the interview, these potential sources were rejected. As the interviews were to be detailed and potentially distressing, I felt it was important that women choose to participate. A voluntary sample was, therefore, decided upon. I began using the methods recommended in textbooks; letters and notices in newspapers and magazines. Whilst there was some response, it was not likely to produce the sample of 60 set for the study. Women had approached me at talks I gave on a variety of topics expressing interest in the research. I, therefore, adapted this to research needs and visited as wide a range of women's groups as possible (for example, community mother and toddler and return to work groups, women's studies groups, nursing and social work training groups). I also adapted a strategy used by several US researchers: a notice with tear off strips which were placed in a community bookshop and a health fair organized by the Community Health Council.[25] Pauline Bart calls this a 'multi-varied approach to purposive sampling'.[26]

The majority of volunteers came as a result of the talks I gave. As one of the effects of sexual violence is decreased trust, it is not surprising that women are wary of volunteering to take part in a project about which they know very little. Several sociologists have stressed the importance of establishing and maintaining trust in sociological research.[27] Face to face contact with the researcher offers the interviewee the possibility of an initial assessment of the researcher's 'trustworthiness'. This was confirmed when several women revealed, during follow-up interviews, how they had tested me out before agreeing to be interviewed. 'I'm reluctant to talk to people about it . . . It was several weeks before I decided to approach you. I thought I'd sum you up first' (laughs).

All women expressing an interest in the research were sent a letter explaining the aims of the project and what participation would involve, a return letter to arrange the first interview or state their reasons for not participating, and an information sheet on support services. By far the majority of those who expressed interest were interviewed. There were, however, some practical problems getting back in touch with some of the young women from pre-nursing training and several women from one of the return-to-work groups withdrew. I was later informed by the tutor of the latter group that those women who had told male partners about the prospective interview had been 'persuaded' not to participate.

Before I began interviewing, I had devised a sampling system which involved interviewing four groups of 15 women: 15 with self-declared experiences of rape, incest and domestic violence (45 in all) and a comparison group of 15 women who did not have to have experienced sexual violence in order to participate. The possibility of a control group which could only include women without experiences of sexual violence was rejected for two reasons. First, one aim of the project was to investigate the range of women's experiences. Second, the absence of experiences could only be assessed by actually doing an interview. Several recent studies have highlighted the problematic status of control groups.[28]

After ten interviews, I became more concerned to document the range of sexual violence women experienced and more aware of the fact that women may not necessarily define incidents of sexual violence as rape, incest or domestic violence. The sample was, therefore, reassessed. The self-declared groups were reduced to 10 in each and the comparison group increased to 30. The 60 interviews were coded according to whether the woman had volunteered on the basis of having experienced rape, domestic violence or incest (three groups of 10 women) and, in the case of the comparison group, whether or not they had, during the interviews, discussed an experience which they defined as rape, incest or domestic violence (two groups of 15). Where tables are presented they reflect this coding: the thirty women in the self-declared groups appear in columns headed R (rape), I (incest), DV (domestic violence) and the thirty women in the comparison group are split between C1 (women who did define an incident as rape, incest or domestic violence) and C2 (women who did not).

Whilst this sample is limited by the fact that it is self-selected, there was a considerable range within those interviewed with regard to age, class of origin, marital status, work experience and sexual identity. There are, however, two important qualifications to its representativeness. Most importantly, by far the majority of women interviewed were white British. Two women of mixed race and two white immigrants were interviewed. The areas in which the interviews were done have very small ethnic minority communities. I spent considerable time wondering whether I should deliberately seek Black women participants outside these geographic areas. For a number of reasons, some of which I would now reconsider, I decided against doing this. In order to take account of the issue of race I have taken care to search out research where race has been addressed and I have read the work of Black women on feminist theory and sexual violence. The second qualification is that a larger percentage of the sample than the population in general had had some kind of further education.

My interviewing style reflects that used by other feminist researchers; a rejection of the 'objective' aloofness and the refusal to enter into dialogue.[29] It is difficult for me to envisage being detached when I remember how shaken many women were during or after the interviews. Many commented that they had never talked through their experiences in such depth before and on a number of occasions interviews had to be stopped because women were visibly distressed (all chose to complete the interview). I often spent as much time talking with women informally as in recording the interviews. These conversations ranged from specific requests for information, to reflections on aspects of the interview, to discussions of preliminary research findings.

Interviewing and transcribing the tapes was much more time-consuming and emotionally draining than I had anticipated. I had little idea of how complicated and frustrating these activities could be. For example, several interviews were done with young children in the room, all of whom insisted on playing with or shouting into the microphone, and several women had speech patterns which meant parts of sentences were inaudible.

Interviewing is a skill. My skill developed over time as I sensed where to ask a further question, when to just listen, and where to leave space for women to think. It is not just talking, although a good interview may feel like a stimulating conversation. It involves the interviewer being aware of a number of things at the same time and juggling priorities. After transcribing several tapes I became aware of how problematic it is to directly transpose the spoken to the written word. Mishearing one word can change the meaning of a whole passage of speech, and meaning in the spoken word is often conveyed by tone of voice and gesture. Several women also commented on this when discussing reading their transcript. In order to retain as much of this meaning as possible I developed a method for coding expression and tone of voice (see the Guide to transcription of interviews on p. vii above). Whilst transcribing I also noted any questions or points that required clarification on a follow-up sheet and wrote any more general insights or questions on file cards.

When copies of the transcript were sent to women, a note was included asking them to note any corrections, qualifications or additions they wanted to make. Follow-up interviews were done with 47 women. Each of these interviews began with a series of questions about participation in the project, reactions to reading the transcript, whether or not there were any changes women wanted to make and whether or not they had remembered anything in the intervening time. Questions specific to each woman's first interview followed.

Almost 75 per cent of the women had remembered additional incidents of sexual violence, or aspects of incidents they had discussed, between the original interview and the follow-up. Several women made detailed comments and revisions on the original transcript; one woman sent me her transcript 18 months later and added important information which she had not trusted me with at either of our two formal meetings. No one felt the interview had been a negative experience; 85 per cent described it in very positive terms and felt that they had learnt things through their participation. A number of women stated explicitly that they valued having the transcript, both as a record of the past and a marker for the future.

'Actually I'm quite surprised, I've found it really helpful. I can't think about it so talking is the only way of admitting it ever happened . . . I have never talked in that concentrated way before . . . I think I like myself a lot more, I feel quite brave really.'

'I felt a lot better after I'd talked about it because it's been a lot of years and I've never really talked openly about it to anyone.'

It is in the style of interviewing, the return of the transcripts, and the content of the follow-up interviews that my feminist research practice is reflected. The return of the transcripts meant that the women who participated controlled the content of their interview. Follow-up interviews allowed what Shulamith Reinharz calls 'joint interpretation of meaning' to take place,[30] and I was able to assess the impact of the research on women. The value of these aspects of research practice were evident in the importance women placed on seeing their experiences written down. It enabled recognition of their strength in survival and a documenting of the positive changes they had made in their lives.

It was during our second meeting that many women asked questions about whether their experiences were 'typical' and asked me to describe the most important things emerging from the research. This enabled discussion of the themes and analysis I was developing. I did not assume that women would want to take part in this process, but the interest in it suggests that there may be ways of making this a more formal part of research methodology. One possibility I would now consider is a third meeting in which the researcher discusses with small groups of participants preliminary findings and analysis.

I should note that for several of the women who had never talked through their experiences with anyone before, participation in the research raised difficult issues and I felt I had a responsibility to offer what support I could. I put four women in touch with each other on the basis of their similar experiences and three women went on to join a local self-help support group. A number of women stayed in touch with me for some time after their interviews were completed. They phoned or wrote letters, either telling me that a problem we had discussed was now resolved or wanting to discuss some recent event. While I always felt touched by the trust these responses demonstrated, there were times when I also felt overwhelmed by the emotional demands. I was constantly aware of how important my grassroots feminist involvement prior to the research had been. It had prepared me, in part, for the fact that some women might need support after doing the interviews and provided me with knowledge of, for example, the law and housing that I was able to pass on.

Analysing the transcripts was a lengthy and laborious process. I rejected the traditional method of cutting up copies and filing them thematically very quickly as answers to questions often contained passages relevant to several themes. I developed a system of numerically coding answers which meant that the basic information in all the interviews was condensed and available in a relatively accessible form. As there were no pre-set categories and responses to code from, each interview was analysed twice so that categories which emerged from later transcripts could be checked against those analysed earlier. By using coloured highlighter pens, it was relatively easy to distinguish the sub-samples from one another on charts which included all 60 women's responses. From this process I built up less complex summary tables. For example, each specific incident of sexual violence women recalled was written down and this formed the basis of the life-cycle chart which appears in chapter 4. Throughout the analysis I respected women's own definitions of their experiences. This resulted in the use of two new categories 'pressurized sex' and 'coercive sex' and the development of the concept of 'the continuum' (see chapters 4 and 5). By the time I ran through the transcripts to check the coding I had decided on the basic themes I wanted to focus on, all direct quotations which related to these themes were written on file cards.

By this point, I had heard each tape twice, read each transcript at least four times, and the information extracted from them had been recorded in a number of different ways. Writing up the project involved using the file cards containing ideas and quotes in conjunction with the numerically coded tables. The concepts used and the themes I have chosen to focus on emerged from and are grounded in the experiences of the women interviewed.

Reflexive experiential analysis

I have already noted the importance for feminist researchers of locating themselves within their research questions. Shulamith

Reinharz has documented her journey through a variety of sociological methods to what she calls 'experiential analysis'.[31] She argues that rather than ignoring our own feelings, responses and experience, we should focus on these human responses as they are precisely what enables us to understand social reality. This chapter ends, therefore, with some selected examples of the impact of doing the research on me, and how paying attention to my own experience resulted in important shifts in understanding.[32]

Vulnerability

I began the project by reading extensively. Very soon I felt overwhelmed by an awareness of male violence. Many research methods texts recommend this 'immersion' in the topic but they seldom reflect on the impact this might have on the researcher. I became more conscious of how surrounded women are by images, comments, jokes and real events connected to sexual violence. It became impossible to watch television, read a newspaper, go out to the cinema or a pub, travel, walk alone or even at times have a conversation without being reminded of this in some way. I began to notice instances of sexual violence in books and films that I had previously enjoyed.

I became increasingly concerned about my own safety. For the first time in years I felt scared walking alone at night. I resisted this fear, told myself that it was irrational, that I was no more at risk than six months previously, that everything I knew about male violence told me that women had more to fear from men they knew in their own homes than from strangers. As I began interviewing I was more directly reminded of the threat and reality of sexual violence. This was the period when extensive media attention was given to the 'Yorkshire Ripper' murders and several rape cases. When I visited Leeds, I sensed an atmosphere of fear amongst women. Jalna Hanmer's and Sheila Saunders' Leeds study found that during this period 83 per cent of women restricted their movements (18 per cent were already not going out alone, or at all, at night).[33] This increased awareness of how strong the fear of attack can be and what enormous effects this can have on women's freedom was a product of all these factors. All women develop coping strategies in order to live with their level of fear, but these are tenuous – changed for women in Leeds by the actions of one man (aided and abetted by the police and media), for me by doing research.

As I listened to women's descriptions of incidents of sexual violence, many of which occurred in the context of their having challenged men, my fear focused on a particular man with whom I had had several political confrontations in the past and who had explicitly threatened me once at a party. Coincidentally, he seemed to appear regularly in places where I was. I occasionally felt I was a character in a thriller and that he knew where I would be. I understood then that the threat of violence is certainly not limited to unknown men in the public sphere but is present in explicit or complex and subtle ways in many of the interactions women have with men.

The impact of the threat of violence was 'brought home' in another way much later in the project. The ex-husband of a woman who had contacted the local refuge group got access to my home phone number and address. He harassed me for over a month and during one phone conversation threatened to kill me. The response of the police to this was, to say the least, unhelpful. I was angry at how easily my sense of safety in my own home could be undermined. He knew where I lived, knew my phone number, possibly even what I looked like and what my movements were. All I had was his name, and the knowledge that the local police felt his desire to find his ex-wife was more important than his threat to my life. I understood how threatening and disturbing so called 'nuisance calls' are and how women living in violent relationships have to cut off from the violence in order to survive as I shifted from feeling scared and vulnerable to refusing to think about about might happen, as it restricted my life too much.

The cumulative impact of all these experiences resulted in the realization that the constant threat of violence in a woman's life could result in extreme emotional distress which was unlikely to be recognized by any professionals from whom she might seek support. I often felt my fear would have been defined by many as paranoid and irrational, and, in fact, at times I attempted to convince myself that this was the case.

One aspect of the issue of vulnerability was specific to my daughter, then ten. As I read more about incest and child sexual abuse I became increasingly distrustful of all men. Accepting that my suggestion that most women experience sexual violence in their lifetime also applied to her and her friends, another generation of women, distressed me and I became concerned to protect her from what seemed, at that point, almost an inevitability. The comments from women about the warnings they had been given in childhood and how confusing these were meant that I tried to discuss carefully and honestly with her what abuse was, that men she knew might try to abuse her trust, and that if anything did happen she should tell me.

Whilst working through these personal issues and trying to come to terms with the literature on child sexual abuse, I saw how easy it is for men to choose to define children's openness and affection as sexual. How easy it is to abuse children's trust that adults know what is right. Adults, particularly adult men who assume the right to discipline children in violent and/or humiliating ways, have enormous power over them. I understood how this power is reproduced through the denial of children's rights, to knowledge, autonomy and choice.

Remembering

Whilst interviewing and transcribing, buried memories of my own emerged: I remembered five separate incidents of assault or harassment from my childhood and adolescence. The fact that this also happened to a woman who transcribed several interviews, and to many women when they read their own transcripts, resulted in my paying attention to how common the forgetting of painful or confusing experiences is.

The experiences I remembered from childhood were all ones which I did not understand or was confused by at the time. I identified with the women I interviewed when they talked about not having the words to tell anyone, or even understand, what was happening. This in turn led me to explore, in much more detail than I would have done otherwise, the process of defining sexual violence (see chapter 6). I realized the power of naming, and why much of the work done by feminists around violence against women has been to name and redefine forms of violence.

Personal relationships

I had anticipated that listening to women's experiences of sexual violence would affect me emotionally. I did not expect to be affected by the discussions of childhood and family relationships that began each interview. My reactions were certainly linked to my personal history; I grew up in a Catholic, working-class, extended family; my mother died when I was 12.

Coming to discussions of mother/daughter relationships without a mother, yet being one, undoubtedly gave me a particular perspective. I either reacted with envy when women talked of developing close relationships with their mothers or felt upset if women were negative and judgemental about their mothers. In trying to understand these responses I realized how I had cut off from my feelings about my mother's death. This occurred at the same time as I was trying to make sense of the immense amount of mother-blame in the literature on incest. I slowly came to see the trap that most mothers are in and why some (but by no means all) abused young women blame their mothers. To children, mothers are powerful and children develop unrealistic expectations of them. Mothers are expected to know, in an almost telepathic way, when something is wrong and to be able to solve the problem. When, for whatever reason, children feel their mother fails to understand or protect them, they may experience this as betrayal. Incest survivors are certainly not the only women who feel betrayed by or angry with their mothers.

At this point, I was beginning to look at forms and experiences of violence in terms of a continuum (see chapters 4 and 5). I noticed how many women's fathers were controlling, seductive and/or physically violent: father–daughter incest being an extension of this much more common and acceptable pattern. Feminists have been surprisingly silent about fathers, almost without noticing reinforcing the traditional psychological view that mothers are the all-important influence in children's lives. I suspect that fathers play a crucial role, particularly in relation to daughters; they lay the basis, subtly, coercively or violently, of our fear of male anger and, therefore, our awareness of the risks of challenging men.

It is impossible to describe in words the emotions and reactions that doing this piece of research evoked, and I have only selected a few examples here. It is just as important, though, to make clear that there was another side to this experience: positive feelings and interactions that were sustaining. The completion of the project was, in part, the result of trust that many of the women who were interviewed placed in me and their interest in, and support for, the research in general and me in particular. It was extremely important that the interviews contained both a record of victimization and of women's strength in survival.

Moving between the interviews and my own experiences and reactions was an integral part of the research methodology. Had I 'tuned out' these responses I would probably not have noticed or fully understood the importance of aspects of women's experience of sexual violence.

2

A central issue: sexual violence and feminist theory

In this chapter I explore how sexual violence has been explained and located within feminist theory, paying particular attention to the proposition that male violence has a critical role in maintaining women's oppression. In the final sections I build on other women's work to develop our analysis of the links between different forms of sexual violence and suggest a feminist definition of sexual violence. While recent historical research has revealed that men's abuse of women and children was a key issue in the last wave of feminism,[1] the discussion in this chapter is confined to recent feminist theory and practice.

Laying the foundations

Three classic works, Kate Millett's *Sexual Politics*, Susan Griffin's 'Rape, the all American crime', and Susan Brownmiller's *Against Our Will* exemplify three feminist approaches to theoretical writing.[2] The first is based on detailed critique of men's writing, the second builds on personal experience and the third researches and analyses an aspect of women's experience that malestream thought either ignores or trivializes. All contain analysis and concepts which have been developed in subsequent feminist theory and research on sexual violence.

Kate Millett uses the concept of patriarchy to describe a social and political system in which men control, and have power over, women. She argues that women's subordination by men has been a feature of the majority of (if not all) past societies and exists across different cultures and socio-economic systems today. Most of her attention is directed towards explaining how patriarchy persists in societies such as the USA, where legal reform has given women equal civil and political rights and in which women have access to education and the possibility of financial independence. She illustrates how patriarchy is reproduced within the family and by the state, ideology and culture. A crucially important, although often neglected, aspect of her analysis is that control in patriarchal societies, as in all political systems, ultimately rests on force.

The term patriarchy has become a contested one, particularly in British feminist theory, and there have been a number of suggestions that it should no longer be used.[3] Like Sylvia Walby, I would argue that it is impossible to understand, let alone theorize, women's oppression without the concept.[4] Criticisms of particular formulations, or specific uses of the concept, do not invalidate the concept itself. As Walby writes: 'These critics move from pointing out very real and important deficiencies in accounts of patriarchy to the false conclusion that all accounts of patriarchy must necessarily suffer from the same problems.'[5] Rather than abandon the concept which names the systematic oppression of women by men, feminist theorists should build on previous insights in order to develop more complex accounts of patriarchy.

The most fundamental criticism has been that patriarchy is a universal concept which obscures historical change and cultural difference. There are, however, definitions of patriarchy which do not make such assumptions. Adrienne Rich's definition, for example, draws on Millett's analysis, but acknowledges that both the forms of patriarchal control and the amount of power women have within and across societies varies.

Patriarchy is the power of the fathers: a familial–social, ideological, political system in which men – by force, direct pressure or through ritual, tradition, law, and language, customs, etiquette, education, and the division of labour, determine what part women shall or shall not play, and in which the female is everywhere subsumed under the male. It does not necessarily imply that no woman has power, or that all women in a given culture may not have certain powers.[6]

This definition, and Diana Gittins',[7] defines patriarchal relations in terms of gender and age relations based on power. Rather than removing the power of the father from the analysis, as some (including Sylvia Walby) have suggested, it remains a central focus. Definitions of patriarchy have tended to focus on

relations between men and women and/or relations between older
and younger men. The relations between men/women and
children are seldom specified, or are seen to be only relevant to a
type of family form which is no longer characteristic of western
industrial societies. Evidence from my research in the chapters
which follow suggests that the power of the father is still an
important factor in the structure of familial relationships.
Retaining the age relation within a definition of patriarchy is
necessary if we are to develop our understanding of how the
position of women and children within both households and
wider structures of social relations are connected. For example,
defining households as embodying complex and, at times, cross-
cutting power relations based on gender and age enables us to
understand and theorize sexual abuse of boys by adult males,
physical abuse of children by mothers (both based on age-related
power) and physical or sexual abuse of mothers by sons (a
transgression of the age relation via the gender relation).
Cumulative power (for fathers) and powerlessness (for daughters)
are as evident in the structure of the family as in the complex
structuring of social relations involving gender, class and race.
Furthermore, two studies have suggested that the power and
authority of the father is a continuing factor structuring gender
relations in paid employment. [8]

In making force and coercion a central aspect of her analysis,
Millett drew on political theory which defined politics in terms of
power relations: force being the overt use of coercive power by
the dominant group as a resource of last resort. Defining
patriarchal relations as political foregrounds the use of force and
the control of women's sexuality as essential features of patriarchal societies. [9] A number of writers have developed Millett's
insights.

Marilyn Frye [10] suggests that forms of control which remove
options and appear to involve co-operation by the subordinate
group are preferred in all hierarchical systems: an argument
which echoes Antonio Gramsci's analysis of hegemony, and
Hannah Arendt's contention that force is only used when power
is in jeopardy. [11] Violence is used only when other methods of
control have failed as its usage makes coercive power explicit and,
therefore, increases the possibility of resistance. Implicit in this
analysis is that use of explicit force/violence is in fact a response
to the failure of, or resistance to, other forms of control. It is in

this context that I argue that male violence arises out of men's power and women's resistance to it.

Most political theorists maintain that the monopoly and use of force by those in power has to be legitimized. Historical studies have revealed the extent to which forms of male violence were legitimized by law and tradition.[12] In some countries the legal system and social norms still sanction certain forms of male violence. In a number of countries feminist campaigning has undermined much, if not all, of this explicit legitimation.[13] Where such change has taken place, however, studies of the practice of social agencies and legal systems demonstrate that implicit forms of legitimation remain whereby only the most extreme cases and forms of sexual violence are criminalized.[14]

Susan Griffin's analysis builds on the influence of the threat of rape in her life. She argues that rape is not a sexual crime but a violent, political act; the threat of rape functions as a form of social control which affects all women. Several writers have developed her thesis that a 'male protection racket' exists whereby individual men are supposed to protect women from all other men; women become dependent upon the goodwill of their male protector, and more vulnerable to abuse by them.[15] This short polemical article also contains many other themes which later writers have expanded on in analysing sexual violence: the social construction of masculinity and femininity; the connections between rape and heterosexual intercourse; and the ideological processes through which women are blamed for men's violence.

Susan Brownmiller drew on both Griffin and Millett in her attempt to 'give rape its history'.[16] She maintains that rape is the primary mechanism through which men perpetuate their dominance over women through force. She expands on Griffin's analysis of rape as a form of social control. The threat of rape, and the fact that it does happen to some women, creates a climate of fear; all men benefit from the fact that some men rape women. Recent research has questioned the grand sweep of Brownmiller's analysis across cultural and historical boundaries as the incidence of rape within different cultures varies.[17] The factor which is seen to account for the difference, however, is the level of male dominance within a society; higher rape rates correlating with greater male dominance. Anne Edwards points out that, at times, Brownmiller, unlike Millett or Griffin, draws a distinction between 'deviant' and 'normal' forms of heterosexuality.[18]

A decade of activism and debate

Whilst Millett was attempting to place the use of force and violence within a wider discussion of patriarchy as a social and political system, Griffin and Brownmiller appear to suggest that rape was *the* most important form of patriarchal power and control. In fact, much theoretical discussion of sexual violence, up to the late 1970s, either focused exclusively on rape or used rape as the paradigmatic example of men's use of violence to control women. During this period, many activists built alternative services and support networks for abused women and children and campaigning drew attention to the issues of domestic violence, child sexual abuse and sexual harassment. It was only towards the end of the 1970s that a body of feminist research emerged which documented the incidence of a number of forms of sexual violence.

In contrast, feminists who were also committed socialists were far more concerned with the gendered organization of production in explaining women's continuing oppression; little attention was given, or importance accorded, to direct physical coercion.[19] For example, Kate Young's and Olivia Harris' attempt in 1978 to develop an analysis of women's oppression which was not culturally specific, suggested that, whilst 'unmediated physical violence' might be the predominant form of control in tribal societies, in more complex societies economic and ideological forms of control take precedence.[20] Their contention that the use of overt force by men has declined has been questioned more recently by Alison Jagger, also a socialist feminist: 'research has revealed that physical force plays a far larger part in controlling women than had previously been acknowledged.'[21]

In the 1980s, feminist researchers and theorists have attempted to draw together the experiences of the previous ten years and have returned to the basic question of the role of force and coercion in the continuing oppression of women. Rape no longer has a privileged place in analysis as the full range of men's use of force and coercion has been acknowledged.

Lisa Leghorn and Kathryn Parker attempted to pick up Millett's grand project of developing a theoretical framework for analysing women's oppression that can be applied historically and cross-culturally.[22] They integrate discussion of the role of force in women's oppression within a framework of 'sexual economics'. It is one of six factors which they see as determining women's position in society; the others being control over fertility, the division of labour, access to resources, networks between women, and political power. Rather than presuming the relative importance of one or more of the factors this framework is used as the basis for detailed analysis of eleven societies. It remains an open question as to which factor or particular combination of factors are determinate in any particular society at any historical moment. Sexual violence is one factor in maintaining women's oppression. Its centrality can be culturally and historically variable (as indeed it may be in individual women's lives). Whilst the authors themselves limit their study of 'sexual economics' to whole societies, the framework could usefully be extended to examine the position of individuals and groups of women within particular societies. Leghorn and Parker's analysis represents the bravest attempt so far to integrate a range of feminist concerns into a theoretical system which is not deterministic, reductionist, historically bounded or ethnocentric.

Instead of arguing in abstract terms about the centrality of particular aspects of women's oppression, we need to begin to explicate how they connect within systems of patriarchal control and with other forms of oppression. This necessitates examining whether and now women's oppression is structured differently across historical time periods and within and between cultures. One interesting hypothesis to explore in relation to sexual violence is that it becomes more prevalent when women as a group (and as individuals) resist other forms of patriarchal control. The incidence of sexual violence will, therefore, vary in direct relation to the collective (and individual) resistance of women to patriarchal oppression.

Alongside the broad sweep of theoretical perspectives which attempt to locate the place of sexual violence in women's oppression are analyses which focus on sexual violence itself. Most of these discussions draw on feminist analyses of power, sexuality and social control.

Power

The concept of power has been the focus of much discussion and debate within political science and sociology, although analysis has predominantly been limited to power in the public sphere.[23] The feminist statement that 'the personal is political' has directed attention to the existence of power within intimate relationships. Just as power at the state level includes a range of possible forms of control over others, including invasions of privacy and the legitimate use of force, so it does at the interpersonal level. However, power in feminist analysis *is not a property but a relation* which structures interactions between men and women in all areas of social life. The fact that women, unlike other oppressed groups, are expected to live in intimate contact with those who have power over them, not only respecting but also loving them, makes women's subordination both pervasive and insidious.[24] Solidarity between and organizing of women as a group can be undermined by the isolation of women within particular households and/or relationships.

Much feminist theory considers the power men have over women by virtue of being men as fundamental or primary. That power is reinforced by men's occupation of other social roles which are accorded specific forms of authority: for example, husband, boss, father. This combination of levels of gender power has been used to explain the particular power dynamics involved in battering, sexual harassment at work and incest.[25] Whilst certain groups of men have far more power than others by virtue of class and/or race privileges, they always have more power than their female counterparts.

Nancy Henley and Jo Freeman have outlined the many ways gendered power relations are present in everyday interpersonal communication, including physical touching, joking and linguistic patterns.[26] Power carries for dominant groups the right to initiate and refrain from intimate physical contact. In ethnic relations power is reflected by the tendency for whites to refrain from intimate contact, although this tendency is overridden when white men want sex with Black women. Physical differences which are defined negatively in other contexts here become 'exotic' and 'sexy'. In gender relations power is reflected in men's intrusive touching of women and their prerogative of initiating social and sexual encounters.

Hilary Lips, in her analysis of the psychology of power, emphasizes that dominant groups/individuals can use anger or aggression as a power resource in a routine way as the risks of reprisal are relatively small.[27] Two feminist academics, Caroline

Ramazonoglu and Sheila MacIntyre, have documented their experiences of verbal and vocal violence and sexual harassment within academic institutions.[28] Both accounts illustrate that men's gender power overrides other power differences including those between female staff and male students and that men's routine use of aggression in these contexts tends to be directed at women who refuse to accept subordination. As individuals, women may resist such behaviour but having minimal access to power resources we are seldom able to change institutional ideologies and structures which legitimize, or fail to challenge, routine exercises of power by men.

These feminist insights reveal the complex ways power structures everyday encounters between men and women, and the extent to which intrusion and aggression may be a routine feature of these interactions. The manifestation of men's gender power through the rotuine use of aggression against women is connected to 'non-routine' assaults, such as rape, which are extensions of more commonplace intrusions. This analysis underpins my use of the concept of a 'continuum of sexual violence' (see chapters 4 and 5).

The connections feminists make between everyday interactions and what would legally be defined as an assault bring into focus a further aspect of power. Stephen Lukes' concept of a 'third dimension' of power specifically addresses the question of who benefits from the routine, institutionalized, unchallenged exercise of power, and stresses the importance of the power to define.[29] Elizabeth Janeway has suggested that one of the 'powers of the weak' is to refuse to accept the definitions of the powerful.[30] A central feature of feminist work around male violence has been to challenge male definitions. Feminist theory and practice has, over the past two decades, shifted attention from only those forms of violence where physical harm and injury are obvious, such as rape and battering, to more 'taken for granted' forms, such as sexual harassment. In extending the definition of sexual violence, feminists have challenged men's power to define and drawn attention to the role of male-dominated legal systems in constructing and reinforcing limited definitions.[31] We have also recognized that it is men, as a group and as individuals, who benefit from limited definitions of sexual violence which function to distinguish a small group of 'deviant' men from the 'normal' majority.

Feminist analyses of male power reveal a complex and multi-levelled process, located both in interpersonal relationships and within social structure and ideology. That the exercise of power brings with it the possibility of resistance has been implicit in much feminist theory to date. Sue Wise and Liz Stanley centre their discussions of sexual harassment in everyday life on the interaction between men's daily intrusions into women's 'feelings, thoughts, behaviour, space, time, energies and bodies' and the many and varied ways in which women resist and fight back.[32] Jeff Hearn's and Wendy Parkin's discussion of the 'dialectics of power' represents a further example of analysing resistance as potential within all power relations.[33] Frameworks such as these, which accommodate both the range and routine nature of men's use of power and women's resistance to it, capture the both complexity of patriarchal power and the possibilities for change.

Sexuality

There are two interlinked aspects of feminist theory which connect analysis of sexuality with male violence: first, the proposition that male control of women's sexuality is a key factor in women's oppression; and second, that sexuality as it is currently constructed is based on men's experiences and definitions, which legitimate the use of force or coercion within heterosexual encounters.

One of the major disagreements between feminists is the location of the primary site of women's oppression. Catharine MacKinnon presents the most complex formulation of a strand of radical feminism which sees sexuality, broadly defined, as occupying this position.

Feminism fundamentally identifies sexuality as the primary social sphere of male power. The centrality of sexuality emerges not from Freudian conceptions but from feminist practice on diverse issues including abortion, birth control, sterilization abuse, domestic battery, rape, incest, lesbianism, sexual harassment, prostitution, female sexual slavery and pornography . . . producing a feminist political theory centering on sexuality; its social determination, daily construction, birth to death expression, and ultimately male control.[34]

Whilst having much sympathy with this view, a number of Black feminists and feminists of Colour have suggested that sexuality does not have the same significance for women in all cultures, or all women in a particular culture. These critiques do not question the importance of sexuality in gender relations but assert that other forms of inequality may be the primary organizing focus for certain groups of women.

The definition and depiction of women as primarily sexual beings has increased this century, particularly in western capitalist countries. What has been called 'the eroticization of dominance'[35] has been perceived as central by a number of white, middle-class, western women. Whilst classism and racism inform these definitions and depictions and undoubtedly affect white working-class women and Black women, other forms of oppression may be experienced by them as more urgent. In fact, multiple levels of oppression may fuse into a complex totality which makes their separation problematic in both theory and individual experience. This is reflected in Ruth Hall's discussion of 'racist sexual violence' where she argues that, for Black women, assaults by white men often involve the fusion of racial and sexual violence.[36]

It is not, however, merely the distorting effects of racism and classism which led feminist theorists to give such a central place to sexuality. Diana Gittins suggests: 'It is in sexual relations that the essence of patriarchy . . . becomes manifest'.[37] Adrienne Rich has attempted to integrate an analysis of sexual violence within a broader framework of the enforcement of compulsory heterosexuality.[38] She argues that heterosexuality must be examined, historically and cross-culturally, as a social institution within which a variable range of forms of control, coercion and force are used by men to ensure sexual access to women.

The concept of sexual access, as used by feminist theorists, refers to the range of processes through which women are defined as sexual objects available to men. These processes are legitimized through a naturalistic ideology of sex which presents heterosexuality as the only 'normal' form of sexual practice and male sexuality as determined by biological 'drives'. The concept has been applied by feminists in two related contexts.

First, it is argued that men assume sexual access to women they do not know (or with whom they have slight acquaintance) by, for example, making sexual approaches or remarks. The extreme form of this is sexual assault or rape by strangers. Diana Scully's and Joseph Marolla's research on convicted rapists suggests that many of the men saw sex as a male entitlement and the justifications they offered for their actions were 'buttressed by the cultural view of women as sexual commodities, dehumanized and devoid of autonomy and dignity'.[39] Extending this analysis, it has been suggested that men sexualize all relationships with women. This is implicit in Catherine MacKinnon's analysis of sexuality as the main area through which men express power over and attempt to control women. The increasing entry of women into the public sphere of work and the revival of feminist campaigning for sexual equality has undoubtedly been accompanied by an increased public sexualization of women throughout the mass media. Several feminist researchers have suggested that increasing demands from women for greater autonomy and equality will increase sexual violence in the short-term as men attempt to reassert their dominance; Diana Russell and Laura Lederer see the recent increase in the sale, availability and acceptability of pornography as a patriarchal response to campaigns for women's liberation.[40]

The second context in which the concept of sexual access is used is within intimate relationships. Here the focus is the assumed rights of men to sexual access with wives and lovers and, in some cases, to daughters. There are remnants of the historical status of women and children in men's proprietorial attitudes which are most clearly legitimized in marital rape exemption clauses. Sexual access, like other resources, is determined by relational power. The more power a man can claim over a particular women, the greater his claim to exclusive access. The greater his perceived right to exclusive sexual access, the more likely it is that some level of sexual aggression will be considered legitimate.[41]

Feminist analysis of the social construction of sexuality has directly challenged naturalistic, biologically determinist theories of sexuality whilst acknowledging that gender currently determines, to a large extent, beliefs about and experiences of sexuality. Nancy Hartsock maintains that 'sexuality in our society is defined almost exclusively in masculine terms and, moreover, hostility and domination are central to the construction of masculine sexuality'.[42] Masculinity, as it is currently constructed in western culture, draws on notions of virility, conquest, power and domination and these themes are reflected in gender relations and heterosexual practice; sex and aggression are linked for most men. To suggest otherwise, Hartsock argues, is to recreate the myth that heterosexual relationships are based on intimacy and mutuality, disguising the reality of hostility and domination that feminism set out to challenge.

A shift away from the feminist challenge to previously 'taken for granted' perspectives on sexuality is evident in some of the current focus on pleasure. A number of feminists, strongly influenced by sexual liberation perspectives and/or psychoanalysis, argue that there has been too much emphasis on danger and too little on pleasure in recent feminist theory and practice.[43] The issues raised by other feminists, namely that 'pleasure' is a problematic concept for women in a context in which for many men pleasure coincides with endangering women and where male ideology encourages women to see fear, pain and power over others as potentially pleasurable, are seldom directly addressed. These theorists seem to want to reassert the western emphasis on sex as the most important site of pleasure that many feminists questioned in the early 1970s. The sexual liberationist influence is evident in the assertion that women have a 'right' to 'pleasure'.[44] The concept of a 'rights' and the unproblematic usage of terms such as 'pleasure' and 'desire' represent a return to an individualistic stance and the implicit suggestion that we possess fundamental characteristics which can be abstracted from social circumstances.

Social control

Feminist analysis of power and sexuality leads to an understanding that social control is the purpose, and may also be the outcome, of gendered social relations. The threat and reality of sexual violence may result in women developing strategies for self-protection which result in apparently voluntary limitations of mobility, territory and encounters. It is also the case, however, that the threat and reality of sexual violence may prompt both individual and collective resistance to men's power.

Betsy Stanko's recent discussion of women's greater fear of crime extends the focus on the threat of rape to the many forms of sexual violence women experience and/or fear.[45] She shows how women's lives are structured around personal safety and is currently researching the range of 'precautionary strategies' which women employ. Whilst not all women live in constant fear, many of women's routine decisions and behaviour are almost automatic measures taken to protect themselves from potential sexual violence. Michele Cliff describes the constant presence of the threat of sexual violence in women's lives as 'the force that does not kill' and likens women's lives to a state of siege.[46]

A number of feminists have used the terms terrorism and/or colonization to describe the impact on women's lives of sexual violence.[47] Kathleen Barry's analysis in *Female Sexual Slavery* demonstrates how her definition of sexual slavery, developed whilst studying forced prostitution, applies equally to a range of forms of sexual violence.

Female sexual slavery is present in *all* situations where women or girls cannot change the immediate conditions of their existence; where regardless of how they got into those conditions they cannot get out; and where they are subject to sexual violence and exploitation.[48]

She stresses that her use of the term 'slavery' is not rhetorical but, describes 'an objective social condition of sexual exploitation and violence'. Like Catharine MacKinnon, she defines male control of female sexuality as the foundation of patriarchal societies and the result of this is sex colonization.

Female sexual slavery, in all its forms, is the mechanism for controlling women through the sex-is-power ethic, either directly through enslavement or indirectly using enslavement as a threat held over all other women. This is the generalized condition of sex colonization. Enslavement or potential slavery is rarely seen as such by either its aggressors/potential aggressors or by its victims/potential victims. That is the subtlety of long-term sex colonization.[49]

Jill Radford, in developing the analysis of how sexual violence functions as a form of social control, has called it a form of policing.[50] She argues that much of men's interaction with women involves routine behaviour of the type that characterizes police work: watching, supervising, segregating and changing women's behaviour. The state's role in policing women is, in her view, residual, confined to defining the limits of acceptable behaviour and deciding which women are legitimate targets for male sexual aggression. MacKinnon, on the other hand, sees the state as having a critical role in western patriarchal societies where, she maintains, it has become an institutionalized agency of male control over women.[51]

Social control is a predominant theme in much of the sociology of deviance, attention in the main being directed at the role of state agencies in defining deviance and implementing law and order and control policies to police the population. Stephen Pfhol's 'power-reflexive view' is a good examples of the radical perspective which argues that deviance is socially constructed and usually contains within it some form of resistance to the prevailing power relations: 'Deviants never exist except in relation to those who seek to control them . . . they only exist in opposition to those they threaten and those who have enough power to control against such theats.'[52]

Feminist analysis of sexual violence presents this perspective with some difficult questions: specifically, who defines deviance, who has power to control, and whether abusive men are the agents rather than objects of social control. Men's actions are often defined by women as abusive without being reported or labelled as such by anyone else, yet women do not have the power to control either the threat or reality of sexual violence. Feminists understand that social control is men's purpose when using sexual violence against women, a process in which the failure of state agencies to define such behaviour as 'crime' is implicated.

Despite arguing for a more complex and interactive analysis of power, Pfohl's fails to apply this to gender relations, resulting in the all too familiar refusal to accept the culpability of abusive men for their actions: 'The violent spouse is likewise understood as harvesting centuries of structurally denied power through an explosive personal search for physical power over another body.'[53] The obvious fact that women have been excluded from structural power to a far greater extent that men is conventiently ignored, as is the fact that individual violent men, and men as a group, may benefit, at least in the short-term, from their use of violence.

The inherent problem in this type of analysis resides in the political nature of deviance being defined only in terms of challenge to the powerful and in a liberal refusal to name any behaviour as inherently 'morally' or 'ethically' wrong. Both sexual and racial violence are attempts to maintain, rather than challenge, existing power relations; both demonstrate that social control is not the monopoly of the state and both ought to be unacceptable forms of behaviour in any society.

Specifying the links between forms of sexual violence

One of the primary aims of my research has been to explore the links between different forms of sexual violence, and this concern underlies the discussions in later chapters on sexual violence as a continuum and on how women define, resist, cope with and survive their experiences. Here I want to use two examples to demonstrate these connections: the similarity of both the myths and stereotypes surrounding forms of sexual violence and of the institutional responses to abused women and girls.

Male ideology surrounding discussion of sexual violence was a focus of challenge for feminists in the early 1970s. Yet the ideas within that ideology remain widely held: a backdrop against which women make sense of their experience and within which much public discussion and response takes place. Mildred Daley Pagelow notes that the common-sense ideas and stereotypes about rape and domestic violence are 'so similar that the names of the crimes could often be transposed without loss of meaning.'[54] Table 2:1 illustrates how a number of these common-sense ideas apply across rape, domestic violence and incest.

These somewhat simplified examples highlight a number of commonalities which can easily be extended to other forms of sexual violence. They function to minimize the assaults, as does defining obscene phone calls, sexual harassment and flashing as 'minor'. They reveal underlying attitudes which may have as much impact on how women see their own experiences as on how others respond. The first two myths imply that women either want or deserve the violence they experience, and they combine with the fifth and sixth myths to remove responsibility from men for their actions. The third and sixth myths make individual histories the explanation of violence and suggest that its incidence is restricted to certain types of personality and/or particular social groups. The fourth, and to some extent the first two, deny that an offence has occurred. The fifth suggests that women/girls could easily prevent sexual violence, either through their own resistance or in the case of repeated assaults by the same man by making an official report.

These ideas combine, interact and lead to stereotypes of which men commit sexual violence, which women/girls it occurs to, at the same time as offering a form of causal explanation. They may

Table 2.1   Common myths and stereotypes about sexual
violence

Myth	Rape	Incest/sexual abuse	Domestic violence
1 They enjoy/ want it.	It wasn't rape only 'rough sex'. Women say no when they mean yes. Some women enjoy rape.	Girls get pleasure from it. They don't object so they must like it. If it happens more than once they must want it to.	Some women are masochistic, seeking out violent men. Women don't leave so it can't be that bad.
2 They ask for/deserve it.	Women provoke by the way they dress, by 'leading men on'. They take risks by going out alone, accepting lifts.	Girls are seductive or precocious.	Women provoke men by nagging, not fulfilling household 'duties', refusing sex.
3 It only happens to certain types of women/in certain kinds of families.	Women who live in poor areas; women who are sexually active; women who take risks; women who have previously been abused.	Girls who come from problem families; large families; isolated rural families; girls who are precocious; whose mothers were abused.	Working-class women; women who are 'bad' housewives; women who saw or experienced violence as children.
4 They tell lies/ exaggerate.	Women make false reports for revenge, to protect their 'reputation'.	Girls fantasize about incest, accuse men of sexual abuse to get attention.	It wasn't violence only a fight. Women exaggerate to get a quick divorce.

Table 2.1 (continued)

Myth	Rape	Incest/sexual abuse	Domestic violence
5 If they had resisted they could have prevented it.	An unwilling woman cannot be raped. If there are no bruises she must have consented.	They should/ could have told someone.	If they had fought back it would stop the man, they are abused because they are weak and passive. They should have reported it.
6 The men who do it are sick, ill, under stress, out of control.	Abuse of alcohol/drugs, mental instability, childhood experiences cause men to act violently.		
	Hostility to women. Psycho-sexual dysfunction	Wife not sexually available. Deviant sexual arousal. Abused as a child.	Witnessed or experienced abuse as a child. Pressure of work/ unemployment.

deny the violence, normalize it or pathologize the offender and/or the abused woman, resulting in both the deflection of responsibility from men and the denial of women's experience. The impact of these ideas on women is further explored in chapter 6 in relation to defining sexual violence and in chapter 8 in relation to self-blame. Their influence is also evident in the response of the legal system and statutory agencies to women or girls who have been abused.

Linda Holmstrom's and Ann Burgess' study of 146 women and girls who reported rape to a US hospital emergency room provides an excellent illustration of this last point.[55] They maintain that both the response of the police and the decision to prosecute by the district attorney were directly related to stereotypes about rape. In the rapes of adult women, cases were prosecuted if the woman had been forced to go with the rapist, if she was a virgin, if she was 'emotionally stable', if she appeared 'upset' when the rape was reported, if the rapist was a stranger, if a weapon was used by the rapist, and if there were other charges against the rapist. Cases tended to be dropped if the women was perceived to have 'taken risks', if she had gone with the rapist willingly, if she was unmarried but sexually experienced, if she had emotional problems, if she was calm when making the report, and if she knew her rapist. These same attitudes informed the responses of most of the medical staff who saw their role as discovering if a 'real rape' had occurred. In the 18 trials that resulted from the 146 reports, many of the myths and stereotypes in table 2.1 were used to discredit the woman's testimony.

The pattern that Holmstorm and Burgess documented, of stereotypes surrounding rape resulting in cases being filtered out of the criminal justice system at each stage so that only a small proportion of reported assaults result in charges being made and even fewer result in convictions, has been confirmed by a number of US and Canadian studies and in a recent UK research project.[56] Cases of domestic violence are screened out early on in the process through police practice of minimizing assaults through defining them as 'domestic disputes'. Police practice in the UK and the USA has been based on a policy of mediation rather than one of law enforcement.[57] In the few cases that do reach the courts in the UK, small fines are the usual penalty.[58] Whilst the occurrence of an assault is acknowledged, it is defined as unimportant. Similarly, throughout the 1983 parliamentary debate on the death penalty, there was an insistence that domestic murder is of a different order to murder in the public sphere; the comments of members of parliament reflected a common understanding that domestic terrorism and domestic murder are less serious crimes, and less deserving of severe penalty, than international terrorism or murder in the streets.

New strategies developed in the USA to deal with incestuous abuse have provided a further route away from prosecution. It has become common practice that the courts mandate therapeutic treatment, often for the whole family. Where treatment programmes are completed, all criminal charges are dropped. This model has found powerful supporters in the UK.[59] In the USA, similar 'diversion programmes' are in use in relation to domestic violence.[60] Feminist campaigning to get assaults on women and girls treated as crimes have resulted in adaptation within the legal system and the establishment of new routes away from criminal prosecution.

Several writers have suggested that rape is the only crime for which 'provocation' is an acceptance defence. Documentation of recent UK cases of domestic murder and domestic violence have shown that in these cases too 'provocation' is common as a mitigating plea.[61] The supportive work of the London-based Incest Survivors Campaign has involved attending court cases. They too observed that provocation by the girl, or her mother, was accepted as evidence in mitigation of the abusive man's responsibility.[62] Here the idea that women or girls 'ask for' abuse is elevated to a legal concept. Further research is needed to establish just how widespread the use, and acceptability, of pleas of provocation are in cases of sexual violence that reach the courts.

Many research projects have revealed similarities, across both a range of agencies and a number of countries, in the way in which women who have been abused are responded to. Two themes predominate: a failure to recognize sexual violence or, if its occurrence is known, a failure to respond appropriately with support, advice and, where necessary, protection.[63] Two groups of researchers, one based in the UK and one in the USA, have argued that the lack of training, results in workers falling back on the common myths and stereotypes outlined above.[64] The influence of these ideas on practice is immense. The inadequate response of statutory agencies has been researched in most detail in relation to domestic violence. In every study which has included questions on help-seeking, women's dissatisfaction with the 'help' they receive is evident.[65] The extent, severity and impact of violence is not taken seriously, and the many barriers which make leaving abusive relationships difficult are often ignored. Responses tend to consist of suggesting ways in which the woman might change her behaviour rather than of any attempt to challenge, let alone change, the behaviour of violent men.

A network of feminist services for women and girls who have been abused has emerged in many countries precisely because of the inadequacies in the responses of statutory agencies and the extent to which myths and stereotypes are reflected in their practice. Alongside these alternative services, campaigning work challenging definitions, myths and stereotypes has been undertaken to encourage change in public attitudes and practice within statutory agencies.

Towards a feminist definition of sexual violence

A considerable amount of attention has been paid in feminist writing and campaigning to challenging limited definitions of particular forms of sexual violence. Kathleen Barry's definition of 'female sexual slavery' is, however, one of very few attempts to link a number of forms of sexual violence within a broader definition. It does not, however, cover all possible forms of sexual violence as it is intentionally limited to situations where women are trapped in relationships or situations where they are repeatedly violated.

One way of developing a feminist definition is to examine the range of behaviour that feminists have included within the category of violence in the light of the dictionary definition of the word. The *Oxford English Dictionary* defines violence as involving damage to the self. The damage may be physical, emotional, psychological and/or material. Violation can be of the body, of the mind or of trust. The exercise of violence involves the denial of the victims' will and autonomy. Interestingly, this definition emphasizes the impact on the person violated, making little reference to the imputed intentions of the violator.

Clearly, acts committed by individual men which result in physical, emotional and/or psychological damage are covered by this definition. It is also possible to include institutional or socio-structural factors. Miriam Hirsch, for example, includes medical violence in her book on male violence.[66] She sees male control of the medical profession as denying women autonomy and resulting in particular forms of abuse that damage women physically and emotionally. The recent discussion of 'the feminization of poverty' raises the possibility of defining gendered economic deprivation as violence which results in material damage.[67] Whilst the dictionary definition could accommodate a wide range of actions on the individual and societal levels within the category of violence against women, such a wide definition is likely to prove less than helpful in developing feminist analysis. All forms of male power, individual and institutional, are potentially definable as violence.

I intend to explore a definition in terms of the conjunction of the words sexual and violence (see also chapter 5). Kathleen Barry herself begins from this premise in a more recent article.

'Crimes against women are defined as those acts of violence which are directed at women because of their female sexual definition.' However, in her development of this theme she arrives at a much more limited definition than is implied in the first sentence: 'In committing a crime against women, sexual satisfaction, usually in the form of orgasm, is one of the intended outcomes of sexual violence for the aggressor who unites sex and violence to subdue, humiliate, degrade and terrorize his female victim.'[68] Here sexual violence is restricted to only those forms of abuse where ejaculation is possible or intended, where power is used to get sex. Like Sue Wise and Liz Stanley, I would argue that much sexual violence uses sex to get power.[69]

Dorothy Klein maintains that a feminist definition of sexual violence must distance itself from legal codes which focus on the extreme and less frequent forms of violence, thereby obscuring 'the subtler and more pervasive forms of abuse of women which are woven into the fabric of our society'.[70] Cross-culturally, words describing women's bodies or sexuality are often used as insults, often containing associations with hurt and devaluation.[71] Sandra Bartky maintains that language and images which portray women as inferior are the result of stereotyping, cultural domination and sexual objectification.[72] She notes that such attitudes and images are habitually used in everyday life and function to deny women autonomy; there are few places where women are safe from threat, insult or affront.

The social meaning of pornography and whether or not it constitutes a form of sexual violence has been the most contested aspect of the analysis of violence against women within feminism.[73] In fact, the debate has focused less on the content and meaning of pornography and more on its importance as an issue and the strategies some feminists have suggested for opposing it.[74] Whatever an individual feminist's perspective on these issues, few dispute that pornography presents women as objects available to be acted upon by men and as enjoying rape or coercive sex. It is also incontrovertible that the pornography industry has grown rapidly over the past ten years. Within this debate, however, there is disagreement about how pornography should be analysed.

Andrea Dworkin and Robin Morgan argue that pornography represents the ideology of patriarchal domination.[75] This analysis is premised on seeing men's attempts to control women's sexuality as the fundamental basis of patriarchy. Feminists who question this analysis are likely to see women's place in the social organization of production and reproduction as the determining factor in women's subordination. Elizabeth Wilson, for example, questions the connection between pornographic images and acts of sexual violence implicit in Robin Morgan's phrase 'pornography is the theory, rape is the practice'.[76] Much recent feminist opposition to pornography has, however, focused on the fact that, whether or not causal connections between it and acts of sexual violence can be proven, it constitutes a form of sexual violence in itself.

To complicate the issue of definition further, a feminist definition must be sensitive to woman's perceptions and understandings. Whilst the definition I have come to is rather lengthy, it does attempt to reflect both the extent and range of sexual violence and to include women's perceptions within it. Sexual violence includes *any physical, visual, verbal or sexual act that is experienced by the woman or girl, at the time or later, as a threat, invasion or assault, that has the effect of hurting her or degrading her and/or takes away her ability to control intimate contact.*

More connections

Feminist analysis sees all forms of sexual violence as involving the exercise of power, functioning as a form of social control by denying women freedom and autonomy. Men's power over women in patriarchal societies results in men assuming rights of sexual access to and intimacy with women and in certain levels of force, coercion or abuse being seen as justified. This theoretical analysis was shared by many of the women interviewed, an illustration of how feminist analysis arises out of women's experience.

'It seems very much tied up with the power that men have over women. It is a sexual power because that's the difference between us and it's that they abuse. There's something about the kind of communication that goes on in sexual relationships that I think is different. Like, with a friendship, I can't imagine anyone resorting to violence.'

'I'm sure it's to do with keeping control and keeping power. I suppose most men consider it their right to be able to take sexual pleasure.'

'It's a matter of men wanting to prove that they have power over women . . . or that they do have power and showing that they can do as they please.'

'There's something about relationships with men, about me needing to be placatory, expecting or fearing a lot more pressure to change or to be a certain way, and that only had to be reinforced once or twice for that pressure to be there.'

Sexual violence as I have defined it is a major factor limiting women's options and choices. Heterosexual relationships and encounters are the site where many women experience patriarchal oppression most directly and intensely; they are also a site of resistance and struggle. Marilyn Frye defines oppression in the following way:

something pressed is something caught between or among forces and barriers which are so related to each other that jointly they restrain, restrict and prevent the thing's motion or mobility . . . Women are caught like this, too, by a network of forces and barriers that expose one to penalty, loss or contempt.[77]

3

The knowledge explosion: an overview of previous research

If I had begun this research project in 1987 the thought of reviewing the existing literature on sexual violence would have produced mild hysteria. Since the late 1970s there has been a 'knowledge explosion' – an explosion which might be unfamiliar to many readers in Europe as it has occurred primarily in the USA and much of the evidence for it can only be found in journals available through university libraries. Traces of it can, however, be discerned elsewhere: in the surveys conducted by several British women's magazines, in numerous articles reporting on new findings and innovative policy approaches in magazines like *New Society* and *Community Care* and professional journals including the British police's *The Job*. Concrete examples of the remarkable shift in the USA include: the establishment of governmental agencies on rape and domestic violence;[1] publication of proceedings of federal and state investigations and hearings and commissioned research;[2] the existence of research units specializing in this area;[3] and the establishment in the 1980s of two academic journals, *Violence and Victims* and *Sexual Coercion and Assault: Issues and Perspectives*.

This knowledge explosion is one concrete result of feminist insistence that sexual violence is an important public issue. There are indisputable connections between the raising of issues within the Women's Liberation Movement, a feminist response (campaigns and the provision of services for abused women and girls), and the subsequent increase in publication of popular books on the topic, articles in newspapers and magazines, the issues appearing on television and within films, the commissioning of research, and institutional change such as law reform and revised agency practice. The number, extent and time-scale of these changes and the sequence in which particular forms of violence become public issues have, however, varied in different countries.

The outcome of this dramatic shift is that for each form of sexual violence there now exist ever-increasing amounts of papers and books based on empirical research, reviews and comment- aries, theoretical perspectives, and specialist discussions of legal and/or treatment responses. Since this would be impossible to reflect in a single chapter, I intend to offer the reader an overview of the knowledge explosion in research on rape, domestic violence, incest and child sexual abuse, and point to some of ways in which research findings and perspectives have been influential outside academia. As research on each area has a specific history, each will be discussed separately but in relation to common themes: offenders; experience; incidence; attitudes; agency response; and avoidance and prevention. Studies of the immediate and long-term impact of sexual violence are reviewed in chapters 7 and 8.

The majority of recent studies originate in the USA. Whilst I will highlight research done in the UK, it should be understood that far less has been undertaken there. Moreover, the studies that are available remain at a preliminary stage, thus cross- cultural comparisons are problematic. It is even more difficult to make comparisons with other countries, either because there is minimal published research or because that which does exist is not publicly accessible.

Whilst ploughing my way through what now fills a four-drawer filing cabinet, three book shelves and a card-index system with almost 2,000 entries, I began to notice that particular ideas or statements within individual articles were taken up, almost without question, by later writers. In one sense this is not surprising as most research projects refer explicitly to previous studies, attempting to replicate, extend or challenge them. But what I noticed was more than this. I suspected they were examples of what Richard Gelles has called the 'Woozle Effect': 'Simple empirical results or statements are repeated by many authors until the statement or finding gains the status of a "law", without so much as a single bit of additional data being collected.'[4] In order to trace this process I developed a method for listing all the empirical studies of specific forms of sexual violence in chronological tables. Within each table, summaries of methods, size and source of sample, links to previous and later studies and theoretical framework were recorded. Whilst initially done on paper, the tables were transferred onto a computer database using a spreadsheet program.[5] This method enabled me to explore examples of the 'Woozle Effect' and note shifts in research topics, methods and theoretical frameworks. The method and the computer software represent a useful resource to anyone wishing to analyse a body of literature systematically.

Research on rape

Until 1970 there were few published studies on rape, and the majority of what existed focused on rapists. The increased attention to rape followed publication of several sociological studies and the politicization of rape by feminists. One response of the US government to feminist campaigning was to sponsor research and the majority of US studies I will refer were funded by one of three federal bodies. This availability of funding is, therefore, a determining factor in the dramatic increase in research (on all forms of sexual violence) in the USA. A cynical reading of the knowledge explosion would attribute a causal role to research dollars rather than to any increase in understanding or concern amongst non-feminist academics.

During much of the 1970s, three main topic areas predominated in research on rape: women's experience of and response to rape; attitudes to rape; and how the criminal justice system responds to and processes rape reports. By the late 1970s, four other specific areas were increasingly being addressed: incidence; the long-term effects of rape; marital rape; and male sexual aggression.

Offenders

Pre-1970, and some current, studies of convicted rapists reflect an interest amongst criminologists, psychiatrists and sexologists in sex offenders and sexual 'deviance'; the main question posed by the latter two groups being which type of offender/offence was 'sickest'. Rapists were, in fact, seen as the most 'normal', as rape is not defined as a deviant sexual orientation (as compared to, for example, child molestation or exhibitionism). Much of this research has involved the use of psychological tests in order to construct 'personality types' characteristic of men who commit particular offences. Typologies are then presented in which aspects of personality are seen to constitute causal explanations of offenders' actions.[6] In most of these studies a psychoanalytic framework underlies the analysis (many of the authors were in fact clinicians reporting on their own patient populations), rape being conceptualized as an individualistic act, a symptom of an underlying psychopathology. The most frequent explanation proffered is that rapists are 'weak and inadequate' men, revenging themselves on women by whom they feel dominated.[7] The rapist's mother and/or wife is often accorded a determinate role in creating the personality problems which 'cause' men to rape.[8]

Whilst there have been some methodological improvements in research on convicted rapists, the medical/psychoanalytic approach still characterizes much research. For example, one recent approach uses controlled psychological tests and experiments directed towards finding 'objective measures of the urge to rape' or evidence of 'deviant sexual arousal'.[9] Commentaries on the study of convicted rapists have pointed to the inadequacies of this framework. Findings are often contradictory and inconsistent.[10] Whilst intending to arrive at a definitive 'rapist profile', there are now over 50 subtypes of rapist within the literature.[11] Finally, there has been a singular failure to isolate any pattern of personality characteristics or life experiences which are causally linked to rape.[12]

These inadequacies are even more glaring when one takes into account the non-representativeness of convicted rapists. Conviction is likely to be confounded by many other factors (for example, race, class, previous convictions, the nature of the assault). Daniel Smithyman has undertaken the only study of undetected rapists, although women's testimony and the studies of sexual aggression also provide data in this area.[13] The men Smithyman interviewed came from a much broader socioeconomic range than the prison population and their justifications and explanations turned much more on their own 'needs' and gratification. Few felt either remorse or that their actions had had negative impacts on their life or their self-image. The implications of the tunnel vision of researchers who limit their studies to convicted rapists can be further illustrated by the failure of the 'deviant sexual arousal' school to account for the substantial numbers of their control groups who are aroused by rape depictions or to relate their findings to a series of similar experiments with male college students which founds that a substantial percentage were aroused by rape depictions.[14] The fact that a substantial proportion of the male population appear to have 'deviant sexual arousal patterns' needs to be addressed and explained.

There are, however, a few researchers who have gone beyond the medical/psychoanalytic framework. Diana Scully and Joseph Marolla suggest that the accounts of convicted rapists should be viewed as 'vocabularies of motive'.

[Convicted rapists] have learned the attitudes and actions consistent with sexual aggression against women. Learning also includes the acquisition of culturally derived vocabularies of motive, which can be used to diminish responsibility and to negotiate a non-deviant identity.[15]

They are critical of research which fails to problematize rapist's accounts, arguing that this merely reinforces 'the vocabulary of motive that rapists use to excuse and justify their behaviour'.

Nicholas Groth is the only medically trained researcher who has developed a broader social explanation of rapists' actions in terms of power and control.[16] It is probably not a coincidence that he was involved in collaborative work with Ann Burgess and Linda Holmstrom who were studying the impact of rape on women. He has also highlighted one example of the 'Woozle Effect' with regard to studies of convicted rapists: that they are not recidivists. He maintains that this 'fact' is recreated by defining recidivism as repeated conviction for the same crime, thus making an untenable assumption that all rapes are reported and all reports result in conviction.[17] Groth asked two groups of convicted offenders (rapists of adult women and child molesters) in a confidential questionnaire to record any offences for which they had not been convicted or which had not been detected; 55 per cent of the sample admitted an average of five other offences. He regards this as an underestimation!

There has been little sociological study of rapists, and most of the studies to date have attempted to demonstrate that rapists are different to the majority of the male population. The direction of future research must focus on the prevalence of rape and coercive sex and recognize that the majority of rapists are not convicted.

The experience of rape

The publication of Menachem Amir's *Patterns in Forcible Rape* in 1971 marked the emergence of sociological studies of rape which also took account of the victimized woman.[18] His Durkheimian methodology has been seriously challenged as the patterns he discusses are based on the treatment of police records as 'social facts'. For example, there is no discussion of why cases are 'unfounded' (a US legal term, sometimes called 'no-criming', meaning that detectives decide that the reported events are not to be recorded as crimes). Nor is the possibility that there may be important differences between rapes which are reported to the police and those which are not acknowledged.

Amir was also much influenced by victimology, investigating the victims' role in crime. Perhaps the most influential, and most criticized, aspect of his analysis is his use of the concept of 'victim precipitation'. Drawing on Wolfgang's study of homicide[19] but, unlike this work, failing to offer a clear definition or statistical evidence to support his claim, Amir concludes that 19 per cent of the rapes in his sample were 'victim precipitated'. He then compares these rapes to the larger group. This is a circular explanation; the factors which distinguish the two groups are the ones used to define victim precipitation in the first place. Linda Curtis, using FBI records and a wide definition of 'victim precipitation', could only place 4 per cent of rapes under this heading.[20] Very few researchers since 1975 have suggested that women provoke rape.

Ann Burgess' and Linda Holmstrom's *Rape: Victims of Crisis*, Diana Russell's *The Politics of Rape* and Pauline Bart's 'Rape doesn't end with a kiss' mark the emergence of a body of research, informed by feminism, which draws primarily on women's experience of rape.[21] From these studies, and many others that were to follow, a picture emerged of the 'facts' of rape: the range of circumstances in which it occurred; the nature of the assaults, including the use of force and weapons and the sexual acts women were forced to engaged in; the relationship of the rapist to the woman; and the immediate impact on women. Just as convicted rapists are not 'typical' rapists, it has become increasingly obvious that reported rapes are not 'typical' rapes. As studies increasingly used either random samples or samples of women who had never reported their rape to any agency, it became clear that women were far more likely to be raped by someone they knew than attacked by a stranger.[22]

Burgess' and Holmstrom's work is significant in two respects. It was based on a hospital crisis programme and the sample of women and girls have been followed for over five years. The three books and numerous articles published to date represent the largest output from a single project in the field, in which the legal process, theoretical issues, and the long-term impact of rape have been discussed.[23] However, the enduring legacy of their work has been their development of a three-phase model of response to rape first proposed in 1970.[24] Despite academic criticism on methodological and conceptual grounds,[25] the 'Rape Trauma Syndrome' and the treatment responses Burgess and Holmstrom suggested have been the basis of much crisis provision since the book was published. The influence of their work can be illustrated by two examples. First, it has resulted in an increased recognition by the police and medical profession, at least in the USA, that there is no one immediate reaction to rape. Prior to Burgess' and Holmstrom's demonstration that women may respond in a 'controlled' way, women reporting rape who did not display visible distress were assumed to be lying. Second, discussion of the 'Rape Trauma Syndrome' has become an accepted part of expert testimony in court cases, again primarily in the USA, including those where women take revenge on their rapists.

As the findings on the 'facts' of rape accumulate, it has been increasingly suggested that there may be important differences in women's experience of rape. One group of researchers propose differences between adolescents and adults[26] although their findings have been disputed.[27] Linda Davis and Nicholas Groth suggest that rape of older women tends to be accompanied by extreme physical violence.[28] Increasing attention is being paid to how class and race inequalities affect women's experience of and response to rape.[29] One researcher has suggested that sexual orientation has implications for women's response to rape; he found that lesbians blamed the man whereas heterosexual women tended to blame themselves.[30] Studies are also emerging on the incidence and effects of multiple experiences of rape,[31] and on how women manage to resist and avoid rape.[32]

Incidence

Estimates of the incidence of rape have, for the most part, been based on official reports or victimization studies. Studies specifically designed to investigate the prevalence of rape in random groups of women have only been undertaken in recent years. Two such studies, using self-administered questionnaires with samples of women college students, recorded prevalence rates of 10.2 per cent and 26.2 per cent. The latter study also recorded a 25 per cent incidence for attempted rape.[33] Lower figures emerged from two telephone surveys with representative samples of women: 8.2 per cent and 5 per cent.[34] Ruth Hall's is the only published UK incidence study.[35] It involved a self-administered questionnaire completed by 1,236 women and recorded prevalence figures of 17 per cent for rape and 20 per cent for attempted rape. The highest figures, 41 per cent of a random sample of women experiencing rape or attempted rape, are contained in Diana Russell's research.[36] She has suggested that the disparity in findings are attributable to methodological differences. She is not simply referring here to the merits or otherwise of surveys or face to face interviews but also to the attention researchers pay to the wording of questions (see chapter 1).

One particular application of incidence findings has been the calculation of rape rates. Whilst acknowledging the limitations of their data-base (US victimization surveys), two researchers have made important contributions to this area of research.[37] Both reject the previous basis of calculation (10,000 of the general population, that is, including men), insisting that calculations of rape rates must be based on the population at risk: women and girls. Both conclude that, on the basis of their data, US women who were 16 at the time of their analysis have a 20 to 30 per cent risk of experiencing rape or attempted rape in their lifetime. Diana Russell, using empirical data from her own random sample, suggests that the risk is closer to 40 per cent.

Attitudes to rape

The studies of attitudes to rape are extensive and the majority draw on methods and theoretical perspectives (attribution theory and Just World theory) from within social psychology. The predominant method involves written vignettes, audio tapes or videos in which certain variables are altered, particularly the status of the woman and the circumstances of the assault. Statistical factor analysis is used to assess the importance of variables in relation to allocation of responsibility for the assault.[38] Samples are overwhelmingly students but two studies have extended the method to other populations.[39] In many of these projects, attitude to women and attitude to sexuality scales are also used. Despite contradictory findings on variables such as the woman's attractiveness, some common findings have emerged. Men tend to blame the raped woman more than women do, and victim-blame and believing myths about rape are linked to traditional attitudes to women and sexuality.

Like most research on rape, little conceptual or theoretical development has emerged from these studies. Few researchers have reflected on the limitations of the methods used, whether in fact they do tap attitudes to rape. This area of research is basically examining underlying definitions of, and ideologies surrounding, rape – the process by which women become 'legitimate victims'[40] – but these issues are seldom addressed directly.

Agency response

Whilst there is a considerable literature, particularly from the USA, documenting innovations in medical and counselling provision, research has been limited to assessing how the criminal justice system (police and courts) responds to and processes rape reports. Studies using a variety of samples and methodologies have reached the same conclusions. Rape cases are systematically 'screened out' (dropped) at each stage of their investigation, from the recording of the rape as a crime through to sentencing. The explanations offered are also similar, hinging on the perceived likelihood of successful prosecution. These judgements reflect 'common-sense' assumptions about rape victims and offenders and where and how rape takes place. For example, rapes by strangers in which a weapon is used and the woman resists are far more likely to be prosecuted.[41] A recent Scottish study reached similar conclusions.[42]

One study estimated the likelihood of reported rapes in the USA resulting in a conviction for rape: less than 15 per cent of recorded rapes reach trial and only one per cent result in conviction for rape (14 per cent are acquittals or are plea-bargained to a lesser offence).[43] As estimates of the percentage of actual rapes that are reported range from 4 per cent to 40 per cent, this means that *one rapist in 250 to 2500 is convicted*. Given the stress on the extent of under-reporting, it is surprising that few projects have addressed this question directly. Evidence from the USA and UK, however, suggests that women do not report rape because they have little faith and trust in the police or courts, they fear being blamed, and/or their immediate reaction to rape is to try to forget the assault.[44] Women who report do so out of fear, because they want the rapist caught and punished, and/or because they told someone who encouraged (or insisted) on reporting.[45]

Despite the reform of rape laws in many US states in response to feminist criticism of the definition of rape, standards of proof required and treatment of women in court cases, only two projects have attempted to assess their impact.[46] Both suggest that, in terms of conviction rates, the changes have had little effect. No assessment has been made of whether or not women's experience of the court process has been affected.

Avoidance and prevention

Three feminist researchers have examined attempted rapes in terms of rape avoidance, shifting attention from the man's 'attempt' to the woman's successful resistance.[47] Whilst finding that women who resist immediately, use 'active' methods of resistance (running away, physical resistance and screaming) and that multiple strategies have a greater chance of avoiding rape, all conclude that there is no single resistance strategy which assures avoidance. Pauline Bart and Patricia O'Brien point out that in their study no woman who was attacked by a man she knew avoided rape.

Marital rape

Research into marital rape is one of the few direct links between research on rape and domestic violence as much of the evidence comes from research on battered women.[48] All of these studies record a substantial incidence of marital rape within groups of women physically abused by male partners. Four studies have examined the incidence of marital rape in random samples of women and findings range between 7 per cent and 12 per cent.[49] Most of these researchers suggest that marital rape may be the most common form of rape, and that it is particularly likely to occur when the woman is being battered by her male partner.

Male sexual aggression

Recent research on male sexual aggression has developed both out of research on rape and the work of Eugene Kanin from 1957 on college student dating relationships.[50] He found a consistent proportion of men admitted sexually aggressive behaviour (20–25 per cent) and a larger proportion of women reported being offended against (50–60 per cent). This approach has recently been extended by two groups of feminist researchers through increased size of samples, inclusion of school students, and explicit linkage with research on rape.[51] As in Kanin's studies, the proportion of women reporting experiences of sexual aggression is higher than that of men admitting to such behaviour. Mary Koss presents a typology of male sexual aggression: of the sample of 1,846 male students, 22.4 per cent were 'sexually coercive' (using verbal coercion to obtain sex), 4.9 per cent 'sexually abusive' (using physical force to attempt to obtain sex), and 4.3 per cent 'sexually assaultive' (using physical force in obtaining sex). She and Kanin point to the implications of their findings for research on rapists. Both regard a percentage of their sample as 'undetected rapists' for whom the medical/psychopathology explanation of rape is inappropriate.

Mary Koss points out that her findings confirm that the double standard is alive and well and that men still view sex as an adversarial contest. Both suggestions are supported by other studies on dating which consistently report that men expect greater levels of intimacy sooner than women whilst also expecting women to set the limits on sexual intimacy within relationships. It is within this contradiction that many men construct their own limit beyond which women forfeit the right to say no.[52]

Unfortunately, this type of research has been limited to samples of US and Canadian school and college students. We do not know if the incidence of sexual aggression that women experience decreases or increases with age, whether or not it takes other forms, or whether or not women in other countries have similar experiences.

Research on incest and child sexual abuse

The literature on child sexual abuse, particularly incest, has a much longer history than that on other forms of sexual violence. This is partly accounted for by the interest of psychoanalysts and anthropologists in 'incest taboos'. These early influences are reflected in the emergence, and shifting of, dominant theoretical frameworks within which research findings are placed. A further contrast with research on rape and domestic violence is that there has been little development in the major themes of research, although there has been some increase in studies of incidence and the long-term effects of abuse.

Offenders

The research on offenders who abuse children follows a similar pattern to the study of rapists. The medical/psychopathological model again results in personality characteristics and/or individual life-experiences being cited as causes of abuse. The most common explanation is 'psychosexual immaturity'; the most recent a version of the cycle-of-violence theory whereby abuse in childhood is seen to account for abusive behaviour in adulthood.[53] The behaviour of wives is frequently seen as a determining factor, particularly where the offence is incest. However, as adult sex with children is defined as deviant, most researchers argue that offenders against children represent a specific deviant psychopathology. Supporting evidence is provided by experimental studies of arousal patterns in which stronger differences are found between convicted offenders and controls than in studies of rapists.[54] A plethora of typologies exist, the majority distinguishing between paedophiles (men whose sexual interest is restricted to children), child molesters (men whose sexual interest includes both children and adult women) and incest offenders.

The factors that have been invoked to explain child sexual abuse have resulted in a range of treatment strategies for convicted offenders including: masturbatory reconditioning;[55]

desensitization;[56] heterosocial skills training;[57] insight therapy;[58] and drug therapy.[59] None report outstanding success.

The major problem with all of the research to date is that, once again, samples are limited to convicted offenders. Convicted child abusers are likely to be the more compulsive and blatant offenders and/or those who have committed more 'extreme' offences (murder, rape or use of excessive force). The only study of undetected offenders is of paedophiles whose 'interest' was limited to boys[60] although there are some papers reporting on treatment programmes for unconvicted incest offenders.[61]

A 'Woozle Effect' finding has been highlighted. Many investigators maintain child abusers use far less physical violence than other groups of sex offenders. One study cross-checked offenders self-reports with court medical reports and found that 75 per cent seriously underestimated the violence that they had used.[62]

The experience of incest and child sexual abuse

Most pre-1970 reports of incest or sexual abuse studies contain inadequate descriptions of method and are based on small clinical samples, often drawn from case files. From 1900 to 1960, 40 frequently cited research reports on incest and/or child sexual abuse were published, originating from ten different countries. They either present case histories in a psychoanalytic framework or use court records and emphasize the causal significance of cultural factors such as overcrowding, rural traditions and 'low morals'.[63] The latter studies were primarily of poor European families. This 'cultural milieu' perspective lost favour as the prevalence of sexual abuse in all social groups was demonstrated.

During this period, a number of important papers were published which have had a great influence on later work. Lauretta Bender's and Abram Blau's 1937 paper was based on clinical interviews with 14 children in a psychiatric hospital ward and a follow-up study was published in 1952.[64] Three themes from these articles have set the terms of debate for later writers: the participation of the child; the lack of long-term negative effects; and the negative effect on children of having to appear in court.

The participation of children in abuse was a central theme in many of the articles published in the 1950s and 1960s. One of the

most revealing papers offers an explicit statement of how
'participation' is defined – more than one incident of abuse!
Thus, 60 per cent of the children are described as 'full
participants'.[65] Nineteen other studies transform the inability of
children to stop abuse into participation and complicity. Whilst
blaming of children has decreased, it is still evident in some
recent publications.[66]

The view that court appearances are damaging to the child is
inextricably linked to the insistence that the long-term impact of
the abuse itself is minimal; only four research reports are ever
quoted to support this latter argument.[67] With the exception of
the Kinsey study, they contain very small samples and make no
distinctions between the impact of flashing and that of rape or
prolonged incestuous abuse. Despite the fact that recent
research on rape and incest consistently reports serious negative
effects both at the time and over time (see chapter 8), some
experts still hold this view and still fail to distinguish between
forms of child sexual abuse:

The minimal damage attributable to most sexual encounters does not
justify extreme reactions . . . In particular, police questioning, appearances in court, family dissension and eventually perhaps the imprison-
ment of a parent, friend or relative to whom the child is strongly
attached are likely to be far more traumatic than the sexual incidents
themselves.[68]

This is another example of the 'Woozle Effect', not to mention
an explicit recommendation that criminal offences be ignored.
No study has been done on the effects of criminal investigation
on children and little attention has been given, until recently, to
making court procedures less distressing. The only study to
specifically address the impact of prosecution for incest found no
differences in the percentage of family break-ups between two
US counties with radically different prosecution policies.[69]

A 1954 study of 11 children referred by the court for
psychological assessment produced further themes that have
informed research to the present day.[70] Family dynamics are
presented as the causal mechanism in incest; fear of separation
unites the whole family in complicity. The mother is depicted as
'dependent and infantile', sexually rejecting her husband and
'unconsciously participating' in the abuse. Abusive fathers have
had 'emotionally deprived and chaotic childhoods'. Each of these

statements is repeated in many later works. Norman Lustig and his colleagues use six case studies to locate these ideas within a functionalist analysis of incest.[71] Incest is a 'family survival pattern' in response to family dysfunction. The sentence beginning to final paragraph is of crucial importance: 'The mother appeared the cornerstone of the pathological family' – it appears in many subsequent articles as a proven 'fact'.

Lustig's article marks a number of important developments in the research literature: emphasis shifts from child sexual abuse to incest; family dynamics rapidly becomes the dominant theoretical framework; and the collusion of mothers replaces the participation of children as a predominant theme. Incest becomes a symptom of another, more significant problem: family dysfunction in which mothers play a pivotal role. This framework has so dominated research on incest that its influence is discernible in recent feminist analyses which focus on male power and control. Marie De Young states: 'Incest is a product of family pathology, and except on the rarest occasions all family members contribute in some way.'[72] Judith Herman maintains that the single factor which distinguished families in which father's were seductive from ones where they were abusive was the behaviour and health of mothers.[73]

David Finkelhor notes that this perspective is based on two premises of family-systems theory: the danger of cross-generational alliances and that all family members collude in family pathology.[74] One review of the literature suggests that the family dynamics approach itself could be seen as an example of the 'Woozle Effect': 'Descriptions of incest families suggest more opinion and less observations, more conclusions than demonstrations of methods used to collect information or support conclusions.'[75]

Whilst many have commented on the controlling and dominant personality of the abusive fathers, describing them as 'domestic tyrants' or 'patriarchs',[76] these observations have not been considered important in explanations of incest until the publication of feminist studies in the late 1970s. Instead, following Lustig, mothers have been the focus of discussion and husbands' descriptions of their wives are often unproblematically presented as research 'findings'. For example, Bruce Cormier suggests that incest is the logical outcome of mothers 'frigid, hostile, unloving' behaviour.[77] There is no awareness that abusive men's opinions

may be 'vocabularies of motive' constructed to justify abuse, or
that acceptance of them involves assuming that men have the
right to expect certain things from wives (particularly sex) which
if not forthcoming make sexual abuse of daughters understable, if
not inevitable. The commitment of researchers to this framework
results in absurdities such as a mothers' death being defined as
'desertion'.[78] Even evidence of physical violence towards wives is
made their responsibility: 'some deliberately got into situations
where they could have been injured physically'.[79] Not only is
incest 'understandable' – so is wife-beating.

It is also asserted that mothers always know abuse is occurring
(consciously, unconsciously and/or preconsciously) and that they
often overtly sanction it. Evidence for these accusations is often
limited to the daughter sleeping in the next bedroom to the father
and daughters shouldering some responsibility for household
tasks. Both of which are probably characteristic of the majority of
nuclear family households. Elizabeth Ward suggests that careful
attention should be paid to the use of language in these studies.
The behaviour of mothers is always represented as active whereas
that of abusive men appears as a passive response.[80] For example:
'The treatment of the mother consists of exploring her need for
violent relationships, and also why she knowingly hands over her
two girls to be molested [and] how her own choices and
unconscious collusions had first set up the process.'[81]

Mothers are also held responsible for not reporting abuse or
taking other action to stop it, despite evidence that the largest
proportion of official reports are made by biological mothers.[82]
The logical outcome of this framework of explanation has been to
define mothers as 'co-prepetrators', as a number of US state laws
now do.[83] It is also explicit in the 1983 US national incidence
study, data for which was obtained from professionals on the
basis of cases dealt with in the previous year. Women appear as
perpetrators in 46 per cent of cases. David Finkelhor and Gerald
Hotaling reanalysed the data and attempted to isolate cases where
there was an indication that a woman had personally abused a
child.[84] Given the lack of clarity in much of the data, they
conclude that their figures of 6 per cent in relation to girls and 14
per cent in relation to boys may still over-estimate the number of
women who sexually abused children.

The dominance of the family-dynamics model in the study of
incest has been extremely influential in the recent development of

treatment strategies. If the cause of incest is family dysfunction, in which all members are implicated, then criminal prosecution is an inappropriate response. A 'humanistic' treatment model based on family therapy developed by Henry Giaretto at the Child Sexual Abuse Treatment Programme (CSATP), San Jose,[85] is now the predominant response throughout the USA and has powerful support in the UK.[86] Jon Conte, an academic who is also connected to a centre providing services for abused women and girls, maintains that there is still no evidence of its effectiveness.[87] Indeed, analysis of the one research project to be based at CSATP suggests that 'success' turns on whether the father's power and control over his wife can be re-established.[88] Findings from several projects that the abused girls may not want the family reunited and get little of benefit from family therapy have been ignored.[89]

Incidence

Incidence research has tended to focus on child sexual abuse within which incest is a particular sub-category. Evidence of the prevalence of child sexual abuse was contained in the Kinsey surveys done in the 1950s; 28 per cent of women interviewed had experienced some form of sexual abuse before the age of 13.[90] Judith Herman maintains that the desire of the Kinsey researchers to promote sexual tolerance resulted in a deliberate reticence on this topic. 'On the subject of incest, apparently, they felt the less said the better. This, in spite of the fact that they have accumulated the largest body of data on overt incest that had ever appeared in the scientific literature.'[91] It was left to feminists working on rape to rediscover the prevalence of sexual abuse in the mid-1970s, and for social researchers to confirm it later that decade. David Finkelhor's 1979 study was ground-breaking, showing a high rate of child sexual abuse in a predominantly middle-class sample.[92] He is amongst those who now maintain that sexual abuse may be the most common form of child abuse.[93]

A number of studies have investigated prevalence within particular populations including hospital admissions, prostitutes, drug abusers, and a variety of clinical populations.[94] A number of studies, using large random and voluntary samples and survey methods, have been published recently which present more accurate and generalizable findings. Of these studies four are based on college student samples and findings range from 8 to 22 per cent of women and 5 to 9 per cent of men.[95] A further four studies are based on random samples, prevalence findings ranging from 12 to 38 per cent of women and 3 to 6 per cent of men.[96] All of the above projects were conducted in the USA. The only comparable UK studies are two based on large voluntary samples of women and one with a smaller sample of female patients on a doctor's list and women students. Ruth Hall and Tony Baker report that 16 per cent and 36 per cent, respectively, of their respondents recalled experiences of child sexual abuse.[97] The other survey records higher prevalence, 42 per cent of patients and 54 per cent of students.[98] A recent Swedish study using a probability sample reports rates of 9 per cent for women and 3 per cent for men.[99] The variation in findings is the result of a complex interaction of a number of factors: the definition of abuse (whether, for example, flashing is included); the age cut-off point (14, 16 or 18 years old); the population studied; the method used (telephone interview, self-report questionnaire or face to face interview); and the sensitivity of the researcher to question construction.

A number of important findings are highlighted by these studies. The vast majority of abusers of girls and boys are male. Much sexual abuse is committed by men known by the child, particularly relatives and family friends, and step-fathers represent a disproportionate percentage of known abusers. Finally, some prevalence findings suggest higher rates in the poorest and most affluent groups. Finkelhor argues that the family-dynamics approach cannot account for the range of contexts and relationships in which sexual abuse occurs. This point is echoed by two researchers who found that abuse of Black US children by relatives is more commonly by non-household members, particularly uncles. Treatment models (and theories) tend, therefore, to be based on the pattern of intra-familial abuse within white families.[100]

Agency response

The majority of literature in this area has focused on the development of procedures and treatment models.[101] To date, few empirical studies of how agencies respond to reported cases have been published, although the plethora of articles in vocational journals is testimony to dissatisfaction with, and confusion about, current practice. Jon Conte notes ruefully that a range of new approaches are being implemented which are neither based on empirical findings nor being monitored for their effectiveness.[102]

David Finkelhor presents findings from a questionnaire distributed to 790 US professionals attending conferences on child sexual abuse.[103] Many were clearly not complying with the now mandatory reporting requirements in the USA and there was little agreement on appropriate responses to sexual abuse within the family. He concludes that responses to reported abuse are still essentially arbitrary, dependent on the varying practice of the agency first approached.

Attitudes

Research into attitudes to sexual abuse is extremely limited, and much of what is available has focused on professionals. Acceptance of family dynamics/dysfunction as the predominant cause of incest and the belief that mothers collude has been demonstrated in two studies.[104] Both maintain that professionals tend to assert what they have been taught or read, even where it is contradicted by their own experience and working knowledge. A survey of 500 psychiatrists conducted in 1978 found that over three-quarters thought that there was little or no negative impact from abuse which involved a single or a few incidents, although a larger percentage (87 per cent) felt abuse over a long period would have a negative impact.[105] Again, widespread support for the family-dynamics approach to incest was evident.

Finkelhor used the vignette method, common in research on attitudes to rape, in his study of a random sample of 521 families with children between 6 and 14 years of age.[106] The factors which determined whether or not an incident was defined as abuse were: the ages of the child and the abuser; the nature of the act; and whether or not the child resisted. A negative impact on the child was not taken as evidence of abuse. The majority of parents had seen an article or programme on sexual abuse in the past year, were aware of its prevalence and the potential negative effects on children. Nevertheless, most had not discussed the issue with their children and those that had tended to concentrate on abuse by strangers.

Avoidance and prevention

As with agency practice, the bulk of the emerging literature in this area concerns the development of prevention programmes. Finkelhor notes the massive increase since 1980 of books, programmes, films and theatre presentations for use in prevention work.[107] Jon Conte has been insistent in calling for assessment and evaluation of prevention programmes, presenting evidence of how poor conceptualization can result in confusion, rather then enlightenment, for children.[108] Two papers based on evaluation of particular programmes reveal that children do not retain new knowledge: for example, that abusers may be known to them or that boys are abused.[109]

Research on domestic violence

As the term 'domestic violence' was not in use until the mid-1970s, specific studies of it date from that point. There was, however, data on violence within marriage in studies of homicide[110] and divorce.[111] The development of research has some similarities to both that of rape and incest. As in research on rape, studies on particular topics have emerged over the past ten years covering: incidence; courtship violence; institutional responses; and women's experience of domestic violence. As with incest, there has been the development of theory within empirical study. Unlike either of the other areas, an explicit debate has taken place within the literature about theory and method.

Offenders

Research on abusive men received little attention until very recently. Since domestic violence is not defined as a sex crime, and offenders are seldom prosecuted unless they have killed or attempted to kill the woman, there are few studies of convicted batterers. The two that exist follow the now-familiar pattern of explaining men's abuse by references to women's personality and behaviour.[112]

Most of the recent studies contain samples from US treatment programmes, participants being both court mandated and voluntary. Much of the discussion in these papers is limited to outlining treatment approaches and data is often limited to men who had completed the programme.[113] One consistent finding, however, is that abusive men under-estimate both the frequency and severity of their violence. One researcher notes that if men's self-reports had been relied on 19 per cent of a group of convicted batterers would be defined as non-violent.[114]

Attempts to evaluate treatment programmes have been hampered by the lack of consistent record-keeping and/or failure to institute internal evaluation.[115] This is ironic since such programmes are increasingly used in the USA as an alternative to criminal prosecution in the belief that they are more effective in preventing further violence. There are two basic treatment models. One is based on social learning theory and concentrates on teaching abusive men non-violent ways of managing stress and anger. The other is based on an insistence that abusive men recognize that they use violence in order to control and dominate their partner; the focus here is on broad attitudinal change.

The experience of domestic violence

Several studies in the 1960s discussed what were called 'sado-masochistic' marriages.[116] Violence was seen to be caused by the man's immaturity and the woman's behaviour. Women are depicted as frigid, hostile, aggressive and the fact that they did not leave is taken as proof that they at least accepted and perhaps even enjoyed the violence. Note the similarity with incest research of the same period: negative descriptions of wives and victims being seen to be responsible, and even willing participants, if they are unable to prevent further abuse.

The increase in sociological attention to domestic violence was marked by two very different publications. William Goode's article 'Force and violence in the family', published in 1971, begins with the statement 'Like all other social units, the family is a power system. All rest to some degree on force and its threat.'[117] His theoretical discussion of violence within families as a socially legitimated power resource, used primarily against women and children, opened the issue up to empirical investigation and laid the basis for the use of resource and systems theory within much of the US research done in the 1970s. A number of researchers have also drawn on the decision-making models of family power in investigating domestic violence; all

ignore the detailed analyses of the inadequacies of this perspective.[118]

In 1974, Erin Pizzey's *Scream Quietly or the Neighbours will
Hear* was published and in it she named violence against wives
'battering'.[119] It is in this book that the experience of battered
women begins to be documented. Whilst journalistic, the book
raised a number of issues that researchers were to take up in
future projects. She demonstrated the extent and seriousness of
the violence whilst also pinpointing the range of factors which
prevented women leaving abusive men. She proposed an model
of intergenerational transmission of abusive behaviour which is
still debated within the academic literature.

Studies published in the mid-1970s were predominantly
epidemiological, focusing primarily on the frequency and severity
of violence.[120] From the mid-1970s, there has been a huge
increase in published research on battered women's experiences.
Over 30 projects have been based on samples drawn from refuges
or crisis lines. In the same period, five projects have been
published based on voluntary samples. It is not clear at this stage
whether or not the experience of battered women who go to
refuges is similar to battered women who do not.

In a number of articles and, more recently, a book based on
research in Scotland, the Dobashes have presented a critique of
previous research and a feminist analysis of battering.[121] In
Violence Against Wives: A Case Against the Patriarchy, published
in 1979, historical analysis and evidence from interviews with
battered women are used to demonstrate that men use violence to
control women.

Two women researchers have developed models of battering
based on women's experiences. Leonore Walker suggest a three-
phase cycle which begins with an escalation of tension, followed
by an explosive violent episode and a subsequent period of calm
and reconciliation.[122] She uses the psychological concept of
'learned helplessness' to argue that, over time, battered women
feel that they cannot prevent violence. She has recently called this
'the battered-woman syndrome'.[123] Mildred Daley Pagelow
distinguishes between what she calls 'primary' and 'secondary'
battering. The former refers to initial or isolated incidents of
violence, the latter to a repetitive pattern of violence within a
relationship.[124] Both see the inadequate response of social
agencies as contributory factors in this process.

Kathleen Ferarro has challenged the focus in most research on physical violence, stressing the importance of emotional and verbal abuse: 'the potency of words and non-violent deeds should not be underestimated in their ability to cause pain.'[125]

Incidence

Within the literature on domestic violence, the study of incidence has often been integrated with study of the dynamics of battering and the development of theoretical perspectives. It is in this context that the debate about method and theory has taken place.

A number of incidence studies have been based on particular populations. For example, two studies found 50 per cent of women with mental health problems were currently being abused[126] and Anne Flitcraft estimated that 18 per cent of all injuries to women seen in a hospital emergency room were the result of domestic violence.[127] These studies, and all random sample incidence studies, have been undertaken in the USA. The latter studies use a research instrument designed by Murray Straus: the Conflict Tactics Scale (CTS).[128] The CTS lists a range of aggressive acts in order of seriousness, beginning with verbal abuse, followed by pushing, through to 'beat up' and assault with a weapon. Respondents are asked to note the 'tactics' they have used and/or experienced. Straus and his colleagues published findings from their own national random sample study of violence in the family, for which the CTS was designed, in 1980.[129] Of the adults, 16 per cent said they had experienced violence in the last year and 28 per cent had experienced violence in the past. Slightly different figures emerge from two random sample telephone surveys using the CTS.[130] Whilst considerable debate has taken place over the CTS itself and the interpretation of the data it produces (particularly that women are as 'violent' as men), it remains the most popular method for incidence research on both domestic and courtship violence.

Criticism emerged within the research community following the publication of an article by Susan Steinmetz on 'battered husbands'.[131] The detailed critique published the same year and subsequent commentaries highlighted important methodological problems with the CTS.[132] The 'tactics' are poorly conceptualized and are not mutually exclusive. The CTS fails to distinguish between offensive and defensive acts and contains no questions on either the frequency or consequences (injury) of violent acts. The scaling implicit in the CTS assumed that all acts within categories are the same, whether they are committed by a woman or a man and whether they are part of on-going abuse or a single event. The hierarchy of 'tactics' implies that pushing and throwing is by definition more serious than any amount of verbal or emotional abuse. The CTS, therefore, provided data on acts of violence abstracted from both the context in which they occurred and their consequences and meaning to the individuals involved. These problems and others have subsequently been confirmed by researchers using the CTS.[133] For example, Ferraro and Johnson used the CTS with four slight variations of method to explore variations in incidence figures in four previous studies of courtship violence. Whilst 41.3 per cent of the young people checked off one or more of the conflict tactics, 70 per cent of this group did not proceed to the section on abusive/violent relationships. These young people clearly did not share the definitions of violence and abuse implicit in the CTS.

Whilst certain limitations have been recently been acknowledged by Straus himself,[134] and the title of an unpublished paper suggests the CTS has been revised,[135] the impact of this poorly designed research instrument has been immense. The work of Straus and his colleagues continues to be regarded by many as the major source of accurate and generalizable data on violence in the family.

Michele Bograd is one of the few researchers to study the effects of method on findings. She used both standardized test measures and in-depth interviews with couples. Differences in men's and women's attitudes to, and definitions of, violence only emerged during the interviews.

This study suggests that abstract decontextualized questions may measure only general and socially desirable perceptions of domestic violence and that instruments should be carefully constructed with attention to contextual factors . . . This suggests that detailed open-ended questions grounded in concrete experiences are the most effective way of exploring persons' everyday understandings of domestic violence.[136]

Despite the limitations of the CTS, the incidence research recently conducted on courtship violence has had an important impact within the research community.[137] The consistent finding that substantial numbers of US college students had experienced and/or used violence in heterosexual relationships has shifted the focus of analysis from the family to heterosexual relationships: 'rather than a broad family violence theory, a theory of violence in intimate adult, heterosexual relationships would be useful'.[138]

Agency response

The failure of most statutory and voluntary agencies to provide protection or support is often commented on in research based on the experience of battered women. The response of agencies to domestic violence has been widely researched in the UK and the USA.

Studies of police response reveal that domestic violence is not seen as 'serious' police work, despite evidence that a high proportion of domestic homicides involve households known to the police for prior violence.[139] Police response has traditionally been one of crisis management rather than law enforcement, a disregarding of the criminal acts that have been committed.[140] One justification for this approach – that prosecution exacerbates conflict – has recently been challenged. In a controlled field experiment, arrest was found to be the most effective method of preventing further abuse.[141] This study, in conjunction with feminist campaigning for assaults in the home to be treated in the same way as assaults outside it, have resulted in a number of US police districts instituting mandatory arrest policies. The possibility of a pilot scheme using mandatory arrest in the UK is currently under discussion in the Home Office. This shift, however, has to be placed in the context of a dramatic increase in the US of court mandated counselling for abusive men as an alternative to presecution.[142]

Studies in the USA and the UK note the tendency for courts to reduce charges in domestic violence cases so that they are tried in lower courts where lower maximum penalties are available. The majority of cases result in fines and/or probation despite evidence of serious violence and use of weapons.[143] Two UK surveys of women in refuges found that enforcement of court injunctions left much to be desired; only a small percentage of women felt they offered any form of meaningful protection.[144]

Studies of social work response in the UK demonstrate that perceptions of battered women are often similar to those expressed in studies of 'sado-masochistic' marriages. Social workers have little understanding of the impact of violence on women or the limited options available to them.[145] Similar attitudes have been found amongst doctors, marriage guidance counsellors, health visitors and advice workers.[146] Anne Flitcraft and Evan Stark have demonstrated the complexity of the medical response to domestic violence, doctors implicitly acknowledge it by treating battered women differently from non-battered patients. They argue that these responses are a critical component in the social construction of battering; by persistently failing to respond to the real problem – violence – whilst treating its effects – 'secondary problems' such as depression – professionals reinforce and implicitly condone men's systematic abuse of women.

Medicine typically identifies these secondary problems as the focus for intervention, attributes the abuse to these secondary problems, and treats the 'multiproblem complex' by reconstructing and maintaining families, in which ongoing violence – and escalating psychosocial problems – are virtually inevitable.[147]

Cath Cavanagh has presented a model of battered women's help-seeking.[148] She shows how women shift from using informal networks for 'supportive help' to approaching official agencies for 'challenging help'. She and other researchers note that many women make considerable numbers of approaches but few responses meet their needs or expectations. The only groups consistently rated positively by battered women in the USA and the UK are solicitors, refuges and women's groups.[149]

Attitudes

Few studies specifically addressing attitudes have been undertaken. Three groups of researchers have used the vignette method: two in a similar manner to rape research (allocation of responsibility)[150] and one to investigate how professionals define violence.[151]. In the vignette studies it was found that women tend to hold abusive men more responsible than men do, and that alcohol is seen in the same way as in similar studies of rape – consumption increases women's responsibility yet decreases that of the male aggressor. The study of the definitions of UK professionals revealed little agreement within and between professional groups. Where there was little evidence of injury and/or the acts were perceived as 'legitimate' (in poorer families or where there was 'provocation'), behaviour was less likely to be defined as violence.

Avoidance and prevention

Three studies have systematically documented the range of strategies battered women use in their attempts to avoid violence before they see help from others.[152] The strategies include running away, hiding, threatening to call the police and trying not to anger their partner. Help-seeking is itself a strategy directed at preventing further violence.

Lee Bowker's research centred on the question of which strategies are effective for women in stopping violence. Whilst he found that leaving was the most effective strategy, his data showed that some women were able to stop violence and continue the relationship. Since the sample was drawn from women who had found ways of stopping violence within relationships, it is difficult to assess how common this is. Pamela Smith concluded from her research with women in a Canadian refuge that the only effective strategy was for women to leave.

Prevention programmes for use with young people are emerging in the USA, modelled to some extent on those used around child sexual abuse but drawing extensively on the courtship violence studies. As yet no assessments or evaluations have been published.

Contrasts and similarities

There are a number of marked differences between research on rape and studies of incest and domestic violence. Few studies of rape use case histories as data. Most studies draw samples from women who have reported rape to either official or voluntary agencies or from specific populations such as students; projects involving random or voluntary samples are the minority. What we know about rape and its aftermath is, therefore, primarily based on women who have reported the incident or sought support. The predominant methods used are either psychological tests, survey research or analysis of agency records. Whilst a vast amount of empirical data on rape has been gathered, very little theoretical development has taken place. Pepper Schwartz notes, in her 1979 review, that 'quite often the research becomes a mass of statistics, figures, profiles and typologies'.[153] There has been little improvement since, the notable exceptions being the work of Joyce Williams and Karen Holmes and Ruth Hall on the interconnections between racism and rape and the recent research on male sexual aggression.

Until the mid-1970s, the majority of research reports on incest and/or child sexual abuse were based on small clinical samples and contained few details of methodology. Whilst most recent studies are based on larger samples and describe the methods that have been used, analysis of findings in relation to incest continues to be dominated by the family dynamics/dysfunction model. Frances Heidersohn sees the popularity of this approach as a further example of the expectation that mothers perform a control function within the family.[154] The responsibility allocated to mothers in relation to incest is similar to that in relation to delinquency and adult male criminality.

The research literature on child sexual abuse displays little of the range of methods and questions evident in research on rape. Few projects have investigated specific questions outside the family-dynamics paradigm (exceptions here being incidence studies and research on the long-term impact of abuse) and, as a result, little attention has been paid to the range of child sexual abuse.

Unlike research on rape and incest, many of the studies of domestic violence have been undertaken in the UK. This may in part be accounted for by the fact that battering first emerged as an issue in this country. In addition, the UK Department of Health and Social Security funded several small-scale projects following the recommendations of the parliamentary Select Committee on Violence in the Family in 1975. This has not occurred in the case of rape and incest.

The response of agencies has also been more thoroughly researched in this area. Nevertheless, apart from the provision of refuges, far less innovation and critical internal discussion of agency practice has taken place than has occurred in relation to rape and sexual abuse. Whilst legal reform has taken place in many states in the USA, no assessment has yet been published.

The debate within the literature on domestic violence has focused on the methodological and theoretical issues raised by the work of Straus and his colleagues. At the theoretical level, it is a dispute over the analysis of the family. The systems-theory approach adopted by Straus and others views the family as a particular type of social system within which individuals are socialized to accept violence as a power resource. Feminist theory stresses that the patriarchal structure of the family legitimizes violence by men, and that male authority within the family is supported by social arrangements outside the family. Men have power within the family before they use violence.

Most research in all three areas is still based on cases reported to statutory or voluntary agencies. This is a major deficiency since one of the most common observations is the extent to which sexual violence is under-reported. Within each of the major areas discussed in this chapter, a particular source of sample has dominated research on women's experience. The majority of projects on rape draw samples from crisis lines, on incest and child sexual abuse from crisis lines and clinical populations, and on domestic violence from refuges. Whilst our knowledge about how women experience sexual violence has increased tremendously over the past ten years, we do not know whether or not these findings apply to women who do not report or use support services.

There has, as yet, been little crossover of research methods and theoretical frameworks between research on rape, incest and sexual abuse and domestic violence. This may, however, develop as studies investigating a range of forms of sexual violence in women's lives emerge.

Whilst each area of research has a particular pattern of historical development, internal debates and favoured methods and explanations, there are also a number of significant shifts of emphasis discernible across research on rape, sexual abuse and domestic violence:

● A shift away from the individual psychopathology models, common in the 1950s and 1960s, which included much 'victim blaming'; from the study of offenders to the study of victims; from epidemiological studies, often based on small clinical samples, to studies based on larger and wider samples, including incidence studies using random samples.

● The development of theoretical frameworks and of particular research questions, such as the study of the effects of sexual violence and attitude studies.

- A widening of the forms of sexual violence studied and, within each form, a widening of the definitions of each type of violence.
- The emergence of debates within the literature on methods and causal explanations.

Future directions

This section could form a chapter in itself as there are many gaps in our knowledge. I will try to draw out some of the major implications from our brief journey through the knowledge explosion.

- There is a pressing need for some of the excellent studies done in the USA to be replicated in other countries, particularly incidence studies concerning courtship violence and male sexual aggression.
- Research must also address whether and how inequalities of class, race, age, sexual orientation and disability influence the impact of sexual violence on and the options for coping with violence available to women and girls; whether these factors affect the response of statutory and voluntary agencies; and whether the accountability of abusive men is dependent on who they are rather than what they did.
- The recent findings concerning the range of sexual violence that women experience suggests that causal explanations which focus on individuals or the family are not capable of accounting for the prevalence of sexual violence. These perspectives also preclude analysis of how forms of sexual violence are linked and what the differences between them are. Attention in theory and methodology must be paid to the possibility that sexual violence is a key feature in the social construction of heterosexual relations.
- Studies of abusive men should not assume that they are necessarily and inherently different from men not publicly defined as abusive. Careful attention must be paid to how abusive men's accounts may be constructed of 'vocabularies of motive' which function to excuse and/or legitimate violence.
- Studies of women's experience of violence should be extended to wider populations, and should cover a number of forms of violence.

- Whilst documenting the negative impact, attention should also be paid to the range of ways women and girls resist and cope with their experience.
- Attitudinal research needs to extend the methods used and focus on how conceptions of women as 'legitimate victims' are constructed and how these inform responses to abused women and girls. It would be an important step forward if these studies began to address how such conceptions and representations can be changed.
- Research and feminist campaigning have resulted in important legal reforms, changes in agency practice and innovative approaches to treatment and prevention. All of these changes must be monitored to assess whether or not they extend beyond a surface response, whether or not they meet the needs of abused women and girls and whether or not they are effective in preventing violence and abuse.

Finally, researchers in this field must take responsibility for the way their findings will be used. The ethics of social research are particularly apparent where the issues studied involved life and death, health and ill-health, safety and danger. Any researcher choosing to study sexual violence must begin with an ethical commitment, a commitment which includes not condoning abuse explicitly or implicitly, seeing the purpose of research as increasing understanding in order that more appropriate responses can be developed, and wanting to contribute to a long-term goal of ending violence in the lives of women and children.

4

'It's happened to so many women': sexual violence as a continuum (1)

As I transcribed and analysed the interviews, it became clear that most women had experienced sexual violence in their lives. It was also clear that the range of men's behaviour that women defined as abusive was neither reflected in legal codes nor in the analytic categories used in previous research. In order to reflect this complexity I began to use the term 'continuum' to describe both the extent and range of sexual violence recorded in the interviews. I used this term, and the developing analysis behind it, in a number of talks given to a variety of women's groups (some were feminist groups involved in work around sexual violence, some were community groups). Many women found it helpful in understanding both their own experience and sexual violence in general.

This chapter will begin with a discussion of the concept itself and then explore its application to the prevalence of sexual violence in women's lives. Chapter 5 complements this analysis using the voices of the women interviewed and explores the range of the experiences within each of the specific forms.

Developing an idea

Several researchers investigating rape have used the idea, if not the actual concept, of a continuum.[1] Lucy Gilbert and Paula Webster's analysis of rape is representative of this approach:

Many rapes merely extend traditional heterosexual exchanges, in which masculine pursuit and female reticence are familiar and formalized. Although rape is a gross exaggeration of gender power, it contains the rules and rituals of heterosexual encounter, seduction and conquest.[2]

Joseph Marolla and Diana Scully use the word explicitly in relation to rapists: 'It is equally relevant to ask if rather than distortion, rapists may not represent one end of a quasi-socially sanctioned continuum of male sexual aggression'.[3] Judith Herman also uses the word explicitly, defining incest as 'Only the furthest point on a continuum – an exaggeration of patriarchal family norms, not a departure from them'.[4]

In each case, specific forms of sexual violence are connected to more common, everyday aspects of male behaviour.[5] The word 'continuum', however, is employed descriptively, the analysis underlying its use is often implicit and its relevance across forms of sexual violence is never specified. Most previous research has concentrated on particular forms of sexual violence in which the samples consist of women who define their experience in terms of a category that has been predetermined by the researcher (see chapter 3). A group of US researchers, commenting on previous studies of rape, suggest that this has resulted in a concentration on the extremes of sexual violence.[6] They note the need for research which explores the range of sexual violence, a task for which the concept of a continuum was specifically designed. The quotation below from a follow-up interview illustrates the importance of documenting this broader range of experiences.

'You asked me if I knew any women who had these experiences. Talking about it afterwards there were a surprising number who had been sexually harassed – none who had been raped. I do feel that's really invisible. We don't say someone flashed at me last night or – so it seems that it's happened to so many women but it's not recognized.'

Betsy Stanko offers a possible explanation for this non-recognition:

Women's experiences of male violence are filtered through an understanding of *men's* behaviour which is characterized as either typical or aberrant . . . In abstract we easily draw lines between those aberrant (thus harmful), and those typical (thus unharmful) types of male behaviour. We even label the aberrant behaviour as potentially criminal behaviour . . . Women who feel violated or intimidated by typical male behaviour have no way of specifying how or why typical male behaviour feels like aberrant male behaviour.[7]

The concept of a continuum can enable women to make sense of their own experiences by showing how 'typical' and 'aberrant' male behaviour shade into one another.

My use of the concept of a continuum is based on two of its

meanings in the *Oxford English Dictionary*: first, 'a basic common character that underlies many different events'; and, second, 'a continuous series of elements or events that pass into one another and which cannot be readily distinguished'. The first meaning enables us to discuss sexual violence in a generic sense. The basic common character underlying the many different forms of violence is the *abuse, intimidation, coercion, intrusion, threat and force men use to control women*. The second meaning enables us to document and name the range of abuse, intimidation, coercion, intrusion, threat and force whilst acknowledging that there are no clearly defined and discrete analytic categories into which men's behaviour can be placed.

My usage of the word continuum should not be taken to imply that there is a linear straight line connecting many different events or experiences. Nor should it be interpreted as a statement about the relative seriousness of different forms of sexual violence. Marie Leidig, the only other writer to use this concept in a systematic way, bases her analysis on a notion of seriousness.[8] She argues that those forms of violence which she places at the extreme end of her continuum, domestic violence and incest, are necessarily most serious and, therefore, have greater negative effects than those at the other end of her scale. Chapters 5 to 8 will demonstrate that women's reactions to incidents of sexual violence at the time, and the impact on them over time, are complex matters. With the important exception of sexual violence which results in death, the degree of impact cannot be simplistically inferred from the form of sexual violence women experience or its place within a continuum.

My perspective is that all forms of sexual violence are serious and that it is inappropriate to create a hierarchy of abuse within a feminist analysis. The 'more or less' aspect of the continuum as I use it applies only to prevalence: that there are forms of sexual violence which most women experience in their lives and which they are more likely to experience on multiple occasions. While these common forms are more likely to be defined by men as acceptable behaviour (for example, seeing sexual harassment as 'a harmless bit of fun'), they are connected to the forms of violence which are currently defined as crimes within the law.[9]

Applying the continuum to incidence

Feminist services for abused women as well as recent research have demonstrated that the incidence of sexual violence is far higher than recorded in official statistics. Furthermore, many incidents which women experience as abusive are not defined legally as crimes.[10] Official statistics and victimization studies are, therefore, of limited use in measuring the prevalence of sexual violence.

The majority of incidence studies have been limited to specific forms of sexual violence and many have been limited to incidents occurring in the year prior to the survey. Only seven published studies have attempted to cover a range of the possible forms of sexual violence that women might experience. Two of these do not provide either incidence figures or details of the sample,[11] and three are limited to investigating the incidence of rape, sexual assault, incest and sexual abuse of children.[12] Whilst two community studies done in the UK in the early 1980s include a wider range of possible experiences, questions were limited to incidents in the year prior to the survey.[13] There is as yet no published study which has systematically asked women about the range of possible experiences of sexual violence over their lifetime.

My choice to respect women's understandings of their experiences means that the definitions of forms of sexual violence in the sections below emerged out of the interaction between women's understandings and the analysis of the interviews. This involved both extending previous definitions and developing two new categories: pressurized sex and coercive sex. Direct comparisons with legal definitions or those used in previous studies are, therefore, in some senses, problematic. This should be borne in mind when figures from other studies are cited. I have not attempted to develop 'new' analytic definitions as it is my opinion that we still do not know enough about the range of male behaviour that women experience as abusive. I have, however, sketched out the parameters of each category in the context of the range contained in the interviews.

The prevalence of 11 specific forms of sexual violence in the lives of the sixty women interviewed is presented in table 4.1 The continuum of prevalence as shown in this table moves *from*

Table 4.1   The continuum of prevalence

Form of violence	Number of women	% of sample
Threat of violence	60	100
Sexual harassment	56	93
Pressure to have sex	50	83
Sexual assault	42	70
Obscene phone calls[a]	25	68 (of 37)
Coercive sex	38	63
Domestic violence[b]	32	53
Sexual abuse	30	50
Flashing	30	50
Rape[b]	30	50
Incest[b]	13	22

[a] This category was added when a woman noted its absence; 23 interviews and follow-ups had already been completed.

[b] These 3 categories include 10 women (17 per cent) who identified themselves as having had these experiences before the interviews.

experiences which were most common in women's lives to those which were least common. The sample of 60 women is small and deliberately not a random one. It is not possible, therefore, to argue that this particular continuum of prevalence has a wider application. Further work needs to be done to assess this. I suspect, however, that the first three, and possibly five, categories would be similarly placed as those most common in women's lives.

In each of the sections which follow, a discussion of the experiences covered by a particular category is placed in the context of brief summaries of previous research and the findings of this project. Whether an official report, particularly to the police, was made is also noted.

The threat of violence

Many women have written about the impact of the threat of violence on women's lives. Most writers focus exclusively on the threat of sexual attack by strangers, particularly rape, which causes women to limit their entry into the public sphere.[14] It is rather surprising that little empirical research has directly addressed the question of the general impact of the threat of violence. Two UK studies, based in London, included some questions on this issue. Ruth Hall found over 50 per cent of women sometimes felt frightened when they went out alone during the day and 75 per cent often felt frightened alone at night.[15] Jill Radford's figures were higher, 92 per cent of women did not feel safe on the street at night and 77 per cent took precautionary measures.[16]

Betsy Stanko, who is currently conducting a cross-cultural study in the USA and UK on gender differences in negotiations of personal safety, suggests that women's greater fear of crime must be examined in relation to the threat and reality of all forms of sexual violence.[17] My interviews revealed that the threat of violence extends much further into women's lives than other writers have suggested, that it is present in many of women's interactions and relationships with men.

In the interviews I conducted, two series of questions specifically related to the threat of violence. One focused on whether or not women felt safe on the street and/or in public and the other, on whether or not they had ever experienced the threat of, or actual, physical violence from parents, siblings, lovers and husbands. The threat of violence was, therefore, discussed in both public and private, stranger and intimate, contexts. References to the threat of violence were also made by women in many other contexts. Because it was so commonly and consistently experienced, it has been placed first within the continuum of prevalence.

Of the women interviewed 75 per cent did not feel safe on the street alone at night. A fifth of women never felt safe; they stressed that this applied to all locations including their own homes. Interestingly, there were few significant differences between women with experiences of rape, domestic violence or incest and those without. That slightly more women who were raped or incestuously abused said they never felt safe reflected that fact that they had been assaulted either in their own homes or during the day. They could not, therefore, define times of day or specific places as more safe. It should also be noted that at least half of the 25 per cent of women who said they felt quite safe in public mentioned that they had a car and that this increased their sense of control. No woman felt safe at all times and in all places.

Remarks made by the women suggested that linking fear to the threat of rape alone is too simplistic. Many women referred to

Table 4.2   Women who had experienced the threat of violence in intimate relationships

	R^a		I		DV		C1		C2		Total	
	N	%	N	%	N	%	N	%	N	%	N	%
Father/step-father	4	40	7	70	4	40	8	53	8	53	31	52
Male lover	8	80	5	50	5	50	6	40	6	40	30	50
Husband	2	20	4	40	10	100	8	53	4	27	27	47
Siblings	2	20	3	30	2	20	1	10	0	0	8	13
Mother/foster mother	1	10	1	10	1	10	1	7	0	0	4	7

^{a} Abbreviations in this and subsequent tables are those introduced on pp. 10–11.

fearing other forms of public male violence such as flashing and sexual assault. It is possible that women's fear is more likely to be articulated in relation to rape because this fear is seen as 'legitimate'.

Table 4.2 reveals that over 90 per cent of women's experiences of the threat of violence from intimates involved males (50 per cent of the siblings category were older brothers). Women were also asked if they had ever experienced physical violence from intimates. In each case, apart from husbands, the threat of violence combined with single or occasional incidents of physical violence was more common than frequent physical violence. Frequent violence being more common from husbands may be partly accounted for by the fact that this group includes women from the domestic violence subsample. It is also the case, however, that if husbands were ever violent they were more likely to engage in frequent violence.

The women I interviewed experienced the threat of violence in relation to individual men, known and unknown, and as a more generalized fear. The predominant response by women, of devising strategies which might enable them to avoid assault, was similar across the private/public and stranger/intimate contexts.

Sexual harassment

There is a considerable range of male behaviour that can be defined as sexual harassment and it can occur in a range of settings. Most studies have been limited to harassment at work or within universities, although several UK feminists have extended its application to aspects of girl's experience in mixed schools.[18] Whilst street harassment, sometimes called street hassling, has been included in some sexual assault laws in the USA,[19] and a bill to make it illegal was introduced in the Indian parliament,[20] there has been little empirical study of this aspect of sexual harassment.

Studies of sexual harassment at work consistently find that it is a common experience for women. The first survey appeared in *Redbook Magazine* in 1976 and 90 per cent of American women responding had experienced harassment at work at some time.[21] A more recent US survey recorded 42 per cent of women experiencing harassment at work in the previous two years.[22] NALGO found 36 per cent of UK female local council employees reported being harassed and another British study revealed that 52 per cent of women managers reported harassment.[23] Extending questions to cover street harassment, Ruth Hall reports that 83 per cent of women had experienced unwelcome sexual remarks, 76 per cent had been touched or grabbed in public places and 72 per cent had been followed in the street by a man.[24]

In order to reflect the possible range of experiences, the interview question in this study referred to harassment at work, in the street and in other public places. Incidents women recalled were mainly in work situations or public places. The harassers were both known men and strangers. A number of women, however, also discussed harassment from ex-partners, friends, male shop assistants and service workers. What underlay these different experiences was that the attention or behaviour of the man was experienced as intrusive, involving unwarranted assumptions of intimacy. Only four of the women interviewed did not recall having experienced sexual harassment. Almost half of the sample spontaneously mentioned that sexual harassment was something that happened to them often. Many of these women spoke of it as a 'normal' experience which occurred on an everyday basis. No incidents of sexual harassment were reported to the police, employers or trade unions.

Pressurized sex

This category was introduced to take account of the fact that women do not simplistically define heterosexual sex as either consenting or rape, between these two is a range of pressure and coercion.[25] Pressurized sex covers experiences in which women decided not to say no to sex but where they felt pressured to consent. It is not possible to refer to previous studies as this category was developed within this project.

Women were asked if they had ever felt pressured to have sex: 88 per cent of women had experienced pressure to have sex and for 96 per cent of them this was a repeated experience; 66 per cent of women experienced it with more than one man. At least 45 per cent of the experiences took place within on-going relationships.

Women were also asked about their first heterosexual experiences. Incest and rape accounted for 13 (22 per cent) of first experiences of intercourse. An additional 12 per cent of women felt coerced by the man. A further 35 per cent felt ambivalent as a direct result of being pressured by the man in question. Over two-thirds of this group of women did not freely consent to their first experience of heterosexual intercourse.

Sexual assault

The term 'sexual assault' was specifically used in a question in order to give women space to discuss abusive experiences that might not be covered by other questions. There are a number of incidents in the child sexual abuse category which women defined as a sexual assault, so the incidence figure of 70 per cent is, in this sense, an underestimate.

A sexual assault for the women interviewed almost always involved physical contact, ranging from being touched by strangers in the street or a crowded train to 18 cases of attempted rape. The distinction between sexual harassment which included physical contact and sexual assault was ambiguous, some women placing similar events in different categories. Interestingly, many women did not restrict sexual assault to strangers. Of the specific assaults women discussed, 54 per cent were by men known to them, including husbands, lovers, friends, relatives and dates. Comparisons with other studies is problematic given the range of experiences that this category includes. Ruth Hall[26] found that 31 per cent of women had experienced sexual assault. It is not clear, however, whether the 20 per cent of women in her study who experienced attempted rape are an addition to this figure or a subsample of the 31 per cent.

Of the incidents women defined as sexual assaults, 60 per cent occurred before the age of 20. The age-related incidence is similar to that for rape, where 50 per cent took place before women were 20. Five assaults were reported to the police, two were reported by the women themselves, two by parents and one by the woman's husband. No case went to court and three women felt that the complaint was not dealt with seriously or sympathetically.

Obscene/threatening phone calls and peeping

For the women interviewed, obscene phone calls covered calls made by strangers where verbal or vocal sexual references were made or harassment from men they knew that included sexual suggestions and threats. Interestingly, a number of women also included series of silent calls which they experienced as threatening and disturbing and had similar effects to calls where explicit sexual remarks were made. Peeping covered intentional watching of women in their own homes and the man was always a stranger. Whilst men women knew also watched women's houses, this was defined as a form of harassment.

At the time of writing, the only detailed study of obscene phone calls is that by Liz Stanley and Sue Wise on calls they received.[27] An article by Juli Goodwin in *The Daily Telegraph* gave figures from a Home Office study.[28] Of the women surveyed 10 per cent had received one or more obscene calls in the previous 12 months. The article also stated that British Telecom have over a third of a million complaints a year about obscene or malicious phone calls. One US researcher found that 83 per cent of his sample of women students had received an obscene phone call.[29]

Of the women interviewed, 68 per cent had received an obscene and/or threatening phone call (percentages calculated on a total of 37, see table 4.1): 36 per cent were series calls and affected other women living in the household; 28 per cent of the calls were silent. A specific question was not included on peeping but six women recalled such experiences when answering other questions.

Two women reported the calls to the police and were told not to worry, that men who made such calls never carried out their threats.

Coercive sex

'Coercive sex' covers experiences which women referred to as being 'like rape'. Specific pressure was always used by the man, often involving the threat of, or actual, physical force. As with pressurized sex, comparisons to other studies are not possible as this category was developed within this project.

Of the women interviewed 63 per cent had experienced coercive sex and 66 per cent of these women experienced it more than once. The majority of the multiple experiences occurred within on-going relationships, of which a number also involved physical violence. A similar, although less marked, pattern emerges as with child sexual abuse. Women with experiences of certain forms of sexual violence, particularly rape, were more likely to define experiences that have been recorded as coercive sex as being 'like rape'.

Domestic violence

Whilst only ten women had never experienced violence in a heterosexual relationship, not all of these women defined the events as domestic violence. In a few cases, the violence was felt to be mutual and was called 'fighting'. In a larger number of cases, violence occurred on a single or few occasions within a short-term relationship. Experiences defined by women as domestic violence took place within the context of marriage or cohabitation and the violence occurred over an extended period.

A number of large-scale prevalence studies have been done in the USA on domestic violence. A national random sample survey estimated that violence occurs in one out of three to four marriages, and that wife beating occurred in 12.6 per cent of marriages.[30] A statewide telephone survey found that 21 per cent of married women had experienced violence.[31] A number of researchers have extended this research to young unmarried couples and reports between two-thirds and a fifth of women students having experienced physical force in heterosexual relationships.[32] Similar incidence studies have not been conducted in the UK, although the Islington Crime Survey found that 22 per cent of assaults were of women by their male partners.[33] This figure is close to the 25 per cent found by the Dobashes in their analysis of Scottish police records.[34]

Table 4.3 records the numbers of women who experienced the threat of or actual violence from lovers and husbands (around 50 per cent in both cases). Of the women who had been married, 76 per cent had experienced violence from their husbands. For 45 per cent of this group of women, the violence lasted for between one and four years, for 40 per cent between five and ten years, and for 20 per cent for over ten years.

Seven incidents of violence were reported to the police. In three cases either children or other relatives made the report. All seven women regarded the action the police took as either useless or negative in the circumstances. On no occasion did the police challenge the man about his behaviour or press charges despite the fact that one woman had an injunction at the time and another was legally separated. Six women obtained injunctions against the abusing men, but the most common legal remedy used by women was divorce. None of the men was prosecuted for violence.

Sexual abuse of girls

This category covers any sexual experiences in childhood and adolescence which women defined as negative that took place before they were 16 and is not recorded in any of the other categories (for example flashing and incest). The incidents included range from fondling through to assaults, and the abusers were known and strangers, adults and peers.

A number of large-scale studies have estimated the prevalence of child sexual abuse. Two early US surveys included flashing and recorded figures of 28 per cent and 35 per cent.[35] David

Table 4.3 Women who had experienced the threat of, or actual, physical violence from lovers or husbands

	R		I		DV		C1		C2		Total	
	N	%	N	%	N	%	N	%	N	%	N	%
From a lover	8	80	5	50	5	50	6	40	6	40	30	50
From a husband	2	20	4	40	10	100	8	53	4	27	28	47

Finkelhor's more recent study excluded flashing and found a prevalence rate of 19 per cent.[36] In the UK two recent studies have assessed prevalence. Ruth Hall found 16 per cent of her sample had been raped or sexually assaulted before the age of 16 and a survey of 19 readers found that 20 per cent of the 3,000 women who responded had been abused by adult men in a position of authority or trust.[37] These studies use different methodologies, sample sources and definitions of child sexual abuse (see chapter 3); all include incest in their figures. Diana Russell has distinguished between intra- and extra-familial abuse, finding a prevalence of 16 per cent and 31 per cent respectively.[38]

Whilst 50 per cent of women recalled sexual abuse that was not recorded in other categories, in order to make figures in this study somewhat comparable with those cited above it is necessary to compile a composite figure including incidents recorded in the rape, flashing and incest categories which occurred before women were 16 years old. This reveals that 72 per cent of the women interviewed had experienced at least one form of sexual violence before the age of 16, 45 per cent before they were 12. Almost 50 per cent of the 43 women with experiences of sexual violence before the age of 16 had experienced more than one form of sexual violence. The frequency of types of child sexual abuse and the relationship between the girl and abuser did vary with age. Fondling and abuse by known men were slightly more common before the age of 12; rape, flashing and abuse by strangers was slightly more common between 12 and 16. In each age group, the incidence of flashing, fondling and touching was greater than for assault and rape.

Two flashing incidents, two rapes, and two sexual assaults were reported to the police. Two women thought that the man had been arrested, tried and convicted but this was never officially confirmed.

Flashing

Flashing includes any deliberate exposure of male genitals to a woman or girl. Incidents women recalled were either directed at them as individuals or at a group of women or girls of which they were a part. Flashing was usually limited to exposure itself but on a number of occasions it also involved verbal threats or masturbation. Whilst the vast majority of incidents were committed by strangers, two of the incidents experienced in childhood were committed by relatives.

Three recent studies found that in groups of nurses and students between a third to a half of these women had experienced flashing and many of this group had had more than one experience.[39] Sandra McNeill found that 63 per cent of her wider sample had experienced flashing and 68 per cent of this group had had multiple experiences.[40]

Of the women interviewed in my project 50 per cent remembered at least one incident of flashing, and 64 per cent of this group had had multiple experiences. Altogether, 76 incidents were recalled, 73 per cent of which occurred before women were 20. Almost half occurred during childhood or adolescence. Four incidents were reported to the police. Two were reported by parents and two by women themselves. No man was charged with an offence.

Rape

If women defined an experience of forced sex as rape it was included in this category. Rapes recalled by women were committed by strangers, friends, lovers and husbands. Most of the experiences involved penetration of the vagina by the penis.

Two recent large-scale studies have investigated the prevalence of rape. Diana Russell found that 44 per cent of a US sample had experienced rape or attempted rape; Ruth Hall found that 21 per cent of a UK sample had experienced rape and 20 per cent experienced attempted rape.[41]

Table 4.4 shows that 28 of the women interviewed (47 per cent) defined experiences as rape. Six of the rapes occurred within marriage. Two women defined two separate assaults as rape. Fifty per cent of rapes occurred before women were 20 years old and this group contained most of the rapes by strangers. Of the rapes occurring after the women was 20, 46 per cent were marital rapes. Research using official statistics or victimization studies suggest that younger women are more vulnerable to rape. The findings of both this project and Diana Russell's suggest that, whilst this may be true for stranger-rape, older women may be more at risk from men they know, especially men to whom

Table 4.4   Women who had been raped

	R		I		DV		C1		C2		Total	
	N	%	N	%	N	%	N	%	N	%	N	%
Raped	10	100	3	30	4	40	10	6	1[a]	7	28	47
Never raped	0	0	7	70	6	60	5	34	14	93	32	53

[a] This woman defined an incident as rape during the follow-up interview, but was not prepared to discuss it in depth. The subgroups were divided on the basis of answering detailed questions on rape, incest or domestic violence.

they were married. As one factor in not reporting rape has been found to be knowing the rapist, this suggests that research based on reported rapes can result in spurious findings. In this study, of the men who raped women 73 per cent knew them in some way and 44 per cent were, or had been, in a close relationship with the woman.

Of these rapes eight were reported to the police: three were reported by the women themselves (two were marital rapes); three women were persuaded to report by their mother or foster-mother; one woman was kidnapped abroad and when she escaped had to contact the police; another woman was left by the side of the road and a lorry driver who stopped insisted on taking her to the police station. The police dropped four of the cases (including the two marital rapes). In one of these, the woman was informed that the man had been found and cautioned but they could not proceed as she had technically consented. Two young women withdrew the complaint following many hours of what can only be described as interrogation. There is no way of knowing how many of these six reports appeared in official statistics nor, if they did, how they were recorded. The remaining two cases went to court. In one, the hearing took place abroad and the woman did not attend; the other woman gave evidence in court. Neither woman was informed of the outcome of the case.

Incest

This was another category where women defined their experience for themselves. Whilst a number of the experiences of sexual abuse discussed above did involve relatives, they have not been included in this section. Incest, as women defined it, involved abuse by either a father figure or a male living in the household. It did not always involve on-going abuse; two women were raped once by their fathers.

Diana Russell found 4.5 per cent of her sample had experienced incest.[42] A survey in the *Australian Women's Weekly* found 3 per cent of respondents had experienced incest.[43] Of David Finkelhor's sample 8.4 per cent were abused by a family member; 1.3 per cent by a father or father figure.[44] In Ruth Hall's survey 20 per cent of the women abused as children were abused by a family member.[45]

I asked women if they had ever picked up any sexual messages in their family; futher questions highlighted whether or not this involved explicit abuse. It transpired that 28 women picked up sexual messages (see table 4.5) during their childhood, mainly from their fathers or father figures. Other relatives mentioned included uncles, grandfathers, a brother and a cousin. Thirteen women defined their experience as incest: six were assaulted by their biological father; two by step-fathers; two by mother's boyfriends; one by a number of male relatives and lodgers; one was assaulted by a cousin who lived in the same household and was treated like a brother; and one by her grandfather with whom she was living at the time.

A large majority of abuse began before puberty; 50 per cent of women had been abused for the first time by the age of eight. Most experiences of abuse occurred over a period of between two and five years, but several were of shorter or longer duration.

Only one woman reported the abuse to the police. She dropped the complaint when the abuser and her mother arrived at the police station.

Table 4.5 Women who picked up sexual messages in their family

	R		I		DV		C1		C2		Total	
	N	%	N	%	N	%	N	%	N	%	N	%
Women who did	4	40	10	100	3	30	5	34	6	40	28	47
Women who did not	6	60	0	0	7	70	10	66	9	60	32	53

Differences across the sub-samples

The sub-samples were not devised in order to do detailed statistical comparisons across them; they were developed in order to demonstrate the prevalence of sexual violence in most women's lives. This was, to a large extent, confirmed by the minimal differences for most forms of sexual violence. Whilst rape/domestic violence/incest was by definition more common amongst women in the self-selected samples for these forms of sexual violence, they were by no means confined to them. Of the 50 women not in the domestic violence sub-group 44 per cent had experienced domestic violence; 40 per cent of the 50 women not in the rape sub-group had experienced rape; and 6 per cent of women not in the incest sub-group had experienced incest.

No differences were evident in the incidence of sexual harassment or pressure to have sex. Slightly more women who had experienced rape or incest never felt safe; this was directly attributable to the fact that they had been abused in their own homes. The other, relatively minimal, differences that emerged are, I suspect, related to how women define sexual violence. Having already defined and named assaults as rape, incest or domestic violence, women were slightly more likely to define (and perhaps remember, see chapter 6) other incidents as assaults. Thus, women who defined an incident of forced sex as rape were more likely to discuss an incident of coercive sex. Women who defined assaults as rape or domestic violence were more likely to recall and name an incident as sexual assault.

One significant difference did emerge across the sub-groups. Women in the incest sub-group were far more likely to recall assaults that occurred before the age of 16 outside the household than other groups of women. I suspect that this finding is in part accounted for by the fact that this group of women were sensitized to recognizing and naming abuse. They were also more likely to remember their experiences accurately as over half of the incest sub-group had spent considerable amounts of time just prior to the interview working through their experiences and this would have aided their recall. Some of the difference might also be explained by the particular vulnerability of girls who are being incestuously abused.[46]

Incidence in individual women's lives

Studies which focus on a particular form of sexual violence, or limit the time frame of the investigation, cannot estimate the extent of sexual violence within individual women's lives. Finding multiple experiences of the same or different forms of sexual violence tend to be incidental and have led to discussions of 'victim proneness' or 'vulnerability'.[47] More detailed studies of the extent of sexual violence in women's lives are needed before such theories can be adequately assessed.

Table 4.6 records each woman's experiences and the age at which they occurred. The threat of violence, sexual harassment and pressure to have sex are not included as they were so common that they could not be recorded as particular events occurring at particular times. It must be stressed, therefore, that the most commonly experienced forms of sexual violence are not recorded in this table. The data on obscene phone calls has also been excluded as it was not available for the whole sample.

This table highlights a number of significant points. The most striking feature is that there is only one woman for whom no incidents are recorded (interview 47). Altogether, 47 women (78 per cent) experienced three or more of the forms of violence recorded in the table. Given that most of these women would also have experienced the threat of violence, sexual harassment and pressure to have sex, almost 80 per cent of the sample had experienced six or more forms of sexual violence in their lives.

The distribution of incidence across the subsamples does not support the theory of 'victim proneness'. Whilst there were women in the rape, incest and domestic violence subsamples who had multiple experiences of the same and other forms of sexual violence, there are also women whose experiences were more or less limited to rape, incest or domestic violence. There were also women within Comparison Group 2 without such experiences but with multiple experiences of other forms of sexual violence. The table also illustrates how, for a number of women, the cumulative impact of a number of incidents occurring close together was an important aspect of their experience.

Table 4.6 Incidence of forms of sexual violence[a] in the lives of the women interviewed (age-scale is non-linear)

Interview number	Age at time incident(s) occurred							Sub-sample
	0	5	10	15	20	30	40	
	(Incident(s) before age 16)				(Incident(s) after age 16)			
1			S[b]		C	DRDDDCDD F*		DV
2		S			V AAR	CC	*	R
3			II			VC	*	I
4				S	A	CVC R	*	R
5		S		IIIII A	F RFDC F A F F*			I
6				R	F F CA DDDR F F*			R
7			F S	SF	C V F*			C1
8				R	A V CFCCF *			R
9			F	S	V ADCDDRDDRCD	*		DV
10			F	CC	ADDF F *			DV
11				S	C A ADDADDDDDDD	*		DV
12				S	DDDDDDDDDDD	*		DV
13			F S S		FA FCCVR C F *			R
14			F		A DDDDDDDDRD	*		DV
15					A DDDCCD	*		DV
16		II			ACVR AVC *			R
17				S	DDCDDCDADDDDDD	*		C1
18				S S F RF	CGDDDRDDD	DDD DDD	*	R
19				F II C	A R *			R
20				F	A C FF F V	*		C2

#		Type
21	C CCC A V *	C2
22	S R DDCDRD *	R
23	CC CCCC F R V C*	C2
24	F A CC DDDDD *	DV
25	F S F F *	C2
26	I S F A C F V CC F *	C2
27	I IIIFIFIIF F S CC V R *	L
28	S V DDDD DDADR *	DV
29	IIIIIISIIF F F F DDDDR *	L
30	S C A *	C2
31	F RR F V F *	C1
32	S S CC R V *	C2
33	IISIII *	C1
34	C V A *	C2
35	S S A V AF *	C2
36	S DDDDDD *	DV
37	IIIIIII A V F *	L
38	F V *	C2
39	R CFDFDDAF *	R
40	F DDDDDDCCDDDC *	C1
41	R CC CACVC *	C1
42	C *	C2
43	A DDDDD A *	C1
44	S AC C ADRDD A *	C1
45	DD R A *	C1
46	CCCC *	C2

Table 4.6 (continued)

	Age at time incident(s) occurred							
Interview number	0	5	10	15	20	30	40	Sub-sample
	(Incident(s) before age 16)				(Incident(s) after age 16)			
47						*		C2
48			S	F	DDDRDCD		*	C1
49		S			C V	*		I
50					VV A A*			C2
51					C	DDDD*		C1
52			IIIII		CCV	*		I
53				F	*			C2
54			ISIIIIIIFIIII	F	CCC	*		I
55					R	*		C1
56				IIIIIII A	R *			I
57			S	F	A FFF A	R *		C1
58			S	II FR	DCCD*			C1
59				DD	CD A R	*		C1
60			S		DD F RF DD F		*	C1

* Denotes the age of the woman at the time of the first interview.

a Experiences of sexual violence are recorded once only. Thus, child sexual abuse includes only those experiences not recorded elsewhere (for example, as rape or flashing). Sexual assault includes only assaults after age 16.

b Experiences are coded as follows: A = sexual assault; C = coercive sex; D = domestic violence; F = flashing; I = incest; R = rape; S = child sexual abuse; V = single or few incidents of violence in a heterosexual relationship.

Part of women's reality

This chapter has focused on the continuum in relation to the prevalence of sexual violence. As this sample is self-selected and at least 50 per cent of women participated on the basis that they had had experience of rape, incest or domestic violence, it would be inappropriate to over-generalize on the basis of these findings. The figures do, however, show clearly that the vast majority of this sample experienced the more common forms of sexual violence; the threat of violence, sexual harassment, and pressure to have sex. These forms of sexual violence were extremely common in women's lives, both in the sense that they occurred to most women and that they occurred on multiple occasions. Nor can the facts that only 17 women did not experience some form of sexual violence before the age of 16, only 10 women had never experienced violence in a heterosexual relationship, and only 18 women had not experienced rape, attempted rape or coercive sex be explained in terms of sample bias. Indeed, table 4.6 suggests that sexual violence is a characteristic feature of all women's lives and investigating prevalence in terms of cumulative experiences within women's lives is of crucial importance.

The commonness of sexual violence was investigated in another way. Women were asked if they had any friends who had experiences of rape, domestic violence or incest. The 60 women interviewed knew 435 other women who had experienced either rape, incest or domestic violence. Only six women did not know a woman who had experienced any of these forms of sexual violence. Women were more likely to know about experiences similar to their own. Through being open about abuse to female friends, women invariably discovered that some had had similar experiences. This was confirmed by the women who, as a result of the first interview, chose to discuss their experiences with women friends.

As this was a predominantly white group of women it is not possible to comment on the suggestions made by a number of US researchers that Black women are more vulnerable to sexual violence, particularly rape.[48] These findings are based primarily on studies of reported rapes and were not confirmed by either Diana Russell's US, nor Ruth Hall's UK, study. Diana Russell suggests that the inclusion of rape by male partners in her study may explain the different findings.[49] The implicit suggestion that Black women are more vulnerable to rape by strangers (rape by strangers being more likely to be reported) is unfortunately not discussed. An alternative explanation for the US figures can be found in the work of Gary La Free.[50] He found that rape reports in which the rapist is said to be Black are taken more seriously by police and prosecutors; Black men are more likely to be charged with rape, prosecuted and convicted. As most rapes are intra-racial this suggests that, in the US at least, rape laws are enforced in a racist way. This results both in Black men being dispropor-tionately convicted and a possibly spurious finding that Black women are more vulnerable to rape. There is no research currently available which would enable the assessment of whether or not this particular form of racist law enforcement also occurs in the UK.

Less than one per cent of the specific events women recalled were reported to the police. A number of these complaints were either withdrawn by women or dismissed by the police and may not, therefore, have been officially recorded. A maximum of five men were charged with offences. These startling figures further underline the fact that the incidence of sexual violence is far greater than is recorded in official statistics. These may under-estimate actual incidence by two orders of magnitude. They also reveal that men who are charged with and convicted of offences involving violence towards women or girls are very much the exception rather than the rule.

5

'It's everywhere': sexual violence as a continuum (2)

The continuum of sexual violence ranges from extensions of the myriad forms of sexism women encounter everyday through to the all too frequent murder of women and girls by men. This chapter documents the range, both of sexual violence as a whole and within each form, through the words and experiences of the women interviewed. To illustrate the point made in chapter 4 – that the categories we use to define forms of sexual violence are not mutually exclusive – sections are organized around particular interconnections. The explicit linkages in the section headings are not, however, exhaustive and references to other overlaps and connections will be made.

The threat of violence in public, flashing and obscene phone calls

These three forms of sexual violence are discussed together as their impact hinges on women's perceptions of what might happen next. Whilst flashing and obscene phone calls are in and of themselves violating, both rely in part for their impact on the explicit or implicit threat of further assault. The link is between the generalized fear that most women experience and forms of visual or verbal violence that accentuate it. All are also unwanted intrusions into women's personal space which transform routine and/or potentially pleasurable activities (for example, a walk in the park, a quiet evening at home, a long train journey) into unpleasant, upsetting, disturbing and often threatening experiences.

The continuum of fear and threat extends from being limited

to particular times, areas or individuals, through to affecting all aspects of women's daily lives. The extent to which it affects any particular women changes over time; the time frame here can be minute by minute, week by week or longer periods. The wariness of women in the public sphere can be heightened by an awareness of assaults in their local area or, more generally, by media reporting on a national level. Whilst actually in the public sphere, the behaviour of individual or groups of men can affect women's sense of safety. Most women recall an awareness of being watched or possibly followed. It is these perceptions and realities that result in women feeling they have to be constantly aware of their environment, watching and checking the behaviour of men they may encounter, trying to predict their motives and actions. Two feminist researchers refer to this as a 'geography of fear' that affects all women and which becomes a 'georgraphy of limitation'.[1]

Whilst having been sexually assaulted is likely to make women feel less safe, all the women interviewed were aware of the threat of violence. The women speaking below had not experienced stranger assault in the public sphere.

'Rape *is* constantly at the back of my mind when I'm in situations where I feel vulnerable.'

'I don't go out at night, I'm a coward, but then it can happen in the daytime. I think we're all very aware these days, through the media, of the very real threat of rape, not just to ourselves but to our own daughters, our friends, our mothers.'

'I definitely don't feel safe when it's dark and sometimes not in the day – and I think that's increased probably in response to the publicity. But I feel that it is a realistic apprehension as well, so although I go out a lot I tend to minimize the times when I will come back in the dark on my own. That's one of my considerations, where would I feel least vulnerable, as well as *being* least vulnerable.'

It is the threat of violence that results in women feeling vulnerable. Media coverage of sexual violence, whilst reporting real events, concentrates on stereotypical forms, predominantly stranger-rape or sexual abuse of children by strangers. Women who had experienced sexual violence in the home, particularly incest, were more likely to feel that nowhere was safe.

'I don't think you stand much chance really, you're no safer whether you're in the house or out of it.'

The threat of violence is not limited for many women to the possibility of rape by strangers but the impact of this generalized fear on women's freedom of movement was extensive.

'I feel it an awful lot in big cities where it's limited my social contacts, even my work, because of my fears of what might happen.'

Flashing is defined by Jalna Hanmer and Sheila Saunders as a form of predominantly visual violence.[2] The experiences of flashing recorded in the interviews revealed considerable variation in the form of the assault. Flashing may only involve a sudden exposure of male genitals; it may be preceded by being followed or be succeeded by being chased. The abusive man may make verbal remarks, of an apparently innocuous kind to get women's attention, of a sexually provocative nature, or which involve explicit threats of further violence. He may also be masturbating. The context in which incidents took place also varied considerably, ranging from the stereotype of a park or street at night, to daytime exposures on trains or buses, in pubs through to the two young women who were exposed to by relatives in their own homes.

'I was abroad and my daughter was having a tantrum and I said "Look I'm going!" and walked off. I turned round to look at her and there was this bloke masturbating *just behind her*. I grabbed her. I almost got violent with her because she was still carrying on. He just *kept following us* and every time I looked round he was *there*. He followed us until we went into this cafe but that wasn't very nice because the cafe was full of men.'

'It was near my house, and at first I didn't realize what was happening. Then he shouted at me, something about rape — I can't remember exactly — and I saw. I started to run and he chased me right into our garden. I thought afterwards how lucky I was that my house was round the corner.'

'I was about 12 and I was in the park wheeling my baby sister in her pram — I was very short-sighted (laughs). This man came along and started talking to me — Did I know where babies come from? — and it wasn't until he was quite near that I realized he was flashing. It was *awful*, very frightening and upsetting. I didn't tell anybody or talk about it. I just went home and brooded.'

'I've wondered whether it was an accident, but he was sitting downstairs playing with himself. He must have heard me coming down the stairs and he didn't stop — so he must have wanted me to see.'

In chapter 4 I noted that many experiences of flashing took place when the women were children or adolescents. Any explanation of flashing must take account of this fact. Do men who expose themselves deliberately seek out younger, therefore more vulnerable, females? Is part of their motivation to be young women's first encounter with an erect penis? Do they get a 'kick' out of terrorizing/confusing/upsetting young women – using their penis as a hostile threat?

Some women had lived or stayed in areas where flashing was a regular occurrence. All were places where women alone or in groups were common: holiday towns in this country and abroad, areas where single people lived, and university or nurses' residences.

'It was so consistent *everywhere* you went — everywhere — on the beach. Even when I went to the toilet in a cafe, when I came out the man made sure he unzipped himself and exposed himself. It was incredible really.'

The difference between how women experienced flashing at the time and how they talked about it in retrospect noted by Sandra McNeill was also evident in this study.[3] At the time, women did not experience flashing as a 'minor' crime. As children, they were often very frightened; as adult women, they felt personally violated and the uncertainty of what might happen next created fear and tension. When women reflect on their experience with the knowledge that nothing else happened and that flashing is not generally taken seriously, they dismiss or minimize the fear and or distress they felt in order not to appear paranoid or to be over-reacting to a 'trivial' incident. The woman speaking in the quotation which follows, like many, began discussing her experience of flashing flippantly, concentrating on the sarcastic comment she made to the man. When considering her feelings at the time, however, it became clear that whilst she was able to react she was also frightened and upset.

'But I shook, I really shook, because I didn't know whether that was going to be a flasher, what it was.'

It is important to remember that although further violence may not be intended women cannot know this until after the event. Indeed, being followed or chased suggests that in some circumstances flashing may be a preliminary to further assault. Evidence from recent studies of sex offenders has shown that many began offending as exposers and moved on to rape, sexual assault and/or sexual abuse.[4] No woman is, therefore, in a position to know at the time of an incident of flashing whether the assault will be limited to exposure. The threat of further violence is, in fact, a very real one.

Obscene phone calls are an example of predominantly verbal violence. Their impact on women is a combination of the invasion of privacy and the explicit or implicit threats of further violence that are made. Whilst abusive callers seldom use the word 'rape' they assume a particularly intrusive form of sexual access to women. It is a form of intrusion which, at least the first time, women cannot anticipate. It is this, alongside the intention to shock, humiliate and frighten women, which makes these calls a form of sexual violence. They are experienced by women both as a specific form of the threat of sexual violence and as violating in themselves. Calls varied over a number of dimensions, some appearing to be random, isolated incidents, others series calls. Some were obviously made by men who knew the woman. The continuum is further illustrated by the fact that women felt equally disturbed by series of unexplained silent phone calls. In some cases, these were more threatening because of the uncertain intention behind them. Women's reactions to silent phone calls have to be understood in the context of the reality of obscene phone calls and the generalized threat of sexual violence.

'I've had silent phone calls and I had to have my phone number changed. It was a series of calls. There wasn't even heavy breathing really and that was quite disturbing. I did put bolts on the door and changed the number.'

The initial reaction to a call which includes verbal abuse is often one of shock. This rapidly changes into either anger, which allows women to respond in some way, or fear. However they responded, all women felt that their personal space and sense of self had been violated.

'I've received telephone calls that feel like a sexual assault. Partly they make me feel really bad because the person knew me — well, knew my name and asked for me — and I had a feeling that it was a boy I was working with. I feel I *ought* to be able to tackle it with him. It just makes me feel very vulnerable. It happens at night when I'm asleep, not many clothes on. It makes me feel quite cross that even though I see myself as a powerful person, when that happens, I feel totally helpless and it makes me feel sick and *frightened* as well.'

'That upset me a lot because I felt that was the ultimate invasion of my privacy for someone to phone in my house.'

It was as much the uncertainty of what the call meant, as the actual content, that concerned women and preoccupied them afterwards. Did the man know them? If their name was used how was it known? Did he know where she lived? If threats were made about other forms of sexual violence, would they be carried out?

'It wasn't the actual fact that he was being obscene to me, it was whether he knew me, or how he got my number. That's the thing that worried me. Whether he actually knew who I was or whether it was at random.'

'I got quite worried about it because I thought he could see me — just because it happened a couple of times just as my husband went out. I thought he was watching from somewhere.'

'That did make me shake and I still don't know *why* it bothered me so much. I think it was because I was pregnant and I was alone in the house. I think what frightens you thinking about it now is that it might be somebody that knows where you live and who might turn up.'

As with flashing, women often felt that they had over-reacted at the time. It is only in retrospect, however, that women can be sure that no further action will be taken by the man. Public references to them as 'nuisance calls' and the practice of agencies such as the Samaritans offering a service to men who make such calls imply that women should not take obscene phone calls seriously.[5] Women are, therefore, encouraged to deny or minimize the impact of obscene phone calls on them. Impacts which range from the immediate distress through to changing phone numbers and locks to, I suspect in some cases, changing their address.

Women also received threatening phone calls which focused on physical violence. These were mainly from ex-partners. They were most commonly experienced by women who had left violent relationships. In these circumstances, the threat of further violence is very real and some men went to great lengths to find women in order to continue harassing them.

'That chap I threw out, he used to do things like that and get his friends to do it too.'

'He would call over and over again saying he was coming to get me and that he had a sawn-off shotgun.'

Answering the phone after an obscene or threatening phone call or during a series of silent calls becomes a frightening experience. Instead of being a useful tool which is often a source of support, the phone now makes women vulnerable and accessible.

Women's discussions of safety and the threat of violence focused on the threat of rape/sexual assault. Yet they themselves were much more likely to have been followed, flashed at or harassed by strange men. It may be that part of women's experience of these events was that it made the threat of rape more real. Alternatively, women may cope with these events by minimizing them through a comparison with how much 'worse' it would be to be raped.

Sexual harassment and sexual assault

The continuum in this section extends from the myriad forms of everyday sexism, 'routine oppression',[6] that women encounter in men's use of gesture and language through a range of behaviour to attempted rape. The point at which sexual harassment becomes sexual assault is not clear. There was a considerable area of overlap in the definitions used by the women interviewed. There was one distinction, however: sexual harassment involved a variable combination of visual, verbal and physical forms of abuse; assault always involved physical contact.

Visual forms of harassment include leering, menacing staring and sexual gestures; verbal forms include whistles, use of innuendo and gossip, sexual joking, propositioning and explicitly threatening remarks; physical forms include unwanted proximity, touching, pinching, patting, deliberately brushing close, grabbing. Any incident of sexual harassment may contain visual, verbal and physical elements.

The most common forms of harassment recalled by women took place at work or in the street. Some women, however, gave very clear examples of similar forms of treatment in other situations. All were experienced as intrusive and involved assumptions of intimacy that women felt were inappropriate and/or involved men treating women as sexual objects.

'He sat right next to me, interviewed me and halfway through he grabbed my hands and started fondling my hands, and I had to carry on the interview with him holding my hands! What could I do — I wanted a job — I was *outraged*.'

'They would put their hands up your back and ping your bra, put their hands inside your jumper. You just used to try and ignore it. Well at that point I did, I've perhaps changed my mind now. It seemed to be part of office culture to be mauled by the older male members of staff.'

'Men at work — commenting on the way you dress, the shape of your legs, the size of your bum, your bust, looking up your skirt every opportunity they got.'

'Some would stand really close, breathe down your neck, put their arms round the back of the chair — that sort of thing makes you feel really uncomfortable. They never did it to the other men in the office.'

'I hate it in the local pub, when they look at you as if they are stripping you . . . . . . or men who sit next to you and want to touch you, I can't stand that.'

None of the behaviour listed above would be defined in law, or by the women themselves, as sexual assault. No doubt, many of the men concerned would defined their actions as either 'just being friendly' or 'harmless fun'. This was not how women experienced them. By defining harassment as normal, men justify their behaviour and when it is challenged are able to dismiss (read redefine) women's perceptions.

Lin Farley suggests that men use particular forms of sexual harassment to discourage women from entering male preserves in the labour market.[7] Such strategies constitute a refusal to treat women as co-workers. This woman was one of the first women to work on the local buses in the town she lived in.

'When I was working on the buses I was harassed. Everybody in the depot considered any woman who worked there as up for grabs or up for comment.'

The way in which this situation developed illustrates one of the indirect ways in which harassment occurs in a predominantly male environment. One driver arranged for her to work with him and constantly demanded kisses and dates which she refused. She then discovered that he had told the rest of the staff that she was an 'easy lay' which resulted in comments and propositions from other male workers. This creation of a 'reputation' was also noted by Lin Farley and is a key theme in recent studies of young women's experiences of sexuality.[8] Once women are defined as 'loose', 'fair game' in men's eyes, future harassment is justified. This process occurs in more explicit ways in a number of predominantly female work roles. The frequency and form of harassment at work depended, to some extent, on how far women's work role was sexualized. Aspects of women's work may be dependent on attractiveness and display: for example, reception and secretarial work. The work situations of women in the sex industry are totally sexualized, and the most extreme examples of harassment at work were experienced by the two women who had worked in the sex industry.

'I wish I had a pound for every time I got called a slag . . . Nine times out of ten you walk onto that stage knowing you're going to be slagged off. The attention that you get is essentially hostile not flattering . . . Whenever groups of men came in, irrespective of their background, they would all behave in a remarkably similar way . . . Some of the things they would say were *really disgusting*. They'd do things like grab hold of a girl and try and push a bottle up her.'

The experience of the six women who had worked as barmaids suggests that this job sits uneasily between display and sexploitation. Each of them felt that sexual harassment was part of the job. Male customers and co-workers assumed the right to make sexual remarks and sexual advances.

'It's part and parcel of being a barmaid, or at least that's the impression your employers give you. And also it goes on from both sides. If you are working with a man behind the bar, he is as guilty of it as the ones in front. You don't have the counter in front of you to stop them either. I'd say about half of the male customers are going to do that. They're going to try it on . . . . . . Some of them were quite disgusting, the things that they would say were really, really hurtful, and you weren't supposed to show it, just get on with the job.'

'Working as a barmaid you get this thing that you are public property, you're the girl behind the bar. If you look at the bar, most of the people there are men and there's that whole sexual undertone a lot of the time.'

The extent to which women's work roles are sexualized and the sex ratio in the workforce affect the forms and frequency of sexual harassment. What men consider acceptable treatment of strippers would not be acceptable treatment of barmaids, and what is considered acceptable in the latter case would not be routinely acceptable in an office. What men are able to get away with in male-dominated environments has to be moderated in mixed sex and women-dominated work situations. Jeff Hearn and Wendy Parkin stress that sexuality and power relations are not isolated actions but structured processes within all organizations; sexual harassment being one explicit way in which they are expressed.[9] Whilst none of the women interviewed referred to it, Hearn and Parkin point out the particular meaning for, and types of harassment experienced by lesbian women in paid work.

Street harassment was a common experience for many of the women interviewed. Through street harassment, men define and treat women as sexual in an aggressive way. Men who do not know women assume the right of intimacy and/or sexual access.

'I experience a degree of sexual harassment I would say sort of once a week . . . . . . it varies in intensity, some I remember particularly, others . . . . . . It depends how you define it, some of what I mean would be just shouting at you on the street.'

'It's something that happens so much — you just experience it on the street all the time. It's almost a background of what going out of doors seems to mean.'

'In England they have this favourite thing of "Cheer up love", which I find very annoying. It's usually when I'm thinking about something and I find it very intrusive. Someone I don't know saying pay attention to me. Although it's maybe a very minor form, it's extremely annoying.'

The final quotation illustrates the continuum of experience very clearly. For women, sexual harassment ranges from physical assaults through to what, on the surface, appear to be innocuous remarks. The meaning behind the remark, the fact that through it men deny women the choice of which individuals to interact and communicate with and the intrusiveness of the encounter are what defines this, for women, as harassment. The expectation that women should be paying attention to and gratifying men, rather than preoccupied with their own thoughts and concerns, underlies this kind of intrusiveness.

Several women commented on a particular form of harassment of young women; the way men (strangers, friends of the family and relatives) seemed to enjoy embarrassing adolescent girls by commenting on their bodies.

'When I was an adolescent I used to blush very easily. *Men* would make comments and *they knew* I would blush. Then they would comment on that! It was excruciatingly embarrassing.'

There were many examples of other encounters that women defined as sexual harassment. Two women recalled being fondled by male nurses in mental hospitals. Seven women defined ways they were treated by male shop assistants as forms of sexual harassment; men's behaviour here ranged from verbal sexual innuendo to extremely patronizing attitudes. Women also defined aspects of the behaviour of male friends as harassment.

'I was harassed once by a friend at a party who I knew was married. He really went on and on as if I was really flattered!'

'All my husband's friends used to try it on to see how far they could get.'

The incidents recorded in the sexual assault category clearly reflect the continuum of experience ranging from being touched by strangers in the street, which other women defined as harassment, to attempted rape. One end of the continuum within sexual assault shades into sexual harassment; the other into rape. What characterized sexual assault for women was physical contact and the intention of the man concerned.

'Just *last week* I was cycling along when somebody reached out of his car, grabbed my bottom and tried to shove me off my bike, which is very sexual and aggressive.'

There were a number of examples of men abusing their professional status, including an optician, teachers and driving instructors. Some of these incidents were defined as sexual harassment, others sexual assault. In each case, the woman was temporarily dependent on the man's goodwill. This made responding angrily more difficult, as did the fact that the assault was always totally unexpected.

'I agreed to take part in a psychology experiment with a lecturer. When he was rubbing the glue stuff on my hair he stuck his hand down my jumper and it wasn't until I got home that I was *really angry*.'

Women defined two forms of behaviour by known men as sexual assault. The first involved attempted rape; the second the use of pornography by male partners. The majority of attempted rapes by known men involved acquaintances rather than friends or lovers and just under half occurred on holiday.

'It was one of those situations on holiday with friends when everybody pairs off and disappears. I was left with this bloke waiting for the others to come back. I spent the rest of the evening with him. He started to cuddle me and then he pushed and he pushed and he pushed and was trying to have intercourse with me. I spent at least half an hour having to keep him off me. I had a lot of flashbacks to it afterwards when I went back to school, feeling *absolutely petrified*.'

'I now see a lot of my relationship with him as being some kind of sexual assault. He used to use pornography at the same time as having sex with me — it was as if I became one of those pictures . . . . . . That's a much more subtle form of assault.'

'I felt more like an object than anything else, something to be experimented upon. When it was getting really bad he used to come home with all these various contraptions. It was almost like I wasn't involved. I was just a piece of apparatus in an experiment.'

A disproportionate number of women's recollections of flashing, sexual harassment and sexual assault occurred whilst they were on holiday. Indeed, a considerable number took place abroad and some women explicitly referred to the conflicts and contradictions that had arisen for them concerning cultural differences. A few women made overtly racist remarks, suggesting that particular groups of men of Colour were, by nature, more sexually aggressive. These remarks are a variant of a more common tendency to define 'types' of men as potentially violent. In a racist culture, race is easily transformed into a 'type'. In attempting to explain the disproportionate incidence of assaults whilst on holiday, three possibilities occurred to me. The figures may be an artifact in so far as women may be more likely to remember incidents which take place outside of their daily routines and in a context in which they expected to relax and enjoy themselves. Alternatively, women may, in fact, be more vulnerable in situations where they either relax or are unable to refer to and use their routine precautionary strategies. Finally, men may, across cultures, share a construction of foreign women as more vulnerable and/or more 'available'. This suggests that foreign women in the UK would experience British men as more sexually aggressive than men from their country of origin.

Pressurized sex, coercive sex and rape

A number of feminist writers have argued that one of the key problems in 'proving' rape in a court of law is that forced or coerced sex are common experiences for women.[10] This analysis challenges the assumption that all sexual intercourse which is not defined as rape is, therefore, consensual sex. Pauline Bart has developed a continuum which begins from consensual sex and moves through altrusitic sex (women do it because they feel sorry for the man or guilty about saying no), to compliant sex (the consequences for women of not doing it are worse than the consequences of doing it), to rape.[11] I have deliberately separated out consensual heterosexual sex from my continuum – it is a continuum of non-consensual sex. It is both conceptually and politically important to retain the possibility, at least, of consensual heterosexual sex. The categories of altruistic and compliant sex are covered by my category of pressurized sex. The category of coercive sex was introduced to cover experiences women decribed as being 'like rape'.

Paul Willis and Sue Lees have both documented the still existing double standard for young men and women in relation to heterosexual sex.[12] Willis describes boys' attitudes to girls as: 'exploitative and hypocritical. Girls are pursued, sometimes roughly, for their sexual favours, often dropped and labelled "loose" when they give in.'[13] Over three-quarters of the women interviewed recalled being on the receiving end of this exploitative male sexuality during their adolescence.

'He was never violent or anything — but he — it depends what you call violence — pushy in the sense of, you know, when you are a teenager, when you're with your boyfriend there's this constant pressure to go further sexually . . . There's this constant thing about boys needing sex and confusion about how you feel about it.'

'I didn't actually want to stop seeing him but I ended up having to because I couldn't see him and not have sex . . . I can remember quite early on him not taking no for an answer, and then him being very shocked when he saw that I did mean no, I wasn't just so called "messing about".'

'Most boys pressurized girls for sex. I don't think they wanted deep relationships. They wanted a score on their card.'

'Always there was pressure, well most of the time. It was like you had to do something to satisfy them.'

Pressure continued into adult life, as did this sense of obligation to meet men's sexual 'needs'. Specific obligations were incurred for which payment was assumed to be sex when men spent money on women. The situations range from the proverbial dinner for two, to a holiday or paying the rent. Pauline Bart's altruistic sex fits some of these experiences but does not include the sense of responsibility women internalize for satisfying men's desire for sex.

'I used to feel terrible. It's like women feel responsible for men's erections. You're conditioned into feeling that. But I don't anymore, I can say "It'll go down in a minute, don't worry".' (laughs)

'I went on holiday with this man and I *knew* that it was expected of me but I didn't want it. So I just gritted my teeth and did it because it was expected and I couldn't really say no.'

'When I was living with Mark, I'd come home from work and I'd be shattered. I'd just want to go to bed and sleep. He'd start cuddling up and touching me and I'd think "oh here we go again". It was like a *duty*, that was sort of paying the rent. I had a roof over my head and that was what I was expected to pay.'

A further form of obligation existed for women in marriage or long-term relationships.

'There are even occasions in my relationship now when I don't particularly want to . . . . . . I tend to acquiesce more often than not . . . . . . I think that's a problem that women have. We find it difficult to say no, particularly if you feel you've been agreeing, that there's some kind of tacit understanding that you are withdrawing from.'

These tacit agreements and obligations are seldom made specific, which partly accounts for why they are so difficult to challenge. Women often felt unable to assert their interpretations or needs in the face of male assumptions.

In response to a series of questions on attitudes to a variety of forms of heterosexual practice many woman discussed feeling pressured into sexual practices which they did not like, particularly oral sex. Men's consumption of pornography was implicated on a number of occasions in these discussions; either because its contents were used by men as an instruction manual or because men insisted that if a practice was represented in pornography it was 'normal' and 'fun'.

'We used to watch films and he would want me to do what . . . . . . He said that anything that turned you on and involved two people was alright, but I didn't feel it was alright.'

'He wanted to do everything they said in the book.'

'Whatever happened in this magazine we used to have to do it, it was like a manual. I'd think "Oh god, I better read it to see what I've got to do tonight".'

Clearly some of the above quotation shift into the compliant sex category, as most of these women felt the consequences of refusing to participate were worse, on balance, than the consequences of participating. Within relationships, many women recalled times when having sex was a price they had to pay to improve the situation, receive affection, and/or prevent their partner behaving in particular ways that upset them.

'I wanted the cuddles, the touching, but the intercourse was the thing you had to do for that.'

'I had a number of relationships in which I seemed to be under *pressure* and that wasn't what I wanted, but I did want the affection.'

'Generally in relationships I've felt that I've had to do it to save myself the trouble of persuading him not to want it. I would do it because it was easier than spending a whole day with him sulking about it.'

'I knew that if he didn't have an orgasm he would actually be *terribly* bad tempered. He was an emotionally violent sort of person, I knew if I wanted a quiet morning it would be best just to let him . . . . . . My god, I'm glad I got out of that relationship.'

Many women made angry remarks about the impossibility of friendships with men. In their experience, once a certain level of intimacy had developed, men always wanted the relationship to become a sexual one. Some women clearly felt that most of their heterosexual relationships had involved pressure to have sex.

'I believe that you can have men as friends . . . nearly every bloke that comes round here as my friend, they see it that you've got a man here because you want sex, and it's just not like that.'

'Not just one . . . . . . I mean *right from the very beginning* — my first real boyfriend, I didn't sleep with him for five weeks and he thought I was a real dud. It's happened from them on.'

'I felt pressured to have sex by nearly *everybody* I met at university — apart from one who actually did ask. I felt pressured by the bloke I was engaged to, I just felt *obliged* to have sex with him.'

Pressurized sex involved women assessing the costs of refusing sex. Past experience with a man or other men resulted in the feeling that to say no always had negative consequences. Women frequently had sex for men's pleasure rather than their own. Once a sexual relationship was established, the majority of men assumed sexual access; it was not something which involved negotiation and women's right to say no was seldom openly discussed, let alone accepted.

The general socialization of women to place the needs of others before their own and naturalistic models of sexuality where needs (usually male) are given the status of biological urges or drives result in many women internalizing a sense of responsibility for men's sexual pleasure. Hence, women find it difficult to say no to sex. Moreover, they realistically fear the consequences of saying no. In addition, it was obvious that many men assumed the right of sexual access within heterosexual relationships. They clearly also wanted to control when sex took place and what forms of sexual practice it was to consist of. Many women expressed considerable anger when discussing men's hypocritical refusal to respond to women's desire for sex if it was not what they, the men, wanted at the time.

Whilst many of women's discussions of pressurized sex referred to a general experience within one or a number of relationships, incidents of coercive sex were specific events: experiences of forced sex that women did not define as rape at the time of the interview. Men ignored women's physical or verbal resistance; explicit pressure, often including the threat of or actual physical force, was used. The majority of the men were known to the women and much of the difficulty women felt about naming these experiences rape was linked to this fact, particularly if the relationship had included consensual sex in the past. Even these distinctions proved problematic in retrospect. For example, one woman later discovered that what had been consensual sex for her had involved the man making bets about his ability to get her to go to bed with him. Two years later, he coerced her to have sex by behaving in a very threatening way. She, and the three other women quoted after her, illustrate how unclear in retrospect the boundary between rape and not rape was for many women.

'Where do you define rape? The pressure to have sex was so overwhelming . . . I was made to feel guilty. It isn't rape, but *incredible* emotional pressure was put on and I wanted that man out of my room as soon as possible.'

'I didn't say no, I didn't dare to . . . . . . you know you don't want to, but you are still doing it. That's why in my eyes now it's rape with consent. It's rape because it's pressurized, but you do it because you don't feel you can say no.'

'I couldn't call that rape . . . I mean there was that one bad case of it. He'd forced sex on me a number of times, that's what I would call taking a woman for granted.'

'The early time that I would say was — ohh — bordering on rape was a friend of — a married friend in my first marriage. He used to come round and pester me a hell of a lot and I didn't know what to do about it. Basically because my husband was violent to me and I knew he'd *kill* me, he'd blame me as well as the friend when he found out. I was dead scared of the neighbours seeing the car. I didn't have the strength to say fuck off in those days and in the end used to make love just to get rid of him.'

What distinguished some incidents of coercive sex from rape for the women was that they did not resist after a certain point.

'No not rape . . . . . . not in the (sighs) . . . . . . not actually physically forced to have sex, only . . . . . . coerced I think, yes.'

She added later in the interview:

'I remember an occasion where he wouldn't let me get up, and he was very strong. He pulled my arms over my head. I didn't put up much of a *struggle*. I mean I wouldn't have seen that as rape because I associated rape with strangers, night and struggle. I didn't put up much of a struggle, but I *didn't want to*, so in a sense that was rape, yes.'

Three other women who lived with violent men were coerced into sex by one of their partner's friends and lived in fear of him finding out. In each case, the woman eventually told her partner and in each case she was held responsible. This woman is describing what happened after she told her ex-cohabitee:

'We got to the flat and he dragged me into the bedroom and — ohh I just wanted him to go, I just wanted him to get out. Then he forced me into bed, made me have sex with him and he scratched all my back open. Then he got a tin of deodorant and sprayed it into every scratch (sighing and upset) then he started laughing and said "Go and show that to your boyfriend".'

Boyfriends also used a variety of coercive techniques:

'He was a photographer and he took lots of photos of me and they became pornographic. I wasn't aware of that at the time. He'd been giving me lots of drinks. I met him about a week later and he showed me these photos which really threw me. I was very upset and he refused to give them to me. I had to sleep with him to get them.'

As with pressurized sex, some women felt that pornography played a part in their experiences of coercive sex. Again there was pressure to engage in particular sexual practices; in this context, women submitted because the man was also violent. Of the women seven recalled being terrified during sex by their partners fantasies of wanting to watch them being raped. Even if these fantasies were not 'created' by reading pornography, pornography certainly legitimated them and encouraged men's belief that the woman would enjoy it.

'One night he pulled me into the bathroom and he wanted to wee all over me. That's just one of the things. I just can't go into all of them — the things he used to want me to put on. I had to put up with all sorts of sexual deviations those months. I was becoming ill . . . . . . Oh it was just terrible.' (upset)

'His fantasy was . . . . . . for me to be in a gang bang, against my will, so he could be in another room — not actually watching — but in another room knowing I was there with a load of men, screaming and shouting for help. My fear was that it would happen. He often used to say to me "Wouldn't it be nice if you went out one night and got raped and came home and told me about it"!'

The assaults that women defined as rape took place in a range of contexts and the rapists were in a range of relationships to the women. A minority of the rapes were what have been called 'blitz rapes', where strangers took advantage of the fact that women were alone. A far greater number took place in the context of day-to-day interactions with husbands, lovers, boyfriends and fathers. Others were more obviously planned. One man pretended to arrange a modelling session. Another took a woman's purse and ran off with it knowing she would follow him. One woman's ex-boyfriend went out to make a phone call while she was visiting his flat; when she left, his friends were waiting outside and she was gang raped. The two quotation below illustrate two other situations in which women were raped by men they knew. The first woman was staying with a married couple, both her friends, and had been drinking with them during the evening.

'You know that feeling when you're just *out*, I was completely unconscious. The next thing I knew I woke up — I was in bed with *my baby son* — and he was actually raping me *then* . . . . . . I can remember saying to him 'What are you doing!' and he went 'Sssh' — great! (ironic laugh). And he got out of the bed and left.'

'I'd just split up with this boyfriend who had been hitting me and I was feeling quite hurt about it. This friend started paying attention to me and in a way it was a bit of an ego boost. He came round to my house. We were watching tv. Suddenly he was undressing me. I tried to stop him, I was pushing him away . . . . . . in the end I thought "I'll just go dead".'

In both cases male 'friends' took advantage of situations in which women had absolutely no reason, at the time, to suspect what was later to happen.

The assaults by strangers took place either outside or as the result of accepting a lift. Every woman was aware that accepting a lift from a man was a risk but felt safe due to specific circumstances or because the alternatives involved greater risk. For example, a young woman and her friend had missed their last bus home. It was raining and a man offered them a lift. They felt safe as there were two of them.

'He dropped my friend off first and before I could even *think* he'd driven off to this deserted heath.'

Another woman was hitching on the continent with a male friend. The man giving them a lift drove off leaving her friend at a garage.

The forms of sexual practice the rapists forced on women and their use of physical violence also varied. Of the rapes 85 per cent involved forced sexual intercourse, 31 per cent forced oral sex and one woman was raped anally. In eight rapes, considerable physical violence was used by the man. In a further eight, threats of violence were made. In 13 cases the women were held down and one was tied up. Only two rapes involved weapons, in both cases a knife. In two cases, brutal sadistic violence was used. The majority of women became fearful of physical injury when their initial resistance failed to deter their attacker and they stopped struggling making further violence unnecessary. The fear women experienced, particularly when raped by strangers, was fear for their lives although no specific threat may have been made. One woman who decided not to resist for fear of injury recalled a later conversation with a policewoman.

'She initially said "I'd rather be killed than raped" and I said "You must be joking". She thought about it for a bit and then said "Yes, I suppose you're right".'

'He put a knife to me and said if I didn't he'd stab me — well, what do you do — you choose your life.'

One of the many myths about rape is that it is 'a fate worse than death' and this directly links up with the injunction that women should resist throughout. Faced with the reality of rape, women make second-by-second decisions, all of which are directed at minimizing the harm done to them. At the point where initial resistance strategies have failed, the fear of further violence often limits women's resistance. The only form of control that seems available to women at this point is limiting the harm done to them.

Many women had unclear memories of the actual assault, although they had clear memories of the place, the events surrounding the rape and their feelings and emotions. Some had deliberately suppressed the details as a coping mechanism. Other women, whilst they may have remembered more made it clear during the interview, either explicitly or by their manner, that they did not wish to discuss the details of the assault. Of the rapes 85 per cent had taken place at least three years before the interview and 38 per cent at least seven years before, yet recalling details was still painful.

This section has demonstrated that many women experience non-consensual sex on a recurring basis. It is a minority of such experiences that are defined by women as rape. The number would be even smaller if I had applied current British legal definitions of rape to the interview data, and smaller still if we only took into account those rapes which were reported to the police and recorded in official statistics. It is not possible to make clear and precise distinctions between pressurized sex, coercive sex and rape, but the concept of the continuum both validates the abuse women feel and the shifting boundaries between these categories as their own understandings and definitions change over time.

The many statements women made in their discussions of experiences of pressurized sex, coercive sex and sexual assault which implicated pornography cannot be ignored. Nor can the fact that many women also discussed feeling pressured or coerced into looking at pornography, either in magazines or on film and video. I was initially shocked at the extent to which porn videos had become integrated into social events; they seemed to be an automatic part of many parties. Whilst many feminists were engaging in academic debates about the definition and meaning of pornography, many of the heterosexual women I interviewed were having to cope with its unwelcome presence in their lives. Their feelings about this did not reflect a 'prudery' about sex but were grounded in feeling upset at the objectification (and at times abuse) of the women appearing in porn, and by implication themselves, and the reality that their partner expected them to engage in the sexual practices represented. If we are to have honest and frank discussions about pornography in the Women's Liberation Movement they must extend outside our limited networks and include this reality. They can no longer be limited to abstract discussions of censorship and fantasy.

Sexual abuse of girls and incest

The connections between child sexual abuse and incest are in one sense obvious. Many researchers have defined incest as a specific form of child sexual abuse. Within this general linkage, there are also more specific ones. Both may involve a single assault or repeated assaults by the same abuser. In both, the nature of the assaults ranges through forms of unwelcome intimate contact, as discussed in the section on sexual harassment, to flashing, to getting a girl to undress, to touching her body and or genitals and/or getting her to touch the abuser's body, to masturbation and rape. The girl may be gently encouraged, bribed, tricked, pressured, coerced or forced to take part. Whilst in incest the abuser is always known to the girl, many of the examples of child sexual abuse also involved known men. In both cases the abuser may be a peer or an adult, one or two generations older.

In previous sections, examples of sexual violence experienced before the girls were 16 years old have been noted. In this section, I will develop the range of child sexual abuse and demonstrate how incest can be analysed as an extension of patriarchal relations in the household.

Sexual aggression experienced in childhood and adolescence included abuse by adult strangers, acquaintances and relatives.

There were also a number of incidents which involved male peers and slightly older boys.

'I was about 7 and a 12-year-old boy from down the road used to terrorize me. First it was pull up your dress and I wouldn't because I knew what was coming next. It was like a battle of wills for about 15 minutes and I was absolutely terrified . . . My sister and I lived in fear. We came out of school and looked to make sure he wasn't there.'

Many children have memories of being bullied. What makes this situation, and the many similar ones girls experience, sexual assault is the combination of sex and aggression. The next two examples further illustrate this point.

'I must have been about 7 and I was rock-climbing with my sister. She was quite far ahead and two boys who weren't much older, although they seemed to be to me, came up. One of them held a knife at me and I stood against this rock and they had a good feel and then sent me on my way. I was just very aware that I mustn't do anything to aggravte them.'

'I can only remember being there with this big boy. He must have been about 12 — a lot older than me I was only 6 or 7. I was frightened of him because he was threatening to push me down some stairs where there was no banister. Later that day I remember saying to my mum "What does fuck mean?". She went mad, asked me who had said it and I said "Well this boy said he'd give me a bike if I let him fuck me".'

By far the most common category of child sexual abuse, apart from flashing, was assaults by known men. The first woman is discussing an experience with a friend's father when she was 13.

'He wanted to *touch* me and me to touch him, and he wanted me to kiss him. He'd cornered me and I had to talk my way out and get past him and out the door, which I managed to do. He came running after me — it was quite frightening really.'

'I remember uncles coming over and me just feeling uncomfortable about them. Now I know they were rubbing themselves up against me and things like that. I knew it was dirty and horrible and it used to make me shudder — now I know why.'

'When I was around 10 or 11 my aunts fiancé was always touching me up. I just didn't like it. I told him off about it. I know he did it to my niece as well who was younger than me.'

'I was molested when I was about 12 by my godfather . . . . . . I *adored* him, he was a father figure. He'd invite my sister and I to stay in a posh hotel along with his son who was a couple of years older. He would start embracing you, but then get very rough, put his arms right round — I adored this affection. *But then* he started putting his hand under my sweater and holding onto my breast and taking my bra off. I wouldn't get into the lift alone with him *because I didn't want to be molested.* I wasn't terrified but *I didn't* enjoy it. My sister told me recently that he used to come in from his bath either naked or in his pyjamas with his *prick hanging out* (anger and disgust) and he would stand over my sleeping sister and she would open her eyes and be staring straight into this man's penis.'

These women's experiences are similar in some respect to those defined by women as incest in that the abuse involved an extension of affection. There were also a number of incidents involving strangers that women recalled as being very frightening and disturbing.

'We'd built this tree house and this guy chased me into it. He didn't do anything to me but he was shouting that he was going to pull my knickers down and stuff. I remember vividly that it quite frightened me at the time.'

'I've just remembered an experience when I was 12 which *really* disturbed me for about two years. It was only in my twenties that I could even talk about it. I was molested on the underground and the reason it was horrible was because I was at that age where I was old enough to understand and yet I was still a child. This man was sitting opposite me playing with a camera, just started being friendly and talking to me. Being a nice, friendly polite child I responded. He started holding my hand, I thought uhh uhh this is a bit off, but I was *too polite* to snatch it away. It was politeness that made me acquiesce, because he was an adult. He made me feel him up. Looking back, it wasn't that bad, but for me it was the most awful thing that ever happened. I had this repulsion ever after for soft squidgy moist skin, it would remind me of what I felt. I used to think I'd never get married because it put me off men — still now I think about it.'

The woman speaking below was seen shoplifting by a man. He promised not to tell anyone if she went with him to deliver a parcel.

'Anyway, I went to this empty house, being fairly naive and innocent and we went upstairs. He got me to lie on the floor and he did too and was moving backwards and forwards — I presume he was masturbating. At which point, I began to get quite worried and said so and he let me go — which is amazing. I did feel really *awful* afterwards. I remember thinking when I got home that I was really *unclean*, washed, tore off my clothes — I felt really degraded by it. I think I felt a lot of the things women who are raped feel.'

Many women's experiences demonstrated that the impacts of child sexual abuse can be strong and long-lasting and that the physical content of the abuse is not always the determining factor. Little evidence emerged to support the claim made by many writers that it is the response of adults that accounts for the negative impact on children of sexual abuse. Women who told no one were as likely to experience long-lasting effects as those who told someone.

Data were presented in chapter 4 which demonstrated that considerable numbers of women feared violence and/or picked up sexual messages from male family members. Many women had experienced similar paternal controls to those recalled by incest survivors, but were not themselves incestuously abused. Where the control and sexual messages interlinked women were aware of the connection to incest but did not define their experiences as incest. Judith Herman defines this form of father–daughter interaction as 'seductive' and she found it had as damaging effects on women as more overt abuse.[14]

'He very obviously started seeing me as a sexual being . . . I think I was more nervous of him because of the sexual vibes he was . . . I mean, I think he was the central person I was afraid of when I was going through all that terror. I've often thought about what it was he actually did . . . Apart from the initial things, like coming up beside me and putting his arm around my waist, slapping me on the bum . . . . . . When I think about it now there was something very creepy about him . . . . . . a kind of sexual innuendo . . . . . . I think I've blocked a lot out that I could do well now to get in touch with again . . . It comes out in dreams. It really sort of shouts at me in dreams.'

This woman was fearful of what she might discover if she thought too much about her relationship with her father. She was not the only one who felt this.

'I'm sure something happened when I was much younger but I just can't remember. It's like completely blank . . . I can remember when I was older, mild things which I knew were an extension of something else that happened before.'

Other women's feelings were often less clearly connected to overt behaviour but, none the less, they felt uncomfortable. Most of these women resisted attributing incestuous motives to their fathers.

'I don't say he had incestuous feelings. If he did, I don't think he would *ever* have translated it into action. I think some of it was *over-strong* paternal feelings, but I do think there's a sexual undercurrent to that with a girl.'

'It was more of a feeling of something that I shied away from. When he was tickling us or something like that there was some feeling in my mind that this wasn't what it should be.'

'I don't think I ever experienced physical pressure from my father, yet I had similar reactions to those I've read incest survivors have. I don't know where they come from really. Does it just come from that sort of social conditioning of it's a possibility?'

Many women recalled their father ignoring them or being very controlling, critical or verbally and/or physically abusive. Some fathers, whether or not they were sexually abusive, called their daughters whores or sluts. Many women recalled relationships with fathers worsening in adolescence. Much of the conflict concerned girls challenging their father's authority. Many of the incest survivors recalled similar attitudes and forms of control to those common in the lives of women who had not experienced incest.

'I had a very bad time with my father then, having to play the little-daughter syndrome — fights about freedom, what I was and wasn't allowed to do.'

'My father was *always* protesting that he wasn't one of these fathers who had sexual hangups about his daughters. And yet he used to be very hostile to any boys we brought into the house. As soon as we started going with boys he was *absolutely unbearable*. We couldn't talk to him at all. He was *totally dictatorial* and more violent. I remember much more violence to us as teenagers. I can remember cuddling him and very much avoiding being against that part of him. I can remember always making sure that from the waist down I wasn't *actually* against him.'

The majority of women were frightened of their fathers. Some had good reason to be. In the case of others, the reasons why they felt fearful were less clear. Many abusive aspects of relationships with fathers emerged during the interviews; father–daughter incest was the extreme end of a continuum of father/daughter relationships. Where incestuous abuse was by adult relatives other than biological fathers, these men were always in some form of 'social father' relation to the girl: step-father, mother's boyfriend or the adult male in the household. Father/daughter relationships, and the use of paternal authority, are an important area of further research. It is in this relationship that women first see and experience the power that men assume in relation to women and children. Whilst far less common in the interviews, incestuous abuse by peers could be explored in the same way as sexual abuse by peers: that young men see sexual aggression as a legitimate form of behaviour.

The majority of the experiences women defined as incest involved men who were their biological or social fathers. One woman was abused by an older male cousin over a period of about a year, one by her grandfather when she was living with her grandparents temporarily and one woman by a combination of uncles and lodgers. In the first two cases abuse took place over the relatively short period of time that the girl and abuser lived in the same household and in the latter case there was a succession of abusers, rather than abuse over a long period by the same man. There were no examples of brother–sister incest in the interviews, but this form of incest may well be of longer duration as siblings, in most circumstances, live in the same household until they leave home as adults.

None of the women had any idea about the possibility of abuse before it happened to them and ten picked up no signs before the abuse began. Three women also experienced abuse from other male relatives and or family friends. The age at which abuse started influenced the form the initial contacts took. When women were younger, abuse usually began with touching.

'I can remember being touched round — not just lovingly, cuddlingly like you would a child, it was more than that . . . I felt — even then it felt like there was something *wrong* terribly wrong — but I was so young . . . . . . It leaves a mark, I know it does.'

Of these women five defined aspects of the abuse as rape and another three as attempted rape. For several women, the interview was the first time that they had named their experience in this way. Not every woman could remember how long the abuse lasted for. It tended to last longer if it began in early childhood. For two women, it was a single experience of rape, although the threat that it might be repeated remained until they left home. Only the woman who was first approached when she was 15 knew that the abuse was against the law at the time although five other women felt it was wrong from the beginning. For the other women, the abuse began as an extension of affection and it was when either the aspects of the abuse changed or they were older that they too defined what was happening as wrong. When abuse began as an extension of affection women recalled confused and ambivalent feelings. This was either because they wanted affection from the man or because they experienced pleasurable physical sensations.

'I remember my father teaching me how to masturbate when I was four. He said "I'll show you something nice", and it was.'

Unlike the popular stereotype that incest involves treating a child as special and that it is an extension of a close, affectionate relationship, the majority of these women felt that they had virtually no relationship with the abuser or a predominantly negative one before the abuse began.

'He totally ignored me until 11. When I started my periods, he started to sort of take notice. In fact, he took me out for a meal, started to buy me presents. I was quite pleased 'cos he was actually taking an interest in me. Then after that it started.'

Four women did recall at some point feeling, or being treated as, 'special' within the family. For all of them, however, this became a form of bribery and involved aspects of control, such as not being able to chose their own clothes. For one woman, what were seen by other members of the family as treats consisted of her father taking her out for day-trips during which he took photographs of her which he threatened to send away to pornography magazines or pretended that she was a prostitute and he her pimp.

None of the abusers were felt to have positive relationships with the rest of the family. The most positive remark was that they were unpredictable, sometimes they could be loving but they were just as likely to be violent, verbally abusive or threatening – eight were physically violent to the woman, four to her mother, and two to other children. The majority of the physical abuse occurred when women were older and began resisting the abuse or challenging their abuser's authority in other ways.

The majority of women had been explicitly told to keep the

abuse secret. Two fathers told their daughters that their behaviour was normal. The pledge to secrecy that most abusers demanded was usually underlined either by threats of violence or threats that telling someone would upset their mother and/or cause the family to break up.

'Kids are terrible at keeping secrets but, by god, you keep this one.'

The fear of family break-up or of 'abandonment', which many researchers have presented as some sort of unconscious defensive mechanism in families where incest is happening (see chapter 2), was, for this group of women, the result of internalizing explicit threats from the abuser. It is not surprising, therefore, that none of these women told anyone about the abuse whilst it was happening. The reasons women gave for not telling anyone were similar to those women discussed in relation to other forms of sexual violence. They feared being disbelieved or blamed and/or the reaction of the abuser. Several women stressed that they did not know how to tell anyone as they had no words to describe what was happening (see chapter 6). For five women, either the threats about upsetting their mothers or an awareness that their mothers were unhappy and that if they knew they would feel guilty and responsible silenced them.

'. . . I've never forgotten that he said "The next time I'm going to kill you" — so they put the fear of god into you so that you don't tell.'

'Then, the emotional blackmail would start because he obviously realized he had to handle all this. So, it was pressure all the time that I mustn't tell mum, and eventually it was if you tell her then you'll do something dreadful and it's your fault, you wanted this. It was all me you know, so the whole thing becomes a trap . . . . . . It was something I felt I was completely trapped in that I had to do. I felt ashamed and I felt somehow it was something I'd done and if anybody found out everybody would hate me and think I was a despicable person.'

The sense of responsibility and blame that many abusers instilled in girls was reinforced by the general silence that surrounds incest.

Women's feelings about the man during the abuse were either hatred and/or terror.

'I was terrified of him. I used to jump when I walked past him. I never knew what he was going to think up next. It wasn't only physical. It was a mental battle. He used to set up situations in which I was always in the wrong.'

Three women began with more positive feelings but this changed as the abuse continued. The depth of these feelings were illustrated by two women's reactions to their father's death. Both were relieved and felt freed but, somehow, a sense of his presence and the control he had exerted remained.

'I felt as if he was behind me, and I felt as though I was going to get banged in the neck for telling someone — and he's been dead six years!'

'I feel in a way it's been exorcized by his death, although I still think I see him. On the day of the funeral, I thought he had done the whole thing to see if he could get at me.'

One of the most complex issues in this area is the anger many incest survivors feel towards their mothers. Many other researchers have noted that mothers are often held to be more responsible than the abuser and, indeed, many researchers have taken this line themselves (see chapter 3). Whilst by no means all the women blamed their mothers for the abuse, a number had and one still did. In order to understand this response, it is necessary to place it in the context of mothering generally. Several women felt that their mothers ought to have known about the abuse, and three were sure she did, although none had been told directly. As the abuse was so obvious to them at the time, they assumed that it must also be for their mothers. I asked incest survivors to discuss their feelings about mothers in more detail during the follow-up interviews. It became clear that for many women the strategies the abuser used to keep the abuse secret effectively separated them from their mothers. For example, the strategies they used to get sexual access to girls, such as taking over bathtime or bedtime routines, decreased contact with the mother. In some cases, the men deliberately manipulated the relationships between mother and daughter by constantly criticizing their wife. In others, it was the dynamics of the abuse itself that separated mother and daughter.

It is important to remember that mother/daughter relationships where incest is not occurring are not necessarily positive and supportive. Many women who were not incestuously abused had ambivalent feelings about their mothers, seeing them as weak and unable to stand up to their fathers. They also experienced a sense of betrayal when they felt their mothers submitted to their father's authority rather than openly supporting them. Very few women saw their mothers as strong independent women; two of the women who did were incest survivors.

The threat of violence in intimate contexts and domestic violence

The continuum of experience in the case of domestic violence has three important aspects. First, whilst 25 women defined experiences as domestic violence, many more instances of violence in heterosexual relationships were recorded. These were single or infrequent incidents within short-term relationships. For the women interviewed, what distinguished domestic violence from these incidents was that the man and woman were cohabiting and that the violence occurred over time. Second, within the experiences women defined as domestic violence, the severity and frequency of the violence varied, from less severe and infrequent incidents through to repeated life-threatening violence. Taking the continuum beyond the sample of women interviewed, the extreme end of this aspect of the continuum would be murder. Third, the violence that women experienced always involved a variable combination of the threat of violence, emotional violence, forced sex and physical assault.

I have already demonstrated, in chapter 4, that the threat of violence is present in many of women's interactions with men; it was a factor in relationships with fathers, dates, boyfriends and husbands, as illustrated by the women speaking below. These quotations also demonstrate that the threat, as in the public sphere, ranges through a vague, generalized fear to the anticipation of a likely assault.

'I think I overlooked the fear bit of that question. When my father argued with me, which was only rare occasions, I was very, very scared. Whenever he was arguing, he was very much out of control, totally irrational. I was frightened on many occasions.'

'A lot of times I've felt with some men I've gone out with that they could *be very* violent. Some things they would *do*, like they'd grab hold of you — it just frightens me.'

'It's funny because he's a very gentle person, I really don't think he would have hit me — but *I had that fear* . . . . . . so I would be very frightened of challenging him.'

'I didn't know when he was going to knock on the door, what he was going to be like, what mood he was going to be in, whether I was going to get hit . . . . Was he going to scar me for life? Was he going to punch me in the head and knock me out and I'd die?'

The threat of violence in intimate contexts can have the same result as in the public; women question, and often limit, their behaviour in ways that benefit men in attempting to avoid physical assault. The impact on women of threatened violence or a single incident could be quite profound.

'Sometimes he would try and throw me on the bed and pin me down and that's when I got frightened. He used to do it quite jokingly, but actually he's quite strong and I could feel that he meant it.'

'Sometimes I get scared when I see him losing his temper and he *clenches* his fist. That scares me because I can see that it is violence.'

'I remember the tension of becoming aware that I had to notice what I was saying all the time, to make sure I didn't offend him. I had become afraid of him.'

'I always said that if a man I was having a relationship with hit me I'd leave — but I didn't. I was extremely shocked and it made me very quiet and afraid.'

Many women who experienced violence from boyfriends stopped the relationship fairly quickly, if not immediately. If they were cohabiting and particularly if they were married and had children, violence often occurred over longer periods of time. It was not only the increased dependence that affected women but also the greater possibilities of control available to men living in the same household.

'My first boyfriend was quite violent, especially when he was drunk or when he was out of his head. If I didn't want to sleep with him, or we had had a row about where we were going to go . . . . . . It took me a long time to get up the courage to finish with him . . . I was frightened of him.'

This woman's experience highlights a common theme in many interviews; the use by male partners of violence or threatened violence to ensure sexual access to women.

It was clear from many of the interviews that it is not possible to separate physical violence from other forms of control. Control in heterosexual relationships can be multilevelled and violence is one of a range of options available to men.[15] One aspect of the continuum of experience is that other forms of control and aspects of abuse, particularly verbal abuse and pressurized and coercive sex (discussed above), were present in relationships where no, or relatively little, overt physical violence had occurred.

'In my marriage, although he's not violent to me, he is aggressive towards me.'

'He was very good at bringing me down in front of other people. I didn't realize that till some time later.'

'He didn't speak to me for about a month. By that time I was virtually begging him on knees to talk.'

One woman had experienced violence in her first marriage. Whilst her second husband was not physically violent, she clearly felt that some of the ways he behaved towards her were similar to the behaviour of her first husband.

'Again my security has been undermined. He won't let me express myself. He just pooh poohs — you're a non-person, you're negative.'

The remainder of this section will concentrate on the women who defined their experience as domestic violence. All of these women were living with the violent man at the time, of whom 18 were married and seven were cohabiting. For over half of the married women, the man had been their first serious boyfriend. Only two men were violent before marriage, both insisted they would not behave this way once they were married. Only four women had witnessed violence between their parents and most of the rest had never thought about violence in relationships before it happened to them. These figures offer little support to cycle-of-violence theories. Women's understanding of the violence that they did witness as children also challenges this theory. At the time, they understood it as 'fighting'. The few women who, at some point, had seen violence as 'normal' between men and women had not witnessed it in childhood. There was no evidence in this sample that women accepted or expected violence in later life because of their childhood experience.

The point at which violence began in the relationship varied but, for the majority (60 per cent), the first incident occurred within the first year of marriage or cohabitation and for two women during the honeymoon.

'All I can remember is that it was something *so trivial* like he said "That's the fish knife that you use for the fish course" and I said "I know" and he *blew up* (astonishment). He stormed out of the restaurant. I went back to the motel a bit later. He locked the door, became very violent — took the rings flushed them down the toilet.'

For three women, violence did not occur until after the first three years of marriage and one woman had been married for ten years before violence began. In each case, however, other forms of control were used in earlier years, including isolation, verbal criticism, setting standards for childcare and housework (particularly that women should stay at home being 'proper wives and mothers') and forms of economic control.

'Things *really* started to go down hill when I went to university, there's no doubt about that . . . . . . I don't think there'd been any need for him to be violent to me because he had me so much in his control in other ways, financially, at home with the children.'

The frequency of violence varied greatly and two distinct patterns emerged. Seven women experienced violence either weekly or monthly. All the other women described it as either unpredictable or cyclical with relatively long gaps between incidents of severe violence.

'He could go for a *long, long time* without hitting me. Then there would just be a *massive explosion* for no apparent reason.'

'I was never able to tell when — I mean it could go *a year* without anything, then the next day it would happen.'

The fact that were long gaps between violent episodes did affect women's attitudes to the relationship, and their ability to cope. It was not just the physical violence, however, which affected them. The vast majority of the abusive men used threats and other forms of control during periods where there was no overt physical violence. Being violent to objects and destroying women's valued possessions was a reinforcement of the threat of violence to the woman herself.

'He used to fine me if I said anything he considered out of order. All these sort of weird things, trying to get control, power.'

'I had a tremendous amount of furniture in my house smashed, doors and lots of my personal things ruined.'

'He almost burnt my work one time — three years of research and writing. He had lots of my papers out in the garden and the incinerator was burning. I had to beg and plead and agree to various conditions to get it off him.'

The majority of women experienced violence for between two to eight years. The severity of the violence, in most cases, increased over time.[16] This is underlined by the fact that the most common reason women gave for leaving the final time was fear of death or permanent physical damage; nine men explicitly threatened to kill women. Other researchers have suggested that the frequency of assaults also increases over time. This was the case for approximately 50 per cent of the women interviewed.

'*Each* one got harder and harder, I mean the marks . . . . . . one time he hit me *so hard* on the back of the head he broke his own hand.'

'I haven't really talked about how the violence changed, but it certainly did change. There was a young immature pattern to his violence, then there was a more subtle, dangerous — never showing any marks . . . . . . (there were occasions where he could have killed me earlier) — the end was very serious. The last time he battered my head against the wall. I realized that I could easily have ended up as a sort of zombie, just simply by staying there.'

'He used to bang my head against the wall or the floor. I finally left him when I thought he was trying to kill me.'

Every woman experienced physical violence, all but one mental and verbal violence, and 60 per cent were raped or coerced into sex by the abusive man. The link between violence and forced sex has seldom been discussed in studies of domestic violence. Pamela Smith found that 48 per cent of a sample of women from a Canadian refuge had been forced to have sex and 36 per cent had been deliberately hurt during intercourse.[17] Catherine Lynch discusses the continuum of coercive sex as an aspect of domestic violence ranging from single incidents of forced 'regular sex' through repeated incidents to forced 'deviant sexual acts'.[18] Many of the women in this study also stressed the atmosphere of threat and fear in which they lived and the impact of mental violence on them.

'I realized I was under terrible strain the whole time . . . I would be setting the table and I couldn't remember. I'd go into a blind panic about what side the spoon had to be on. It was that sort of detail everyday.'

'Within a couple of weeks, he started snarling at me about the way I laid the breakfast table. It was something *stupid* like the marmalade on the wrong side of the table . . . I got to the stage of wondering about everything, if I was going to get it right or wrong.'

'He definitely sapped my confidence over the years. It's like a drip on your head . . . and I got to believe by the end that I was hopeless at everything, that everything he said about me was actually true. Which is another reason why I didn't leave, because if I was that hopeless how on earth was I going to exist on my own without him . . . . . . That's the ploy of course.'

Questioning women's performance of household tasks was the most common event that preceded assaults. Almost any aspect of women's work in the home could become a focus of dispute and many abusive men felt they should control almost every aspect of household organization, from where the clock stood on the mantlepiece, to how often windows were cleaned, to how the table should be set. The next most common issue which precipitated violence was the man being threatened by the woman's education and/or status, closely followed by arguments about sex and/or sexual jealousy.

'It was normally in relation to something to do with me fulfilling a certain role.'

'Looking back, just by being the person I am, I provoked it because I was educated beyond him and that mattered to him. It didn't matter to me . . . so I didn't even have to do anything.'

Many women found the tension and fearfulness when they sensed a violent incident was brewing unbearable. Some consciously continued an argument in order to get the violence over with and move into a period of relative calm.[19]

'What used to frighten me more was when I knew he was going to do it — the not knowing when. When he was actually hitting me, the fear seemed to go somehow — no, not go. I actually knew it was there. You weren't living on is it going to be now, is it going to be tonight, is it going to be in the morning . . . . . . When it was happening you knew, if you survived, that was going to be maybe a few weeks before the next one, so that was that bit over.'

It is by abstracting incidents of violence like the ones this woman is describing from the context of the history of the relationship and from an understanding of how violence and its threat affects women over time, that researchers and professionals are able to suggest that women 'provoke' violence.

Violence did not always take place in private; eleven of the women's children witnessed the violence. Children often intervened to protect their mothers; three women felt their children had prevented them being killed. Violence also took place, less often, in front of the man's parents or friends and the woman's parents. Threats of violence were often made in public, in social settings. Three men were violent to all their children and four to a particular child, usually a step-child. Three women were hurt when they intervened to stop children being abused. Fifteen men were not known to be violent in any context other than to the woman.

Isolation is a factor often referred to in relation to domestic violence and incest. As with incest, what women said suggested that men deliberately ensured that women were isolated. Women were prevented from seeing friends and family. Only two felt able to go out on their own with friends and many were warned not to tell anyone about the violence. Women were, therefore, separated from potential sources of support. Isolation is not a cause of abuse but is one of the many forms of control abusive men attempted to exert over women's lives.

The reaction of men to their violence varied. Some never apologized; they either ignored the fact that it had happened or justified it in terms of the woman's behaviour. About 40 per cent were initially contrite, promising it would never happen again. As the violence continued, this response tended to diminish.

'He either really didn't know he'd done it or he was very good at making himself believe he hadn't done it.'

'Towards the end, he didn't even feel remorseful. He thought it was his right to do such things to me.'

'I don't think either of them have ever been in the role of the contrite "I'm ever so sorry". It's always been "You asked for it".'

Drawing out the connections

The words of the women interviewed have been used in this chapter to demonstrate the range of experiences within each form of sexual violence, the ways in which the categories shade into each other at certain points and the similarity of the dynamics in a number of forms of sexual violence. For example, incest is usually thought of as a particular form of child sexual abuse but the actual dynamics of incestuous abuse are, in some ways, more like those in domestic violence. The experience of the incest survivor speaking below highlights these similarities: persistent psychological abuse, the ever-present threat of violence, and fear for her life. The fact that after she left home she felt she had to hide from her father in order to be safe is yet another connection.

'He went in for the sort of psychological warfare as well . . . . . . He would do things to annoy me and if I showed any reaction, if I showed no reaction, he'd hit me — I just couldn't win. He would say things like "It took me all my self-control last night not to get the breadknife and come upstairs and knife you". I never knew how far he would go. I just knew that I was in fear for my life.'

To draw together and further illustrate the themes running through this chapter and chapter 4, I will use the experiences of the 60 women interviewed to assess critically the three predominant ways in which forms of sexual violence are distinguished from one another; that violence is physical or sexual; that abuse involves single or multiple events; and that assaults tend to be committed by known men or strangers. These distinctions are often assumed and implicit; only three writers have addressed them specifically.[20]

The first distinction hinges on whether violence is defined as sexual or physical and is most evident in distinguishing domestic violence from other forms of sexual violence. This distinction emerges out of a tendency to assume that violence in intimate relationships is predominantly physical violence. Studies which systematically ask questions about the range of possible aspects of domestic violence are only just emerging but feminists working with battered women have long known that women experience a variable combination of physical violence, sexual coercion and mental abuse. All but one of the women who experienced domestic violence in this study defined aspects of the abuse as sexual; nine defined certain assaults as rape, thirteen as coercive sex and five pressurized sex. Many gave in to men's demands for sex because of fear of further physical abuse. For some women, the forced sex aspects of the violence were the most important.[21]

'It changed from a consenting sexual relationship to a completely dominant one on his part, and very weird peculiar things too. It then got to where he would come in and demand that I went to bed with him and for the first year I fought back, not physically, but I would refuse. Then it got where I would get a good hiding if I didn't do as he said.'

'It was usually if I refused sex that he became violent.'

'I just went off sex completely and then again I think possibly there was . . . . . . Oh god (surprise and upset), it became very coercive actually.'

This last quotation illustrates that women often minimized the sexual aspect of abuse and were surprised, and at times upset, when this emerged during the interview. Furthermore, male sexual possessiveness was one of the most common factors precipitating violent assaults.

'It was sexual, because he was very jealous and he used . . . . . . from very early on the marriage he used to talk about me and other men. Which was a load of rubbish, there weren't any other men, I had no life *at all* outside the kids and him.'

Child sexual abuse, and specifically incest, is often distinguished from other forms of sexual violence, particularly rape, by the suggestion that physical violence is seldom used. Yet, several writers adopting this argument make reference to the importance of authority relations between adults and children, implicitly suggesting that the threat of force ensure children's compliance.[22] This abstract distinction between the threat of and actual physical force is also present in some discussions of rape.[23] There was also strong evidence in the interviews that when girls began to resist incestuous abuse physical violence was used. Of the 13 women in the incest sub-group, eight had also been physically abused. Physical abuse was part of the abuse for all but one of the women for whom the abuse occurred over an extended period of time.

These examples make clear that it is not possible to distinguish between forms of sexual violence on the basis of the violence being sexual or physical. In each form, in each individual assault, both aspects will be present although one may be more dominant than the other.

This analysis has implications for the debate on how rape is defined. A number of researchers and feminist campaginers, particularly in the USA and Canada, have suggested that rape be defined as a violent rather than a sexual crime.[24] For this, two justifications have been given. First, it would eliminate the consent defence and the introduction of women's sexual history in cases that went to court. Second, it more accurately reflects women's experience. Whilst legal reform on these lines has taken place, there is no evidence as yet to suggest that it has had the desired effect (see chapter 3). A number of feminists have recently stressed the importance of not losing sight of the sexual aspect of rape.[25] Catharine MacKinnon argues that defining rape as a physical assault deflects attention from feminist analysis of the links between rape and current male heterosexual practice: 'So long as we say that those things are abuses or violent, not sex, we fail to criticize what has been made of sex.'[26]

The second distinction turns on whether assaults are single events or part of on-going abuse and here rape tends to be contrasted with domestic violence and/or incest. Whilst there are aspects of truth in this distinction, it is not an absolute. Rape by a stranger does tend to be a single assault but many women are raped by men they know. The likelihood of multiple experiences of forced sex increases substantially if the rapist is a woman's husband or lover. Equally, looking at this from the other side, most incestuous and domestic assaults are part of ongoing abuse but there were examples in the interviews of single assaults in both categories. Figure 5.1, based on the experiences of the women interviewed, illustrates this point. The forms of sexual violence at the top are most likely to be single events; the

Figure 5.1   Likelihood of single or multiple assaults

Single assaults ‹———› Multiple assaults

>   Flashing
>   Street hassling
>   Sexual assault
>   Rape
>   Obscene phone calls
>   Sexual abuse of girls
>   Sexual harassment at work
>   Pressurized sex
>   Coercive sex
>   Domestic violence
>   Incest

gradations to the right indicate an increasing likelihood of multiple assaults. The only forms of violence where it is almost always the case that there will be only one incident involving a particular man and woman/girl are flashing and street hassling. Even here, however, there were examples of multiple experiences in the interviews. One woman recalled a man in her community who repeatedly flashed at girls as they came home from school. Another discussed repeated street harassment by a group of young men in her neighbourhood.

The third way of distinguishing between forms of sexual violence is whether the abusive man is known or a stranger. Whilst there are clear differences here, in that incest and domestic violence by definition always involve assaults by men known to the woman or girl, forms of sexual violence that are commonly assumed to be committed by strangers may also be committed by known men. One of the points stressed in much feminist research on rape is that many women are raped by men they know. Within the interviews, there were also examples of flashing, sexual assault and obscene phone calls by men known to woman. Figure 5.2 uses the same method as figure 5.1 to illustrates this point. Forms of sexual violence most likely to be committed by strangers are placed at the top. Those which are always committed by known men are placed at the bottom and to the right.

Figure 5.2   Likelihood of the male abuser being a stranger or known

Stranger ⟵————————⟶ Known

    Street hassling
    Flashing
        Obscene phone calls
            Sexual abuse of girls
            Sexual assault
            Rape
                Pressurized sex
                Sexual harassment at work
                    Coercive sex
                    Domestic violence
                    Incest

The frequency of assaults and the likelihood of the abusive man being known do interact. Multiple assaults are more likely if the man is known, especially if he is related to and/or living in the same household as the woman/girl.

The abuse of trust has been an important theme in the recent research on incest and one group of researchers has suggested that this is one of the fundamental differences between rape and incest.[27] This distinction is, however, based on defining rape in terms of assaults by strangers. Women's perceptions of the impact of their abuse (see chapter 8) demonstrate that the betrayal of trust was an important aspect of forced sex by intimates and domestic violence.

It has been my intention here to show that a number of the taken-for-granted ways of making distinction betwen forms of sexual violence are challenged by women's experiences. This in itself demonstrates the range of women's experiences within each of the different forms of sexual violence. Assaults are always, but to varying degress, physical and sexual. They are committed by men in a variety of relationships to the woman. They may or may not be part of a series of assaults.

Future directions

Whilst the discussion has been limited to exploring the continuum as experienced by the 60 women interviewed, even within this small group there was a considerable range of actual experience. A larger and broader sample would have extended this range even further. For example, the forms of abuse experienced by Black women, lesbians and disabled women could be explored within the concept of the continuum in a way which would both point to the similarities with other forms of sexual violence and keep the particular nature of such experiences to the fore. It is also possible to use the concept for cross-cultural studies; to explore whether the prevalence of specific forms of sexual violence varies across cultures. It is only through fully exploring the diversity and range of sexual violence that we can assess whether and how differences between women affect the experience of sexual violence. Such studies are also crucial in moving discussions about the role of sexual violence in women's continued oppression out of theoretical debate and into the realities of women's lives.

6

'I'm not sure what to call it but . . .': defining sexual violence

In order to live in the world, we must name *it. Names are essential for the construction of reality for without a name it is difficult to accept the existence of an object, an event, a feeling.*
D. Spender, *Man-Made Language*

The issue of how to define sexual violence is an underlying theme throughout much of this book. In chapter 2 some of the myths and stereotypes that dominate public discourse were discussed. I suggested that they result in 'common-sense' definitions of forms of sexual violence which reflect men's ideas and limit the range of male behaviour that is deemed unacceptable to the most extreme, gross and public forms. A clear example of the influence of these limited definitions can be found in both legal codes and legal practice. The dominant male discourse also functions to naturalize and to justify ideologically men's violence towards women and the power relations which underpin the use of force in gender relations.

To name their own experiences women have to question these 'common-sense' definitions, assumptions and justifications. In this process, women often find themselves caught between the dominant discourse and their own experience: a conflict between men's power to define and women's truth. Dorothy Smith argues that this 'bifurcation of consciousness' is an essential feature of oppressive social relations.[1] It is this analysis which underlines feminist critiques of the patriarchal structure and content of language and the discussion of the 'silencing' of women's voices and meanings, particularly in public discourse.[2] Smith goes on to describe what she calls a 'click phenomenon'; a point at which the conflict of meanings becomes so intense that women may come to challenge what they had previously taken for granted and develop a new way of seeing and understanding their experience.

It is the connection between the public male discourse and the silencing of women that has been the target of feminist challenges to 'traditional' definitions of a variety of forms of sexual violence. As Dale Spender (quoted at the beginning of this chapter) points out, where names are not available, the extent and even existence of forms of sexual violence cannot be acknowledged. A vital part of feminist work around sexual violence has, therefore, been to provide names that describe women's experience. The terms 'battered woman', 'domestic violence', 'sexual harassment', 'sexual violence' and 'incest survivor' have all been introduced into our language in the past fifteen years. Naming involves making visible what was invisible, defining as unacceptable what was acceptable and insisting that what was naturalized is problematic.

This chapter will demonstrate the complexity of this process for women who have been abused. Women's negotiations of the tension between the dominant male discourse and their experiential understanding involve a range of possible outcomes; some constitute a form of adaptation to the dominant meanings, others a challenge to them.

Who does the defining

Whilst research on sexual violence is a relatively new area of study, a range of theoretical and methodological differences are already discernible. These differences are reflected in concepts and definitions which involve implicit (or occasionally explicit) references to the theoretical framework underlying the study and the causal factors offered as explanations. It is not just in 'common-sense' ideas that implicit/explicit allocations of blame and responsibility are present. Susan Schecter presents an insightful analysis of how these factors have influenced research on domestic violence.[3] For example, she points out just how many assumptions are implicit in the choice of names/concepts by comparing 'family violence' with 'domestic violence' and 'spouse abuse' with 'woman battering'.

In the majority of studies of sexual violence, minimal attention has been paid to how *women* define abuse and violence; it is all too often taken for granted. Many research projects begin with analytic definitions into which women's experiences are slotted. Many, in fact, depend upon women having already identified themselves as victims or survivors of the form of sexual violence being investigated (as to some extent did this one). But there is a crucial process involving a number of stages which must occur before this. Women must define the incident first as lying outside normal, acceptable or inevitable behaviour and, second, as abusive. Contacting support services or answering research questions involves a third step: naming the experience as a particular form of abuse. To report an incident to the police, the event must be defined by women as a crime.

In chapters 3 and 4, I made reference to the fact that a few researchers had begun to acknowledge the importance of this issue for research findings and, therefore, research design. Two recent studies of marital rape paid careful attention to the wording of questions.[4] However, both of these projects also involved the use of analytic definitions of rape in the analysis of their interview data. As a result, the researchers' definitions did not always reflect those of the women participating.

It was an important principle of this project's methodology that women define their own experience. Care and attention was also paid to the wording of questions so that they did not presume shared definitions. I also asked women who had experienced rape, incest and/or domestic violence how they defined the violence at the time of the assault(s) and whether their definitions had changed over time. Of the 45 women with these experiences, 60 per cent did not define them as such at the time although half of those experiencing domestic violence did so as the abuse continued. These figures are just one small example of how the way we understand our lives is not static. Women's definitions of sexual violence can and do change over time.

Accounting for how each woman defined her particular experiences of sexual violence, both at the time and over time, was beyond the scope of this project. What did emerge from the interviews, however, was a number of recurring themes which influenced women's definitions. They are the focus of the rest of this chapter.

Naming

Access to a word which names one's experience is the first step in defining sexual violence. Even if a name exists and is known to women, the way it is understood varies greatly. The difference between a limited and wide definition of rape, for example, is illustrated by these two women's reflections.

'It wasn't rape because I wasn't screaming, saying no and struggling all the way through.'

'If you are talking about sexual violence — *that is sexual violence*. You take a virgin, you don't rape her. You tell her you love her, she's the most beautiful woman in the world, you want to marry her. You get her absolutely transfixed and then two weeks later you say "Don't touch me!". That kind of violence and rape is of another order.'

It has already been noted that many of the names used in this book, and increasingly in common usage, are very recent entrants into our language. 'Until 1976, lacking a term to express it, sexual harassment was literally unspeakable, which made generalized, shared and social definition of it inaccessible. The unnamed should not be mistaken for the non-existent.'[5] This was underlined by a number of older women who recalled not being able to name experiences, particularly of domestic violence and sexual harassment, which occurred before the mid-1970s. Whilst some of these women had defined the men's behaviour as abusive at the time, none had a way of seeing it as other than as a personal problem. It is the lack of a *social definition* that is crucial. A social definition/name makes clear that others may share this experience, thereby undermining the isolation of feeling that you are the only one. A social definition also suggests the possibility of a social cause.

Access to names came up repeatedly in women's discussions of incest and child sexual abuse. Many told what, looking back, they felt were amusing stories of how as children they had attempted to make sense of what had happened to them. In each case, the woman felt that her limited knowledge of anatomy and sexuality meant that she had no words to describe what had happened. All of the incidents were, at the time, confusing and in many cases frightening. There was a need for them to understand. They drew on what little knowledge they did have, especially if they attempted to tell an adult. The following example refers to an incident of flashing that occurred when the woman was six.

'I've got very dim memories, but I remember it was terrible and coming back and saying to my parents "This man has got a crab down his trousers" (laughs). God, that's what it must have *looked like* to me!'

None of the adults who were told provided the girls with the correct information. It was often not until many years later that women understood what really had occurred. These realizations were often distressing, yet difficult to discuss with others.

'I was sitting with friends — I don't really understand why — I started thinking about this uncle who I hadn't liked sitting next to. I suddenly realized that he'd been touching me up. I wanted to talk about it — I was upset, but also relieved 'cos it made sense now — but I thought everyone would think I was being silly and I didn't know what to say.'

At the time the abuse began, most of the incest survivors interviewed did not know the names of sexual organs. This, coupled with the verbal strategies the abusive men used to rationalize their actions and/or prevent disclosure, gave them very few ways to make sense of what was happening to them. This, in turn, meant that they were less likely to tell anyone else. The two quotations below refer to slightly different experiences of incest. The first woman was raped by her father at the age of nine. The second was 'seduced' by her mother's boyfriend in her early teens.

'I wouldn't have been able to verbalize what had happened to me anyway because I didn't know what had happened to me.'

'I didn't really understand what it was that he was doing. I knew that it was wrong but I didn't understand — I didn't know what sex was so I couldn't call it sex.'

In the following quotation, a woman documents the process, spanning 20 years, through which she named and defined her experience of incestuous abuse.

'I called it not being very nice (laughs). I knew there was something wrong with it. I knew I didn't like it but I don't think I had a name for it . . . The older I got the more I came to see it as abusive, and it's only very recently, in the last year say, that I see it as incest.'

These examples, and many other similar ones not quoted, demonstrate that the first step in any attempt to prevent incest and child sexual abuse must be to give children the knowledge they need to be able to name and define certain forms of behaviour as abusive. Innocence did not protect these women; ignorance made them more vulnerable.

The names that have been applied, particularly to domestic violence, made defining abuse by male partners difficult for some women. The term 'battering' implies actual, and in many women's minds 'serious', physical violence.

'What he did wasn't exactly battering but it was *the threat*. I remember one night I spent the whole night in a state of terror, nothing less than terror, *all night* . . . And that was *worse* to me than getting whacked. That waiting without confrontation is just so frightening.'

'Mental violence is something you can't pinpoint. I suppose physical violence is there . . . . . . but you can't define mental torture, it comes in very funny ways.'

Lack of care in the terms we use to name forms of male violence can result in limited definitions which reinforce the public invisibility of much the range of abusive behaviour men engage in that was documented in chapter 5.

Forgetting and remembering

It is obvious that in order to define and name something one must know that it has happened. The one researcher to mention the issue of forgetting and remembering in relation to sexual violence, Diana Russell, is uncharacteristically dismissive of this aspect of women's experience:

Several respondents mentioned difficulty recalling not simple details, but sometimes entire events. However, it seems most unlikely that they would be totally unable to recall an experience of wife rape, had such an experience occurred to them.[6]

Initially, I, too, was surprised when women told me that they had forgotten abusive experiences for long periods of time. I stopped being surprised when more and more women discussed this, and when both I and the woman who typed several of the transcripts remembered incidents from our own pasts.

Forgetting occurred for a number reasons. Having no words with which to name and, therefore, understand experiences may result in the memory being suppressed. Such memories only become conscious when we have knowledge that enables us to make rational sense of the event(s) and our reactions. This process was most commonly associated with experiences of child sexual abuse. The influence of stereotypical and limited definitions often meant that women discounted or minimized their initial feelings and reactions; assaults were defined as unimportant or 'trivial' events not worth remembering. This process was most noticeable in relation to sexual harassment, flashing and sexual assault. Whilst events may be defined as a form of sexual violence, women may 'choose' to forget as a coping strategy (see chapter 8). This was particularly marked amongst women who had been raped or incestuously assaulted; 58 per cent of women who had been raped and 62 per cent of those incestuously abused forgot the experience for a period of time.

'I just thought of it as "that". I didn't really want to think of it, it was just part of life that I forgot.'

Sigmund Freud also engaged in a process of redefinition. In shifting from a belief in the truth of his women's patients remembered experiences of child sexual abuse to redefining them as fantasy he laid the foundation for much of his theory of psycho-sexual development. His 'truth' resulted in countless women's and girls' truth being redefined as fantasy by analysts whilst at the same time legitimating the legal fiction that 'women and young children are prone to lying.'[7]

Remembering almost always involved some sort of trigger: reading a book or article, seeing a film or watching a television programme, a conversation, dreams, giving birth, experiencing another assault. The first quotation refers to incest, the second to marital rape.

'For a long time I didn't even think about it. It hadn't happened, it didn't exist. If I saw him, it would come into my mind for a split second and it wasn't until — I can remember the exact day. I was working with this group and women were talking about what had happened to them and I was wondering what I could do because I hadn't any experiences like that and I suddenly thought, "Oh yes you have!" '

'I told you events, like the miscarriage, but there was other stuff as well. I had been raped by him, and it came out in a group session. It just came into my head and I started crying and suddenly it all came out.'

For some women, not wanting to see themselves or be defined by others as 'victims' was an important factor in wanting to forget. The shame and self-blame that many women recall immediately following assaults are just two of the common responses to victimization that may prompt women to try to forget. Interestingly, several of the triggers that made women remember were conversations in which negative attitudes to abused women were being expressed.

'I *had* to make him understand, it was really important to me — and to make him stop talking. Like an idiot, I suddenly said "Well, this is what happened to me". I totally freaked out. I suddenly thought "Oh my god, this *is* what happened to me!" '

She, and the other women this happened to, expressed considerable resentment at having to declare themselves 'victims' in order to counter such views.

Women often forget incidents of sexual violence that they did not define as 'serious' and many expressed surprise at the number of instances of abuse they had recalled during the interviews. Doing the interview and reading the transcript also acted as a trigger to women's memories; 70 per cent remembered additional incidents, or details of incidents, between the first interview and the follow-up. The final quotation in this section illustrates that the process of forgetting and remembering can be a complex one.

'While I was ill I was writing because I found it difficult to talk and five experiences came back and I was in a dreadful state, then I forget them all again.'

It was years later that this woman remembered and retained her knowledge of child sexual abuse. The fact that several women knew they had remembered incidents of sexual violence just after their initial interview or whilst reading their transcripts yet could not remember them in any detail at the follow-up interview confirmed that this process involves both remembering and retaining, and that the latter does not automatically follow from the former.

Minimizing

Many women discussed a similar, but different, process which resulted in them not defining what had happened to them as sexual violence. Either the influence of dominant meanings or the desire to not see themselves, or be seen by others, as someone who had been assaulted resulted in the events being minimized.[8] This process, like forgetting (with which it was sometimes associated), was often a coping strategy. It occurred most frequently in relation to the more common forms of sexual violence and domestic violence. A clear example emerges from one woman's discussion of sexual harassment. During the first interview, she made a flippant remark about sexual harassment being a joke. The meaning of her remark was ambiguous – did she think it was a joke or treat it as a joke? In the follow-up interview, it was clear that she chose to define sexual harassment as not serious in order to minimize its effect on her.

'I suppose it's my way of coping, my way of interpreting the situation so that they don't get through to me.'

In minimizing the effect women are also defining a situation as one they do not have to act on – emotional distress and/or outrage are commonly thought of as things we have to 'do something about'. In many of the contexts in which sexual violence occurs women feel unable to act or that all the available options are likely to result in further negative consequences. If the woman speaking above, for example, had complained about the harassment she could well have found herself unsupported and facing a much more hostile attitude from the men she worked with. She assessed those risks and decided that in order to continue her job it was safer to treat the harassment as a joke. Minimizing, therefore, involves squashing the distress and/or outrage so that neither she, or anyone else, is compelled to act.[9]

Jill Radford notes the frequency with which women respondents in a community incidence study prefaced accounts of sexual harassment or sexual assault with remarks such as 'nothing really happened' or 'I was lucky really'.[10] Through comparing one's own experience with something 'worse', such as rape, women feel less threatened and more able to go about their daily lives. Sandra McNeill, in her study of flashing, also argues that women minimize the event in order to limit its impact on them.[11]

Minimizing in order to cope denies the reality of the violence that has been experienced. It is the result of the predominant cultural meanings that define these forms of sexual violence as not 'serious'. In this complex process women also tend to discount their perception of the assault as yet another lesson in what could have happened. Minimizing seldom prevents women being affected and the effects of what is described as 'not serious' may well be.

'It was very confusing to know what to make of it at the time. I had a clash of attitudes — sort of not wanting to make a fuss, because, in fact, I'd got away quite light, but actually feeling quite damaged.'

'Getting away quite light' meant not being raped. The fact that this woman was not raped, however, did not mean that she had not been terrified at the time of the assault, nor did it mean that she was not affected by the experience afterwards. Defining assaults as not 'serious' necessitates minimizing, and at times even denying, the impact of an assault.

Women experiencing violence in intimate relationships often minimized its severity. Very few of the women who had experienced violence once or infrequently defined these experiences as domestic violence and most referred to them as being 'not very serious'. The frequency of violence was the most important factor in determining how quickly a man's behaviour was defined as abusive. Where there were long gaps between violent episodes, women tended to minimize the violence by choosing the focus on the time when it was not occurring and by hoping that it would not occur in the future.

'It was really cyclical actually, really incredible. And the odd thing was that in the good periods, I hardly remembered the bad times. It was almost as if I was leading two different lives.'

'There were long gaps sometimes . . . If it had been continuous battering then I'd have just gone. There were always times of hope.'

Kathleen Ferraro and Norman Johnson adapt the concept of techniques of neutralization in explaining how and why battered women minimize their experiences.[12] One of the factors they highlight is denial of injury. Where there are relatively long gaps between incidents of violence, bruises and marks fade and women focus their attention on the demands of daily life. What they suggest is actually a slightly more complex process whereby women define injury in terms of physical damage. Evidence presented in chapter 5 showed that it is only after some time, or even after women leave, that the impact of abuse on them psychologically is acknowledged.

Limited definitions and stereotypes

Stereotypes of sexual violence undoubtedly affected how many women defined and understood their own experience. These 'common-sense' ideas suggest that sexual violence is relatively infrequent and takes place in particular circumstances to certain types of women. Male offenders are typically thought to have aggressive personalities or to be mentally unstable. Alternatively, they may be seen to be temporarily out of control through the influence of alcohol or drugs. It is implicit that it is relatively easy to distinguish between what is and what is not sexual violence. Many of women's experiences recorded in the interviews did not fit any of the stereotypes which tend to draw on the extreme end of the experience continuum. The further away a woman's experience was from the limited definition offered by the stereotype, the more likely it was that she would not define it as sexual violence at the time of the assault. These stereotypes have also been shown to affect attitudes to rape in general (see chapter 3). One group of researchers, using vignettes to explore how teenagers defined rape, comment,

The closer an instance of non-consensual sex between acquaintances comes to the 'classic' rape – in which the assailant is a stranger and violence is used – the more likely it is labelled rape. The farther it diverges . . . the less likely is the situation to be labelled rape . . . Non-stranger rape, for many, is not rape at all.[13]

The 'classic' rape involves a stranger who attacks a woman late at night in the street and threatens to kill her; the assault involves physical violence and the woman is expected to resist throughout. This 'definition' prevented many women from defining their experiences of forced sex as rape.

'Well I suppose I thought that rape was something that happens to you out on the street, like with a complete stranger.' (ironic laugh)

'For a while I didn't even think it was rape since I'd let him into the house and I knew him. I had this idea that rape was something that happened to you in an alley.'

'It seemed such an unlikely thing to happen and also because it wasn't classic textbook – as I then thought rape was.'

The irony of this last statement is that this women's experience was as close to the stereotype as any in the interviews (there were none that fitted exactly). She was raped by a stranger, outside, but it happened during the day and there was little physical violence. This view of rape also affected how incest survivors defined their abuse.

'I thought rape was a violent act and the woman got hurt, physically hurt . . . When I look back now I feel yes, I must have been raped. But not in the way most people mean rape. I feel I've been raped but it's an 'acceptable' rape.'

'In a way I suppose what happened with my father was almost always rape, wasn't it? It was always against my wishes — yeah, I've never thought of it like that before.'

The stranger-aspect of stereotype, linked to the view that rape is the most terrible thing that can happen to a woman, meant that many of the women who were forced to have sex repeatedly within relationships did not define this as rape. This was also true for women who had had several experiences of forced sex with different men. When women discussed a number of incidents, they often called one rape and the others 'like rape' or forced sex. The factors which determined which incident was named rape correlated directly with aspects of the stereotype. Rape, in relationships where forced sex was common, was the incident in which most physical force was used and/or in which women resisted physically. Where women were discussing a number of incidents with different men, the one named rape was usually the one in which the relationship between the man and woman was least close: an acquaintance or a friend rather than a partner. These distinctions also functioned to prevent women from being seen or seeing themselves as someone who had been raped more than once.

Part of the difficulty in defining assaults by friends, partners or relatives as rape may be that it involves naming a man one has, or once had, positive feelings for as a rapist. Just as there are stereotypes about kinds of women who are raped, so there are stereotypes of rapists and child molesters. The common image is of a 'monster' who is mentally disturbed. These images were seldom felt to be appropriate to women's friends, lovers, fathers or husbands.

The 'common-sense' stereotype of domestic violence stresses its prevalence in the working classes and the personality characteristics of the woman and man. 'Battered wives' are often portrayed as either poor, downtrodden and weak or as nagging women who 'deserve' to be hit. Batterers are commonly thought of as men who have aggressive personalities, are often alcoholic and may be unemployed. The violence is assumed to be predominantly physical, frequent and life threatening. Again, the stereotypes seldom fitted women's experience and prevented many of them from defining themselves as battered women. The starkest example of this was a woman who helped establish a refuge for battered women in her town. At the time, she herself was being abused yet she did not make the conscious connection between her situation and that of the women she was supporting:

'I just thought that the incidents of violence that I — in order to be a bat†ered woman you had to be really battered. I mean OK, I had a couple of bad incidents but mostly it was pretty minor, in inverted commas, violence. I didn't see myself in that category as a battered woman at all.'

Here, minimizing and the influence of stereotypes interact and reinforce one another. Because not all the violence was 'serious' (this woman was most affected by systematic mental abuse), she could not be a battered woman. The class aspect of the stereotype also played a part in her inability to identify with women in the refuge. In fact, several of the women who had professional jobs and/or came from middle-class backgrounds who had been battered chose to be interviewed precisely because they wanted to challenge this view. They were aware that it had prevented them from defining themselves as battered women.

'That image of a battered woman being basically ill-educated, inarticulate and poor is totally misconceived. Not nearly enough is written and talked about women who are not beaten up by drunken husbands every week, but who were in my situation.'

This stereotype also does a diservice to the experiences of many working class women.

The view that battering must include frequent experiences of life-threatening violence affected many women's definitions. This woman, after making the point that the violence was infrequent, added:

'I never used to think *I am being battered*, somebody's being violent to me. Each incident used to be an isolated thing in a way . . . . . . I just thought in order to be a battered woman you had to be really battered.'

Again, the influence of stereotypes and limited definitions is found alongside minimizing.

The fact that a continuum of experience exists within each of the particular forms of sexual violence is obscured by stereotypes which focus on the extremes and/or draw on a limited definition. The further away women's experiences were from these limited definitions, the more likely they were to contain ambiguous elements which made defining them as sexual violence more problematic.

Shifting boundaries

The fact that certain forms of sexual violence are more common and that particular incidents are closer to 'accepted' behaviour formed an important part of the discussion of the continuum in chapter 5. Experiences which were extensions of typical male behaviour were often difficult for women to define as abuse.

As noted in the previous chapter, many men assume intimacy with women working in certain jobs, for example, barwork and waitressing. It is often difficult for women to define behaviour that is accepted, and expected, by customers, employers and, sometimes, female co-workers as sexual harassment.

'They'd chat you up. They'd put their arms around you and press up against you. I always passed it off as being part of the job and never considered it sexual harassment till I left.'

Whilst certain assumptions of intimacy are more acceptable from friends, a number of women commented on the explicit sexual nature of some male friends' behaviour. However, they were all aware that these friends, and other people who were around at the time, would not see this behaviour as sexual harassment.

'I also consider some advances from men in a social context, which maybe they don't see as being, sexual harassment.'

A number of the instances of sexual abuse that women recalled involved extensions of affection which are considered appropriate between adults and children. Women remembered being confused as to why they did not like being hugged or sitting on the knee of a particular male relative or family friend. The majority of women's experiences of incest also began with extensions of acceptable contact.

'I just thought he was really weird. He'd say "Let's do a jigsaw" and when I went to sit down his hand would be there. I just thought it was ridiculous always having to sit on his hand. Then, one Sunday morning, he came into my room . . . . . . and just laid on top of me on top of the bed clothes — of course, I didn't know what was going on — his eyes glazed over and he shook up and down. I mean I thought he was having a fit or something.'

These examples of gender and age relations in which individuals with greater power assume levels of intimacy which shade into abuse illustrate the feminist analysis of the everyday expression of power relations discussed in chapter 2.

The view that certain levels of violence are acceptable within a relationship affected how some women reacted initially to domestic violence. Here, the conflict between a cultural definition and women's experiential reality was particularly marked:

'I thought a few slaps and that were the usual thing to keep a woman down. I hate to say that, but it really is what I thought. I didn't even stop to think for one minute that they really hurt.'

'I think the awful thing was that I didn't see it as being particularly peculiar.'

'I was going to say I saw it as part of the relationship, but that means — I don't think I associate loving somebody with violence, but I could see somehow that sometimes it is part of it. I wouldn't agree with that now but that's how I saw it then.'

This was also the case for some women who were frequently coerced to have sex by male partners.

'I used to give in to the demands all the time — I mean I didn't see them as demands in the sense of pressure, now I do. But then, I just thought it was part and parcel . . . . . . of men.'

The continuum of non-consensual heterosexual sex discussed in chapter 5 illustrates the ambiguity and confusion of many situations for women. A number of themes arising from that discussion are present in the experience of this woman: little force, her limited resistance, and the nature of the relationship between the man and woman.

'I don't know whether to regard it as an assault or not. Last summer, I was hitching to the coast. This man who gave me a lift said "well I know one way you can earn some money quickly". He said if I gave him a blow job he'd pay me five pounds. I didn't want to but he became very insistent and said "I'll give you ten", took it out of his wallet while steering erratically across the road. His manner frightened me *very much*. I didn't know what would happen if I kept insisting no. I thought the best thing was to accept this arrangement, as it might prevent me from being raped or physically hurt — so that's what I did. Though in a way he *forced* me into that situation, it wasn't something I had chosen so in that sense it was an assault.'

She added during the follow-up interview:

'I think it was an assault because I was definitely coerced into doing it. My feelings about it are contradictory — on the one hand, I feel that I perhaps had some choice in submitting to it and on the other I was forced.'

Knowing the man and the previous content of the relationship made defining assaults more difficult. A particularly revealing incident was recalled by one woman. Whilst she defined the incident as rape, the previous content of the relationship made her question her definition.

'We were apart. We'd played at rape before with this tying-up business, so the boundary between that and — but this occasion was *clear cut*. He'd broken in, that was number one and I was angry. He tied me up — but there was this . . . . . . unreality about it because we'd done it so much with my consent. Every time I was saying "Look this is going too far" he was saying "Oh come on, you like it".'

This unreality is repeated each time a woman has to appear in court and her rapist pleads the consent defence.

Being assaulted by someone you trust is counter to the commonly held view that women are assaulted by strangers. If the man is known to the woman, he is also more likely to make known his interpretation of the event, as the man in the above incident did. Men have various techniques of neutralization or vocabularies of motive available to them through which they deny that their actions constitute violence.[14] The first quotation here refers to an attempted rape of a schoolgirl by her boyfriend and the second to domestic violence. The man in latter case also exercised extremely authoritarian control over the children.

'He had *no concept* as far as I could see of what my consent would mean, or how it would be different . . . . . . And the next day, I couldn't believe it! He came to school and he'd bought this box of chocolates and decided that I was wonderful, the "You're beautiful when you're angry" kind of crap.'

'He would sulk and he *would try to* turn the situation round in such a way that *he would* end up thinking that what he had done was justified and that all the rest of us were wrong.'

Any of the many rationalizations men use affect how women see what has happened. In order to define the incident as violence, they have to reject the man's interpretation and construct an alternative.

Two women had been forced to have sex by both a man they knew well and by a stranger or acquaintance. The explicit comparisons they made between these experiences show that, with known men, sexual violence could be explained and even justified whilst assaults by strangers could not be. This goes some way to explaining why women found the latter more disturbing and frightening and were much more likely to define them as rape or assault at the time.

'It made a difference to me because I could not deny what happened to me in the station. I couldn't whitewash it, whereas I could with a relationship. The guy in the station, I didn't even know him. I didn't know why he was doing it to me. I did understand what Al was doing somehow, I knew who he was, I *knew* him — it didn't seem so bad.'

'It was a kind of mental thing the first time too. It was a rape of innocence. I felt totally corrupted after that. With Luke, the second time, although I didn't feel I belonged to him, I know he felt I belonged to him. When he was raping me he was trying to reclaim what he saw as his . . . . . . it wasn't such a terrifying experience because . . . . . . I knew why he was doing it.'

Redefining

Many of the women interviewed had gone through a process of redefining their experiences. The earliest redefinition took place within on-going abuse in relation to both domestic violence and incest. A particular incident, a change in the pattern of abuse, or simply the continuation of abuse over time prompted the change.

Of the incest survivors, two moved through the process of rediscovery and redefinition during the course of the interviews.

The quotation that follows highlights the complexity of redefining experiences of sexual violence, and how painful the process can be.

'The things that I was unsure about were basically the things that I came out with about the incest thing. I hadn't worked that one out *at all* and it just came out. It was really revelatory to me because I'd never . . . I'd always accepted it, that there was something wrong between me and my father, something indistinguishably *wrong* about our relationship, but I had never verbalized it *ever*, but it really came out with your questions. It was only through reading it over that I realized what I'd said, and seeing how hard certain questions were for me to answer and, therefore, recognizing that there were big blocks about certain things. I know now that my father had sexual feelings towards me . . . . . . that the way he was with me, even the violence, was a way of communicating with me sexually . . . . . . but to say that it's incest, I think incest is too much of a decision right now.'

Many women defined their experiences as sexual violence some time after the event(s) in question. The factors women mentioned which prompted their redefinition were remarkably similar to those women mentioned as triggering their memories.

'I just thought of it as another experience of sort of harassment . . . I think talking to a woman I know about it made me see that there were things I was doing that were a direct result of it. She really influenced me to come face to face with what was bothering me.'

'She called it rape that night and that's when I got flashbacks to the occasions with my step-father, and I realized that was rape too. It was all going round in my head at the same time. I was very ill after this and kept passing out.'

Redefining an event and working through what it meant often resulted in women reassessing other experiences. In chapter 4, I suggested that this process might, in part, account for the greater recorded frequency of sexual violence in some women's lives. For example, once an experience of forced sex is named as rape the likelihood that women will define other experiences as 'like rape' increases.

'The first time he inveigled his way into my bed. I think now that could be defined as a kind of rape. I've redefined things like being harassed as well.'

'It was partly as a result of it [a rape] not being so awful that I realized that in some of the situations in which I'd . . . . . . had intercourse with lovers was *not actually* that different.'

When women engage in redefining some of their experiences of heterosexual sex, the direction is precisely the opposite of that which occurs in the public sphere. In the public sphere, women's experiences of rape are often redefined as sex, whereas these two women, and many others, redefined sex as rape or as 'like rape'.

A number of women commented on how the initial interview had made them think about their own experiences far more and a certain amount of redefining happened between the first interview and the follow-up. As had happened with the pilot interviews, seeing their experience written down and thinking more about some of the questions prompted women to reflect on aspects of their experience and to make connections.

'I didn't realize until I started reading this and thinking a bit more about myself in relation to men and everything else. I can look back now and pinpoint times when I've been sexually harassed and I've remembered an incident when I was eight or nine.'

'Only within relationships — but it's still the same isn't it. It's sex with violence, the threat of violence is violence anyway isn't it? It's taken me 18 years to realize that!'

The process of redefinition involved women focusing on their own feelings rather than on stereotypes, limited definitions or the perceptions of others. They were no longer minimizing the assault(s) or its impact on them.

Implications for feminist research and feminist services

Naming and defining experiences of sexual violence is not a simple process for many women, and it may not take place until many years after the event(s). The power of the dominant male discourse was underlined by the fact that even the women interviewed who saw themselves as feminists and had, therefore, access to wider definitions of sexual violence found defining their own experiences problematic. Clearly access to words with which to name experiences is fundamental, especially for children.

It is in men's interests, as the perpetrators of sexual violence, that definitions of forms of sexual violence be as limited as possible. At the same time as women are unable to name their abuse as abuse, men are able to deny responsibility for abusive behaviour. Language is a further means of controlling women.

Defining sexual violence in terms of a continuum, thereby stressing the range of possible forms of abusive behaviour, provides women with a means of defining their specific experience as abuse without necessarily having to name it as a particular form of sexual violence. It provides a framework in which new terms and definitions can evolve and takes account of the fact that the way women define and name their experience may change over time.

The male definitions of sexual violence which are encoded in laws and which underlie the stereotypes are limited and draw on the extremes of the continuum of sexual violence. This means that the range of experiences, both within and between different forms of abuse, is not recognized. It is possible that in attempting to get public recognition of the incidence and seriousness of sexual violence feminist campaigns have, to some extent, reinforced these limited definitions. For example, feminists in Britain campaigned for legal changes around domestic violence in the 1970s. Two major legal reforms resulted: one related to injunctions (protection orders) and the other to housing.[15] Both, however, focus on physical assaults and fail to specify forced sex or psychological violence in the definition of domestic violence. In the case of the Domestic Violence Act, judges have further restricted it in practice to applications in which women can cite evidence of recent assault.

Feminist activists need to pay far more attention to the language we use, both in order that women are enabled to locate abusive experiences within the terms we employ and to ensure that legal reforms widen rather than limit definitions of forms of sexual violence. This means making clear the difference between feminist and 'common-sense' definitions and creating new words where necessary. The fact that so many women found defining experiences of sexual violence problematic means that campaigning around the construction of male-defined stereotypes, particularly in the mass media, must remain a priority, as must continued work to present feminist alternatives to a wider public. Much of the redefinition of experience women engaged in was the result of finding an alternative way of understanding through articles, programmes or conversations informed by a feminist perspective.

The fact that women may not define abusive male behaviour as sexual violence at the time has implications for research design.

The questions asked must allow for experiences which women are unsure how to define. If prevalence is being studied, reference to the commonness of forgetting and minimizing should be made and the impact this will have on reporting must be acknowledged. All estimates of prevalence are likely to be underestimates.

7

Victims or survivors?: resistance, coping and survival

'I survived all of that through my will to live and not be beaten.'

One of my initial aims had been to study the long-term effects of experiences of sexual violence. Yet as a literature on the long-term effects emerged in the early 1980s, I became increasingly unhappy with the assumptions underlying it. Just as most incidence research had abstracted incidents of sexual violence from the context of women's lives, so the impact of sexual violence on women was abstracted from the context of women's actions and perceptions. Much of my unease related to how researchers were conceptualizing 'effects': as discrete physiological and/or psychological changes which could be measured by 'objective' psychological tests. This approach cannot take account of either the range and the complexity of the impact of abuse on women or the fact that women and girls who have been abused are actively engaged in a struggle to cope with the consequences of abuse. By placing women as decision-makers and actors at the centre, the common, although often implicit, assumption that all consequences of sexual violence are, or remain, negative can be questioned and attention can be drawn to the possibility that the process of coping with negative effects may, in the long term, have positive outcomes. I am neither saying nor implying that this process is desirable; only that it is one in which women make choices and act. Just as we are not passive victims at the time of assaults nor are we passive victims in relation to the consequences of abuse.

This change of direction led me to focus on how women cope with violence at the time it is happening and over time, and through this to notice the range of ways in which women resist.

The shift in the early 1980s within feminism from the use of the word 'victim' to 'survivor' echoed my own concerns. The work of a number of Black feminists and feminists of Colour, with its emphasis on strength and survival, were an important source of insight and inspiration.[1] The three concepts that underlie the analysis in this chapter and chapters 8 and 9 – resistance, coping and survival – are discussed below. I will then show how resistance and coping were present in the experiences of the women interviewed by looking at how women avoided rape and the response of women during and immediately after incidents of flashing, sexual harassment, rape, incest and domestic violence. Chapter 8 extends this analysis to the long-term consequences of sexual violence.

Coping

Women's responses to the interview questions on the long-term impact of sexual violence highlighted the fact that it is not possible to distinguish simplistically between effects and the coping strategies that women use. Coping strategies were used during the assaults(s), in the immediate aftermath, and over time. How women coped, and were enabled to cope, directly affected the impact of abuse on them. Indeed, isolating effects is only possible where the violence experienced is a single assault. When abuse occurs more than once, coping responses will already have interacted with effects making their separation almost impossible.

Most discussions of coping have taken place within the parameters social psychology, and a number of insights from this body of work are useful in the study of women's experiences of sexual violence. Coping is defined as the actions taken to avoid or control distress. Women's coping responses are active, constructive adaptions to experiences of abuse. The responses of any particular woman will depend on how she defines her experience, the context within which it occurs and the resources which are available to her at the time and subsequently. He own inner resources and personal situation and the availability of support through social networks and professional agencies affect her coping options. Differences of age, class and race affect access to support networks, knowledge of and access to official or voluntary services and whether or not certain options which require monetary expenditure are possible.[2] The threat of violence often results in anticipatory coping behaviour through which women attempt to avoid sexual violence. The effectiveness of chosen strategies may vary over the short and long term and coping may involve costs to the woman.[3]

By far the majority of research and discussion of coping has, however, been located within the study of 'life events' (events occurring outside the routines of daily life, for example, divorce, serious illness or bereavement) and stress; coping being evaluated through a standard of 'return to normal functioning'. I have argued that this standard is inappropriate in relation to sexual violence, as permanent changes in attitudes, behaviour and circumstances may occur.[4] It is also the case that this standard may be inadequate within the life event field itself. It focuses mainly on 'functioning' (behaviour); coping effectively with daily life. Changes in attitudes, values or aspects of an individual's life that are permanent are neglected or taken for granted. For example, bereavement involves the loss of a valued relationship; 'normal' before the death will not be the same as 'normal' after it.

Resistance

To resist is to oppose actively, to fight, to refuse to co-operate with or submit. It implies a sense of a force, a power or a person which is actively opposed. Resistance is a particular form of coping strategy. It has obvious relevance to instances of sexual violence in which overt force is used and women physically resist. It is not, however, limited to these actions and covers a range of other responses. For example, one intention of men who flash or who make obscene phone calls is to frighten women. Women resist in these situations by refusing to be frightened or to let the fear they do feel be apparent to the abusive man. When men are violent to women who they are close to, they are invariably attempting to control their behaviour in specific ways. Women resist by refusing to be controlled, although they may not physically resist during an actual assault. Resistance, therefore, involves active opposition to abusive men's behaviour and/or the control they seek to exert. Varda Gerhardt suggests that coping may merge into political action where individuals or groups perceive that their distress has a social cause, the solution to which can only be social change.[5] I define this form of coping as a form of resistance – collective resistance.

The extent and form of women's resistance to particular assault(s) is dependent on the circumstances of the event(s) and on the resources that they feel that they can draw on at the time. To resist requires feeling strong enough to take the risk that the incident might escalate; in some situations resistance may prevent or limit violence, whilst in others it may result in greater levels of violence. Women are seldom able to assess accurately which of these outcomes is more likely.[6] Responses are also affected by how strong or angry women feel at the time; on one occasion a woman may respond angrily to harassment and on another she may ignore it.

Resistance is a coping strategy which denies the abusive man certain forms of power over the woman. This is particularly obvious during incidents of sexual violence but it may also be a factor in women's reactions to their experiences over time. For example, the determination of many women to cope on their own after leaving violent relationships is often linked to a desire to regain the power and control over their lives that their abusers took from them.

Survival

To survive means to continue living. Survival refers to continued existence after, or in spite of, a life-threatening experience. It is in this sense that survivors of concentration camps, natural disasters and wars are referred to. Not inconsiderable numbers of women do not survive sexual violence. They are killed by their assailant. Fear of death is a common experience of women during assaults.[7]

Survival is, therefore, continuing to exist after the life threatening experience that is a part of many instances of sexual violence. It is the positive outcome of coping and/or resistance. I use it to refer to physical survival, in that the woman is not killed by the man, and women's physical and emotional survival after the assault(s). In this latter sense too, not every woman survives. Some take their own lives as a direct result of being victimized; many more experience profoundly negative impacts on their lives, such as 'mental illness'. Emotional survival, therefore, refers to the extent to which women are able to reconstruct their lives so that the experience of sexual violence does not have an overwhelming and continuing negative impact on their life.

Victims or survivors?

The focus on coping, resistance and survival reflects the experiences of the women interviewed; it draws attention to the strength women display despite their experiences of victimization through shifting the emphasis from viewing women as passive victims of sexual violence to seeing them as active survivors. The word 'victim' refers to someone who has been killed or destroyed or who has suffered a loss. It is vital to acknowledge that many women are killed by men; many more may feel aspects of their selves were destroyed and many of them experience losses. The term 'victim', however, makes invisible the other side of women's victimization: the active and positive ways in which women resist, cope and survive.

Without this perspective, and given the extent of sexual violence, women can be presented as inherently vulnerable to victimization and as inevitably passive victims. This is exactly the image of women presented in *Bound by Love* by Lucy Gilbert and Paula Webster.[8] Whilst aware of some of the more subtle and complex aspects of the aftermath of experiences of sexual violence, the framework within which these insights are placed is, in fact, a feminist version of the idea that women are masochistic. The authors discuss women's experiences of rape, incest and domestic violence through a 'general theory of the psychology of women'.[9] The underlying theme is that daughter-hood, as currently constructed, sets women up to be victimized. They further suggest that it is 'essential to change the focus of contemporary feminist enquiry from understanding how men become victimizers to how women become their victims'.[10] This in itself is an enterprise many feminists would question. It returns us to pre-feminist perspectives which focused on the behaviour on women and in so doing directed attention away from the culpability of men.

The kind of femininity that is encouraged in girls and young women, through compliance, self-denial, suppression of anger, dependence on male approval and submission to male authority, 'socializes women to accept victimization'.[11] They suggest that, rather than fighting back and being angry with men, women who are victimized 'only hate themselves for being victims'.[12] The core of their analysis is represented in the following quotation.

Made helpless and vulnerable by femininity, women are easy marks for acts of male aggression and rage; we have internalized the feminine stance in our relations to the world and to men, we both expect and accept our violation as inevitable.[13]

This leads them to repeat, albeit in slightly different form, many of the ideas that feminists have been attempting to challenge. In their chapter on incest, we find thinly disguised Freudian ideas which suggest that girls have incestuous wishes and desires and that they enjoy the abuse until they become aware of the taboo. They conclude that, when the abuse ends, young women are relieved 'but also sad and regretful'. The chapter on rape suggests that women who are raped are symbols of defiled virtue which leads them to 'accept defeat as inevitable, one more act of surrender, the last station on the cross of femininity'. Women are 'refeminized' through rape, weakening any desire they may have to be autonomous. In discussing battered women, they suggest that women experiencing violence in intimate relationships are 'more feminine' women who have been 'moulded into tolerant future victims of violence'. Whatever strength they had is beaten out of them and they refer to the theory of 'learned helplessness' in this context.

This 'psychology of women' assumes that all women, all experiences of sexual violence, and the ways in which women respond to them, are the same. None of these assumptions are warranted. Chapter 5 clearly demonstrated the difficulties in generalizing about women's experience of violence. Nor can we ignore the differences of age, class and race which affect how women experience violence and what resources are available to them in coping. Gilbert and Webster conveniently ignore social and material factors; women's oppression is reduced to a psychological process created by childhood experience and based in the construction of personality. Daughterhood becomes a euphemism for oppression and a sense of women's powerlessness pervades the book. The final chapter on autonomy as a solution to sexual violence becomes an idealistic vision since elsewhere in the book there has been no reference to women's resistance, no sense of the numbers of women who seek help to stop violence, who find ways of stopping it themselves or of the active work women engage in to avoid sexual violence in the future and to deal with its consequences. It is precisely these aspects of women's experience that demonstrate that women do not 'expect or accept' sexual victimization, and which provide the basis for women's struggle for autonomy.

The remainder of this chapter, and the following two chapters, document the many and varied ways the women interviewed resisted, coped with and survived sexual violence.

Avoiding rape

A number of the events recorded in the sexual assault and child sexual abuse categories were attempted rapes. In each case, it was the woman's resistance which resulted in them being able to avoid rape. The three examples which follow all involved strangers but the circumstances were different: the first woman was on holiday abroad, the second woman walking home at night, the third was at home.

'He started offering me money to sleep with him. I said no. This went on for a bit and then suddenly he lunged at me . . . . . . I was wearing those old kind of jeans which don't have front zips, which I think confused him rather. I managed to knee him in the balls, which was rather an achievement actually as I wasn't really aware men had balls at the time!'

'I went on fighting and there was this really terrifying bit where he'd got me pinned against the wall, and I'd banged my head slightly so I was feeling kind of woozy and I thought for a minute that I was going to faint. I was *absolutely terrified*: but I managed to get a hand free and I started scratching his face. I think at that point he started giving up and realized that it was going to be difficult to overpower me. Maybe I had made too much noise to risk it. He — I think in total anger — punched me in the mouth and, in doing that, he had to let go of me and I managed to get away.'

'He knocked, I opened the door and he was in. He assaulted me, pulled my nightie up, sort of got me on the bed and pushed me around. I managed to scream and he ran off.'

Physical fighting, running away and screaming were the most common forms of resistance used by women who managed to avoid rape. Pauline Bart and Patricia O'Brien define these responses as 'active' forms of resistance.[14] They suggest that 'active' resistance and using multiple strategies increase the likelihood of avoiding rape. Such responses are, however, not always appropriate or possible. One woman used a different strategy in an extremely threatening situation. She felt she had no choice but to accept a lift from a man she did not like the look of after having been stranded on moorland late at night. During the journey, he suggested she have sex with him.

'I sort of swallowed hard, a cold sweat came over me. It was an old mini and the string handle wasn't there, the window wouldn't wind down. He said "I've got a big knife in the side pocket. If you don't I could always cut your head off and do it." I didn't know what to do so I said "You're just saying that to frighten me", so he produced it! It was about as big a knife as you could get in that pocket — a cutlass I suppose you'd call it. I was terrified! I said "It wouldn't be much fun for you if I was cold" and it seemed to appeal to his sense of humour and he laughed and said "OK I'll take you to your destination" but I insisted on getting out.'

This was not a passive response. She chose the only strategy that seemed possible in the circumstances: verbally engaging her potential rapist. Her resistance, like that of many other of the women interviewed, demonstrates that it is inappropriate to define resistance strategies as being active or passive. *All resistance is active.* It involves making second by second decisions about what strategies are possible in attempting to avoid being assaulted.

Bart and O'Brien's finding that 'active' forms of resistance are more likely to be used when the man is a stranger or acquaintance rather than a friend or lover was confirmed in this study. Undoubtedly, the location (which is more likely to be outside) and the approach of the man (more likely to be a sudden attack) partly account for this. They are also more likely to be effective in the context of an attack by a stranger; whilst many women also physically and/or verbally resisted rape by known men, none of them was able to prevent its occurrence through such strategies. The theory and practice of much self-defence training fails to take account of the different context of rape by known assailants. The only strategy that was successful in preventing forced sex within intimate relationships was to end the relationship.

No particular strategy was most effective in avoiding rape. In similar circumstances, the same form(s) of resistance resulted in the rape being avoided or in men's use of greater force to subdue the woman. It is only by resisting, however, that women have a chance to avoid being raped.

Resistance to and coping with flashing and sexual harassment

In this section, the fact that resistance can take forms other than physical struggle is illustrated further. Resistance to flashing or sexual harassment often involves refusing to respond in the way that men expect. The related issue of women's responses to the expectation that they tolerate pornography is also discussed.

The most common forms of resistance to flashing and sexual harassment were making a cutting remark to the man or calling public attention to his behaviour. Reacting in this way often meant that women felt less violated by the experience. Perhaps because they expressed their anger, they did not internalize feelings of shame or self-blame. The fact that women attempted to take some control of the situation may also account for the differing impact of events on them. The first two examples below describe incidents of flashing; the remainder sexual harassment.

'The first two times I was flashed at I just hurried past. The last time I was with a friend on the tube and he came up and started exposing himself and saying obscenities. I got up and pushed him over and I felt much better because I'd actually done something and because he just shambled off.'

'I was working on a train and I went to the front so I could have a whole table. I was busy working and I looked into the window and saw that this guy had his prick out. I couldn't believe it! My instant reaction was to show indifference and just not respond. Then, I thought we are brainwashed into thinking that exposers are just innocent people, that they are pitiful and we must be sorry for them. So, I went up to the only other person in the carriage and I said "I'd like you to witness the fact that this man is exposing his penis to me and he is trying to degrade me". Then I got really loud and I started shouting, "You think you shock me, your prick does not impress me, I've seen enough. You think you can degrade us or frighten us, we're not going to stand for it anymore." This man looked *absolutely terrified*, sat there trembling saying "I'm sorry, I'm sorry". I went to find the guard to get him thrown off the train, but he must have got off the train at the next station because we couldn't find him.'

'I had my tit grabbed at a party once. I whacked the bloke round the head really hard — the look on his face, *shock* that I didn't enjoy having my tit squeezed by him! But I was scared though, I thought he might hit me back.'

'I was working as a cleaner and the supervisor was always making jokes and insinuations about me. I said something when there was a whole group of women there like "Oh, you're a big stud!" and he was really embarrassed and that stopped it.'

'I was on an underground station, as I walked past someone said "That's a nice pair of boobs" and I turned round and slapped him. I was so terrified that he was going to hit me back — I was absolutely petrified, luckily a train came and I popped into it.'

Several of the women speaking here explicitly refer to their awareness of risk in resisting. Many of the women who coped by minimizing or ignoring the flashing or harassment did, in fact, want to respond by challenging the man's actions, but two factors prevented them from responding in this way: fear of the situation escalating and/or not being able to think of an appropriate response.

'I know we both felt really angry, but we just walked past. Afterwards, we both felt we were stupid not to have said or done something.'

'I can't find a suitably cutting way to respond — I tend to get that knotty feeling inside, part of it is fear of what they might do.'

The threat of further violation implicit in these forms of sexual violence is uppermost in women's minds when they try to assess what the consequences of resistance might be. This is yet another factor they cannot control or predict, although the presence of other people who might provide support or be witness to any response seemed to reduce the perceived risk of the incident escalating. When women did feel able to challenge men's abuse they felt positive about their actions. In discussing why men are sexually violent, many women suggested that the lack of sanctions was an important factor.

Resistance strategies in this context convey the message to abusive men that women refuse to accept or ignore their behaviour. If the strategy involved calling public attention to abuse there was the added component of attempting to make the man in question accountable to some form of community sanction. It was noticeable that once women had resisted harassment or flashing, they were more likely to do so on future occasions.

It is of interest to consider resistance in a rather different context. A number of women mentioned that they had refused to have pornography magazines in their houses or to watch 'blue' films. The increasing acceptability of porn videos within community networks was noted in chapter 5. The final quotation below demonstrates that, in making their objections public, women themselves risked sanctions in their relationships and friendship networks rather than obtaining the support of community sanctions against the behaviour of men.

'He brought one the other day actually and I made him burn it.'

'A set of pornography was brought to our house when we had young children. On top was a picture involving a dog. I felt so sick I burnt them. I can remember thinking how terrible it was and I don't like any of it, I don't want men to see women like that.'

'I went to a party and there was going to be a film shown and I refused — I just didn't want to see it, I didn't want to be there. My ex-husband was the one setting up the projector although he knew I couldn't bear it. I left the party; that caused an upset.'

None of these women, or the many others who made similar remarks, were aware of feminist debates around pornography. They were reacting on the basis of how pornography made them feel. They were resisting attempts to make its presence acceptable within their homes and social life. In making these stands, women took a number of risks. For example, the possibility of being labelled 'prudes' within their friendship network and the probability of a prolonged dispute with their male partner, which in some cases ended in violence.

Rape: resistance and coping

Ann Burgess and Linda Holmstrom suggest that women may use coping strategies that are verbal (screaming, humour, calm talking), physical (fighting, running away) and/or cognitive (deciding to submit to avoid greater injury, cutting off from the experience) before, during and/or after rape.[15] They do not, however, make a distinction between resistance and coping.

Not one of the women interviewed in my study who had been raped passively accepted the assault. Of them 60 per cent resisted physically and the remaining 40 per cent made it clear verbally that they did not want to have sex with the man. Physical resistance was more common when the rapist was a stranger; verbal resistance was more likely where the rapist was known and/or when women feared that physical resistance would result in them being badly injured. The three quotation that follow illustrate the range of resistance in which women engaged.

'He tried to put it in my mouth and that was the wrongest thing he ever did, because I bit it. That stopped him. I bit him that hard that he poured blood.'

'I was quite rational through the whole thing. Very much feeling that I wanted to get away from this without being raped and without being hurt, but primarily without being hurt — it seemed to be the most important thing . . . . . . He just about managed to penetrate me, but then I started pretending I was going to be sick and looking . . . . . . it was again fairly rational but not entirely . . . . . . I managed to make him think I was going out of my mind, acting quite hysterical. He clearly got quite frightened and ran off.'

'I resisted at first, then I just cried, I kind of *lost* the will to resist. In the end, he just said "I'm not going to do this if you are going to cry" and I said "Why didn't you think of that before?" '

An interesting commonality in these experiences is that in each case the women, whilst not preventing the assault, did alter its course by their actions. Six other women negotiated the form of the rape by agreeing to certain sexual acts but not others. None of these women were passive victims. They all refused to allow their rapists to control the event and, therefore, have total power over them.

Other women submitted to the assault to prevent greater physical violence and attempted to control its impact by cutting off during the sexual acts. Opting to submit has been seen by feminists as a form of coping: 'Submission is a way of coping with the reality of being overpowered – that is, it is an act of will over which the victim has control.'[16] When linked with 'cutting off', it could also be seen as a form of resistance: refusing to allow the rapist power over one's mind and feelings, actions that other researchers have called 'disassociation' or 'depersonalization'.[17] This separation of mind and body is a common theme in accounts by women who work in the sex industry; for them it is a coping strategy through which they refuse to be totally objectified in their work.[18]

Many of the women who were raped remembered making a conscious decision to respond in this way and it undoubtedly accounted for the fact that most were unable to recall the rape in any detail. The first two quotation below refer to single events; the third to repeated rapes by a lover. The second illustrates that by deciding to appear totally passive women can sometimes alter the outcome of the assault. It seems that some rapists want women to struggle and resist; when this does not happen, they lose interest.

'I was just really aware that it wasn't my body, it was me and my brain was somewhere else, just staring down at what was happening – it just wasn't real, like it isn't me, it isn't me!'

'I just sort of laid there and he was so sick he just got up and went.'

'I used to struggle before, but then I just stopped, I became totally passive. I kind of didn't see it as sex somehow, I cut off, completely cut off.'

During rape, even when apparently acting passively, women are actively making decisions and choices, taking what control is possible in the circumstances.

In the period immediately following rape, women have to cope with the feelings evoked by being raped. The following ways of feeling (in the order of frequency mentioned) were recalled by the 28 women who had experienced rape: upset, numb, dirty, ashamed, angry, wanting to forget, abused, guilty and fearful. Twelve women's immediate response once they were home or somewhere safe was to have a bath.

'I felt *completely* vulnerable, I felt worthless, like I was shit. I felt like somebody had just kicked me, as though I was completely nothing.'

It is these feelings which result in women wanting to forget their experience, and this was the most common reaction immediately following the assault. By forgetting or minimizing the rape, women were attempting to control its impact on them.

'There was a question about what my immediate reaction was after I was forced to have sex with him and I said I didn't have a reaction. But I was looking back at some things I had written at the time and, in fact, there are pages and pages of poems of anger and just tears. All these things about what he had done to me. I didn't connect the sex in terms of the emotions. I never connected it with myself. It was just something I wrote — it took a long time, maybe two years before I could even think about what happened without blaming myself or feeling really sick about it.'

Women who tried to forget or cut off from the experience were far less likely to tell anyone about the rape. A few women told someone they were close to immediately after the assault but chose not to talk about it subsequently. Two women, however, had virtually the opposite reaction and attempted to confront their rapists in the week following the assault. One woman couldn't find the man. The other did.

'I went back there because I was so angry and I was determined I was going to *kill him* for what he'd done, and for what I'd gone through at the police station . . . . . . He talked to me like I was an old friend! I picked up a bottle and went to hit him, because *he'd destroyed part of me*, he'd violated me. It didn't matter to him, he was laughing!' (angry and upset)

She was prevented from attacking her rapist by her friends, but a number of well publicized cases in the 1970s (for example, Inez Garica, JoAnn Little, Dessie Woods) illustrate that in the period immediately following rape some women take their own revenge and succeed in killing their rapists.

Incest: resistance and coping

Common-sense suggests that children's resistance, particularly if their abuser is an adult, will be limited since they have fewer physical, emotional and material resources to draw on. Yet, over half of the women interviewed who were incestuously assaulted did attempt to resist from the time abuse began. The other group were initially extremely afraid of the abuser or did not define what was happening as abuse.

As with rape, the form of resistance had to be possible and appropriate. This ruled out physical struggle, as all the women were abused by males who were considerably older and stronger. It is, however, possible that girls who are abused by male peers use this form of resistance more often. The most common forms of resistance used by the women involved attempting to control the man's access to them and/or challenging his authority in other contexts. These strategies have been called 'passive resistance'.[19] I regard all resistance as active; it involves making decisions and choices, acting on them and is always aimed at denying abusive men access and control. This girl was not behaving passively:

'He hit me once and I was so sore and got up — this was just about the end of my toleration of the situation and I said "Do you feel better now?'. Of course, that made him worse and he did it again, so I said "Don't worry about it, you'll never make me cry".'

One young woman, after being raped by her step-father, used a variety of strategies to prevent further abuse.

'I told him that, if he ever tried again, I'd tell my mother and he never came back. But each time my mother went into hospital he'd try. One time I wad dead scared you know, and I got bolts and put it on the doors. I used to bolt the door everywhere — bathroom, toilet, bedroom.'

Her resistance prevented further rape. It did not stop her step-father masturbating in the sitting room in the knowledge that she would see him; nor did it make her feel safe from the threat that he might rape her again.

The most common resistance strategy used by women over time was to try not to be alone with the abuser. One woman whose father abused her during access visits developed a particular avoidance strategy:

'I had a very unconscious mechanism of letting it not happen. I used to faint on the station platform and I used to get very bad migraine. So I unconsciously had ways of not actually going to see him.'

A more extreme version of this response, where young women are admitted to hospital with seizures, has been highlighted by two studies which suggest that through 'illness' young women attempt to alert others to what is happening and are able, at least temporarily, to deny access to their abuser.[20]

All but two of the incest survivors had considered running away as a way of permanently denying access to their abuser, but they realized that there was nowhere they could go and/or that they were too young to survive on their own. None of the women interviewed left home before they were 16 years old. The vulnerability of young women when they use running away as an avoidance strategy is highlighted by this woman's recollections; she was about 13 at the time.

'When I say run away — I used to walk up to the beach which was about 10 miles away, I used to spend most of the night out and tell them I'd stayed with friends.'

On one occasion she was offered a lift by a taxi driver when it was raining and she was raped by him.

Two women remembered being aware that the only way they could survive economically before they were 16 was through prostitution. Both decided to remain at home until they could legally leave. Kathleen Barry shows that because young women who do run away have great difficulty finding work and accommodation many are drawn into prostitution.[21] Pimps exploit this vulnerability, initially offering economic and emotional support followed by presenting prostitution as the only viable way of repaying the incurred debt. The one example of this process in the interviews involved a woman who ran away for reasons other than sexual abuse. She was 14 and was befriended by an older man who introduced her to drugs. When she was dependent on the drugs, he suggested prostitution: if she refused to co-operate, she would lose her accommodation, financial and emotional support and drug supply.

The consistent finding that high percentages of young prostitutes have a history of sexual abuse must be understood in relation to young women's lack of material resources and the willingness of men to exploit this vulnerability.[22] All young women who leave home before they are 16, or who are unable to support themselves and find accommodation after they are 16, are vulnerable to this form of exploitation. Young women who are being sexually abused have particular reasons for running away. The lack of support services all too often results in exchanging abuse inside the family home for abuse outside it.

Of the women four remembered being able to stop the abuse themselves whilst still living with the abuser. None of them had a clear memory of when the abuse actually stopped, but each knew that she began to resist in small ways first.

'I remember the first time I made this momentous decision. The decision itself frightened me almost as much as being near him. I remember standing behind him after I'd made this decision and sticking my tongue out and of course he caught me (laughs). But he didn't do anything much about it, and I thought "Oh good", and that's how I started.'

'It got into a period of fending him off and that's the period that's vague — I don't know how I did it, got it through to him that I didn't want it anymore. I know that by 14 I'd got rid of it, but then it was replaced by actual violence.'

Here again the risks of resistance are clear. Most of the incest survivors who challenged their abusers' authority were then subjected to physical violence but by not acting passively they undermined their abusers' confidence in not being detected and the sexual abuse stopped.

Most of the incest survivors felt that certain adults, particularly their mothers, should have picked up on the fact that there was something wrong from their behaviour and the hints that they gave. All of them had wanted someone to pick up on and stop the abuse.

'I'm still very closely tied to my adolescent self who just wanted it to stop. I find it hard to untie myself from that self even though I know it's a totally childish, illogical and unrealistic wish.'

It is this need that feeds into the feeling that the mother ought to have known and ought to have done something to prevent the abuse, a feeling that many researchers have used to blame mothers (see chapter 3).

The coping responses that women recalled during abuse were similar to those of women who were raped, the most common being 'cutting off'. Many instances of abuse took place in the girl's bedroom, after she had gone to bed. Pretending to be asleep was both a form of resistance, in that they hoped it might prevent abuse, and a way of cutting off if abuse occurred.

'I'd be in bed and hear the sound of his trousers and he'd sit down and I'd pretend to be alseep. You think if I pretend to be asleep nothing's going to happen — but it does.'

'I think I used to shut my mind off to it.'

Another woman would lie rigid on her stomach so that her father could not touch her breasts or genitals. As with experiences of rape, not allowing the abuser total control by attempting to limit the frequency, form and/or impact of the abuse was an important feature of young women's resistance.

The feelings women recalled immediately after assaults were

remarkably similar to those discussed by women who experienced rape: they felt abused, angry, numb, raped and dirty (in the order of frequency mentioned). For the majority of women interviewed, the abuse occurred repeatedly and this affected their feelings and behaviour. Of the women six remembered living with a sense of fear and threat, four felt their schooling was negatively affected, four had regular nightmares and three said that during their adolescence they had a nervous breakdown. One woman conceived and had the child which was later adopted.

A number of coping responses were directly linked to these impacts. Four women felt that their disruptiveness or their inability to concentrate at school were directly related to the experience of abuse. (This pattern was also common amongst women who were raped before they were 16 by men not living in their households.) Being disruptive was an attempt to communicate that something was wrong or to express their anger and frustration.

'It just made me so disruptive in school. It does amaze me when I think about it now, how nobody detected it. People don't really know how it affects you . . . . . . I'm going to have to go back and do all that learning again.'

Being unable to concentrate in or remember the content of lessons, was a direct result of trying to forget or cut off from particular instances of abuse. In erasing whole days or periods of time from their memory, they also forgot other things, including what they had learnt in school. All of these women were angry that their education had been affected in this way and amazed that their behaviour was either ignored or punished.

Slightly more women used school as an escape from the abuse. It was, for this group, one of the few places where they felt safe. Feelings of fear and threat did not dominate their thoughts at school and they concentrated on gaining qualifications in order to be able to support themselves and thus leave home. This difference in response was neither attributable to class nor previous achievement at school. It also demonstrates how dangerous it is for professionals to rely on visible 'signs' as reliable indicators of whether or not a child (or woman) has been, or is being, abused.

Many of the early researchers on child sexual abuse used

Freudian concepts of incestuous desire and childhood sexuality to explain sexual abuse. Children who acted 'provocatively' after the abuse was discovered were seen to have invited the abuse by behaving in this way before the abuse had occurred. It is slowly being acknowledged that 'sexual acting out' is the result, rather than the cause, of sexual abuse. The persistence, however, of the view of the child as the initiator of incest is illustrated by this psychologist's response to a woman, made two years before her interview with me.

'He said "You must realize that you can't blame other people, you must have been a very sexual child." '

None of the women interviewed felt they had behaved in a sexual way before they were abused and only two women recalled behaviour following abuse that could be defined as 'sexually acting out'. Both were abused from an early age and had the same explanation of their behaviour. The form of abuse practiced by their abusers resulted in them experiencing confusing feelings of sexual arousal that they did not understand. In retrospect, both recalled being sexually stimulated but never being allowed to have an orgasm. They were, therefore, 'left with all these feelings'. Both responded to this by compulsively masturbating, often in 'inappropriate' situations such as school. They saw this reaction as attempting to 'get rid' of these confusing feelings that they did not understand.

As with rape, young women did not passively accept incestuous assault. Despite the fact that they were children, were living with the abuser, were sworn to secrecy and/or warned of the terrible consequences if they told anyone, many of them resisted. It is seldom mentioned in studies of incest that young women manage to prevent further sexual abuse whilst still living with the abuser nor is sufficient attention given to the strategies young women use to attempt to limit the abuser's access to them or to challenge his authority over them.

Domestic violence: resistance and coping

Most women's initial response to violence in intimate relationships was shock and a desire to forget that it had happened. When violence was repeated, women's responses increasingly included resistance and coping strategies. Trudy Mills, in a study of ten battered women's coping strategies, suggests that their responses are directed at either avoiding violence or limiting injury. Like other researchers, she does not distinguish between resistance and other forms of coping, referring only to 'episodes of defiance'.[23] It is through resistance that women challenge the abusive men's attempts to control and abuse them and, as in all other forms of sexual violence, risk further injury.

The patterns of physical resistance which emerged from women's accounts varied from woman to woman as well as for the same woman over time. Only one woman physically resisted during every violent episode. Many women resisted physically at first, but stopped when they felt this increased the severity of the man's violence, although some returned to physical resistance just before they ended the relationship. Several women began to resist physically towards the end of the relationship.

'I wouldn't let him clout me without me clouting him back. Afterwards, someone said to me "Perhaps if you hadn't have hit him he wouldn't have hit you". I said "So I've got to sit there and take it — no! I'm not having him hitting me and getting away with it". But it would get that he would *pummel me so much* with his fists that I couldn't hit him back no more.'

'When it first happened I used to retaliate and it was always worse if I did.'

'At times I would give in and agree with him. But then I suppose I had enough spirit not to want to live like that and would react violently against it. I don't mean that I would lash out at him, but it would come to a stage where he would strike me and I would have a go back at him.'

'In the beginning I used to hit back. I couldn't accept that someone could hit me and I wasn't allowed to do anything about it.'

'I think because I was sticking up for myself the hidings got harder. I think that's what it was, he wanted to show that he was still my *governor*.'

By retaliating, women were making a statement to themselves and to the man: that they did not accept that he had a right to abuse or control them. It is also clear, however, that each time women chose to resist physically the risk of more severe injury was great.

The most extreme form of physical resistance is when women kill their abuser. Angela Browne interviewed 42 women charged with murder.[24] She suggests that the violence these women experienced was more frequent, more severe and involved more forced sex than that experienced by battered women who do not kill their abusers. Most of the women she talked to felt that their lives were threatened and had no faith (often on the basis of past experience) in being able to escape the man or find protection. Their experience of battering was a constant process of reassessing what they could cope with; each reached the point where she felt she could neither escape and live nor survive within the relationship. It is at this point, Browne argues, that women may kill their abusers.

The response of the women interviewed to the constant threat of violence and the control abusive men attempted to assert over them fell into one of two patterns. These patterns were not consistent throughout all abusive relationships but, rather, were different strategies that women chose. Most women had used both at some time, and there were times when aspects of both were present in women's behaviour. The first strategy involved refusing to be silenced or controlled by the man.

'I always thought "Damn you I'm not going to give in, I'm not going to back down", especially when there was that threat.'

'I used to think to myself, perhaps me saying "I'm going to" used to rile him, but then I used to think he doesn't ask me if he can do so and so, so *why can't I*.'

'He was always threatening me. Me being me, I wouldn't do whatever it was because I wouldn't let him do that to me. I used to fight against it all the time. As far as I was concerned, I'm a person, I could do what I wanted, I didn't want anyone telling me what to do.'

These women were aware that by challenging men and by refusing to be controlled they risked a violent response. It is undoubtedly this refusal that is referred to as 'nagging', 'asking for it' and 'provocation'. This logic of reversal of responsibility was used consistently by abusive men to justify their violence, and is often the basis of professional responses to battered women.[25] The assumption is made that, if women did not behave in this way, the violence would cease.

The second response pattern, discussed below, shows that this is not the case. As the comment below illustrates, it also denies the costs to women of this 'alternative'.

'I suppose you might be able to prevent it by suppressing so much of yourself, learning to avoid the kind of behaviour that precipitates it. But then that in itself is a form of violence.'

The other response to continued violence was to try to avoid conflict, not challenge the man, accept his demands, *in order to prevent violence.*

'The best way to avoid it was to show *as little reaction* as possible . . . . . . Even though I didn't feel I loved him at the time, I *hated* him (anger), I was saying that I loved him. I had to be the absolute *perfect* housewife . . . I wouldn't *dare* argue with him or challenge him — for fear of my life actually.'

'You kept the house tidy, you got the children out of the way, you got meals ready when he walked in . . . all sorts of pandering about, women's skills you know. I got quite skilled over the years, I never knew when it was going to happen, it was just avoidance.'

'I just tried to be kind of self-effacing in every sense — you know, if I make myself invisible he won't see me to hit me.'

'I would just be quite passive, try not to provoke him verbally or physically. I would just do anything he wanted me to do, try and be calm and pleasant just to try and avoid it or if there was a warning I would flee the house.'

These avoidance strategies did not prevent violence recurring although it is possible that, in some cases, they may have limited its frequency. It is a mistake, however, to regard this as a more positive strategy than challenge and resistance since the long-term cost to women's sense of self has to be balanced against any gains in avoiding physical violence in the short term. Indeed, many women abandoned the 'appeasement' strategy when it became clear that it did not stop the violence. Only five women said that they had never used avoidance strategies to try to prevent violence. Most women used combinations of resistance and avoidance strategies. The choice of particular responses varied according to how strong or fearful women felt at the time and whether or not they were seriously considering leaving.

This focus on resistance and coping strategies calls into question two American feminist approaches to domestic violence. Mildred Daley Pagelow has suggested that battered women have a more traditional attitude to women's role.[26] This view of battered women neglects the forms of resistance that persist in women's behaviour despite the probable consequences, and it arises from a fundamental misreading of avoidance strategies. Whilst women may appear to be accepting of men's demands, this was a conscious coping strategy which they used to try and avoid violence. It was not a desire to be the perfect wife and mother. If traditional attitudes are involved in battering, it was not abused women who held them in this sample but their abusive partners.

The application of the theory of 'learned helplessness' to battered women, popularized by Leonore Walker, does not reflect the experience of the women interviewed in this project either.[27] There were individual women who were afraid to challenge their partners. There were periods of time or particular incidents for other women when they coped by being passive. There were also periods of time when women recalled feeling numb and unable to act or react. The fact that, for many women, their resistance increased before they finally left, seriously questions the suggestion that women become progressively more passive and accepting. One of the women interviewed suggested a stage theory of responses based on her own experience.

'The last two times I resisted again, I'd been through this acceptance stage and I decided I wasn't going to accept it and I resisted and I got hurt worse. Then I thought I shall never let it happen again.'

As her initial physical resistance resulted in more severe violence, she adjusted her response to coping strategies, such as not challenging the man and trying to fulfil his expectations of her (what she refers to as the 'acceptance stage'). When these strategies did not prevent the violence, she began to resist again and, very soon after this, made the decision to leave. I use this example not to suggest that this model fits all women's experiences of battering but to point out that what has been defined as 'learned helplessness' is in fact a form of coping in a situation where women feel their options are severely limited.

All the women I interviewed who had been battered had thought of leaving and, eventually, every woman did leave. A number of women had run out of the house to avoid violence on particular occasions. Over 50 per cent had left and then had been forced to return. Three factors accounted for the majority of returns: there was nowhere safe to go; the man found her and either persuaded or forced her to return; and the fact that she had left her children behind when she left. No woman mentioned wanting to return.

The aspect of coping most researched in relation to battered women has been what Cath Cavanagh has called help-seeking.[28] Many researchers have noted the numerous ways in which women attempt to stop the violence before they decide to leave the relationship, including seeking outside support. Cavanagh's changing pattern, from initial contacts within informal networks for supportive help, to increasing contacts with formal agencies for challenging help, was discernible amongst the women interviewed. This process begins from the point when women define the violence as abuse and want to end it. Initially, they want to talk, to have their feelings validated and to discuss possible ways of ending the violence but not the relationship. When these strategies fail, women increasingly approach statutory agencies hoping that some form of sanctions on the man and/or other options for themselves will end the violence. Within this general pattern, however, each woman's help-seeking was slightly different. It varied according to how she defined her situation, which networks and agencies she felt were open to her, who she felt might be supportive, and to what extent the man had insisted that she not tell anyone. Both the range of contacts and women's dissatisfaction with the response were similar to those found in previous studies.[29] Only solicitors, close women friends and, in two instances, refuges were felt to offer effective support.

The decision to leave the relationship was made only when a range of resistance, avoidance, coping and help-seeking strategies failed to prevent the violence and/or when women felt their lives were threatened by the continuing violence. Many women find ending unsatisfactory relationships difficult, those relationships which include violence are at the extreme end of a spectrum. Leaving a violent man is a process in which women weigh the balance of fear and hope; it is both a decisive moment and the outcome of a long process of coping and re-evaluation.

'When a woman's ready to go, she's gonna go and not until.'

'It was purely financial problems and I think also gathering up the courage to do something which would publicly admit that I had made a mistake. I think it takes time to move into that frame of mind.'

'I was really afraid that he would actually injure me. It was also partly that I had started to tell people what was really going on.'

The fact that so few women were given real support which encouraged or enabled them to leave further complicated each woman's decision. Many women had to ensure secrecy and protection before leaving was a realistic possibility.

'I couldn't get away from him. He'd follow me about, if I did disappear he'd come after me, find out from other people where I'd gone.'

'I knew if I went to friends he would find me and he would have created merry hell. *I knew that when I went it had got to be somewhere where he couldn't find me,* or if he did find me I would have sufficient protection.'

Leaving was complicated further by the effects of abuse over time: 19 women were severely depressed, two had nervous breakdowns and six either attempted or contemplated suicide. Women lived in a state of constant tension and fear: 13 feared they would either be killed or permanently injured by the man. Yet, despite the threat of violence and the actual beatings, the isolation most women experienced, the failure of requests for support, the effects of depression and, in most cases, limited material resources, all these women left. This, in itself, is powerful evidence that women do not accept or 'want' violence.

Pamela Smith, in her study of women in a Canadian refuge, has drawn out the aspects of battered women's actions that she defines as survival strategies.[30] She concludes, as did the women I interviewed, that the only strategy that is effective in stopping the violence is to leave the man. For some women, leaving is a technique they use in the hope the man will change. For two of the women interviewed, this proved effective. For most women, leaving was an end in itself.

Keeping the complexity of women's experience

It would be unwise to draw out from the many responses women had to similar and different experience of men's violence any generalized lessons or guidelines concerning resistance or coping strategies in specific situations. Nevertheless, there are aspects of women's experiences which should be stressed.

Despite being in fear for their lives, or that incidents might escalate, many women chose to resist sexual violence. Resistance included physical struggle, verbal challenge and refusal to be controlled by abusive men. Some women's resistance resulted in the avoidance of rape or a particular incident of abuse. Other women altered the course of the assaults. For some women, particularly battered women, continued resistance often meant that they experienced more severe violence.

If resistance failed to prevent violence, or when women chose not to resist physically, they engaged in coping strategies through which they attempted to limit the impact of violence on them. Minimizing and cutting off from the violence was the most common response. More limited coping options were available where women were living with their abuser and/or when they were children at the time of abuse. The immediate impact of experiences of sexual violence was similar across the different forms of violence.

Certain perspective within victimology imply or state explicitly that 'victims' have some responsibility for their experiences. Even where this is not the case, the predominant image of a 'victim' includes a sense of passivity and powerlessness. This image is reinforced by the all too frequent tendency for many of the resistance and coping strategies women and girls use to be reinterpreted as implicating them in the violence. For example, if a woman physically resists and is severely hurt, she is told she should have acted more passively. If, on the other hand, she decides not to resist she is seen as accepting the violence! Clearly, this is a no-win situation – *whatever choices women make, they are likely to be told that they should have done the opposite.*

The many forms of resistance to, and coping with, victimization are active responses requiring strength and determination. This woman is describing her reactions to reading her interview transcript in which she discussed three abusive relationships. Note her stress on how important it was for her to see her behaviour in a new way:

'What came through to me was . . . . . . seems all through my life I've been trying to fit into this mould and all the problems I've had have been me kicking against it. But not knowing what it was I was kicking against . . . . . . just *resistance* (sighs) . . . . . . and I feel so angry that I couldn't see it until now.'

It was through the process of doing the interview that this woman connected her resistance and the violence that accompanied it to a wider analysis of gendered social relations based on power and control. Her experience, and that of the other women interviewed, highlights how sexual violence centres around men's power and women's resistance to it.

I hope that this chapter has done something to redress an imbalance I perceive in both research and some feminist theory. Most research on sexual violence has neglected, or indeed at times misread, the acts of resistance and challenge that women and girls take which display strength and determination. Much feminist theory has centred on men's all too frequent use (abuse) of power and control and, in so doing, has paid insufficient attention to analysing and documenting women's persistent and consistent resistance to it. It is precisely this lack which has been the focus of some Black feminist critiques[31] and which has made possible a recent strand of feminist analysis which suggests that feminists who work around sexual violence produce a pessimistic vision of 'women's common and inescapable victimization'.[32] In recognizing, documenting and validating the many and varied ways in which women resist sexual violence it becomes possible to move away from 'victimism' towards an understanding of the complexity of women's experiences of sexual violence.

8

'It leaves a mark': coping with the consequences of sexual violence

'Now *I realize how much it has affected me. It wasn't good enough* just to get out *of that situation.*'

Every experience of sexual violence has consequences for women. What these impacts are and their short- or long-term nature cannot be simplistically inferred from the particular form of sexual violence women experience. Different forms of sexual violence may have similar impacts; the same form may have different ones. Current and past experiences of sexual violence often interact resulting in a cumulative impact;[1] a recent incident often triggers memories of, and similar reactions to, previous assault(s). The particular circumstances of an assault may result in specific impacts, as this woman's experience illustrates:

'I was 17 and being fitted with contact lenses. The optician was touching me up and it was very uncomfortable and embarrassing and it's meant that I've never actually worn my contact lenses.'

I use the word 'consequences' rather than 'long-term effects' to emphasize that there are a range of possible impacts, some of which are physical, some emotional/psychological, some behavioural and some material. The word 'effects' tends to be limited to changes in individual psychology, whereas the aftermath of victimization also includes subsequent events and circumstances which are precipitated by, or attributable to, assaults. Whilst these are not direct 'effects' they can be conceptualized as consequences.

I stress again that my approach involves locating the consequences in the context of the active process of coping which all women who have been victimized engage in. This approach necessitates looking at the complexity of women's experience; not separating the 'effects' from how women cope with them and recognizing that through coping with profoundly negative impacts women may make choices and come to understandings which they value positively. This analysis contrasts sharply with much of the recent research on the 'long-term effects' of rape and child sexual abuse where 'effects' are conceptualized as negative changes in women's feelings and behaviour which can be isolated from one another and studied using psychological tests.[2]

The difference between these two perspectives can be illustrated by considering the concern in much 'long-term effects' research with 'heterosexual adjustment'. Most research on the impact of rape and child sexual abuse notes that it often has a profound impact on women's attitudes to sex and men.[3] The implicit assumption that all impacts of sexual violence are, by definition, negative, results in explicit suggestions that support/treatment for women who have been victimized should enable them to overcome these reactions. Women should, therefore, be 'helped' to readjust to 'normal' heterosexuality. This uncritical labelling of women's responses to victimization as 'negative effects' leads Mary De Young, for example, to suggest that incest survivors who become lesbians do so as a result of being 'so traumatized' by the abuse.[4] The possibility that incest survivors might choose lesbian relationships and see this as a positive choice which was influenced, but not determined by, their experience of abuse is ignored.[5] Similarly, many researchers label some of women's responses to victimization as frigidity or promiscuity, ignoring the male-defined assumptions implicit in these words and their place within a system of negative cultural meanings surrounding women's sexuality. Later in this chapter, I will show that women's responses are better understood as a chosen period of celibacy ('frigidity') and a choice not to make emotional commitments in relationships with men ('promiscuity'). I will also argue that, rather than a 'negative reaction', women's distrust of men is a healthy and self-protective response to the reality of sexual violence.

The 'long-term effects'

It is only in the past six years that the long-term impact of sexual violence has become a research topic. By far the majority of published studies have been undertaken in the USA; most draw on methods and theoretical frameworks from within social psychology and are limited to either rape or incest/child sexual abuse. The primary focus, to date, has been to discover what the effects of victimization are, the most commonly cited being 'heterosexual adjustment' and areas commonly associated with deviance (drug/alcohol abuse, prostitution and suicide).

While some of the early studies of incest and child sexual abuse referred to negative impacts, researchers have felt obliged to prove that there are long-term effects in the face of accepted received 'wisdom' that child sexual abuse seldom involves a long-term negative impact (see chapter 3). Until the mid-1970s, the predominant focus was on 'frigidity' and 'promiscuity'. 'Promiscuity' remains the most commonly cited impact and areas relating to sexual behaviour still receive the most attention. Other consequences which have been noted in studies since the mid-1970s are, in order of frequency cited: depression, suicide attempts, loss of trust, loss of self-esteem, vulnerability to further victimization, drug abuse, prostitution, pregnancy and flash-backs.[6] Only one study presents aspects of adjustment to experiences of sexual abuse in positive terms, noting that survivors tended to be more independent and self-accepting than the control group.[7]

The largest body of research on the impact of sexual violence focuses on rape. Many of these studies are designed to assess treatment needs and/or treatment programmes following the dramatic increase of support services in the USA during the 1970s. In the mid-to late 1970s, most studies emphasized the Rape Trauma Syndrome (see chapter 3) but increasingly this has been replaced by the study of specific short-and long-term effects using structured psychological tests at regular intervals after the assault. The two most commonly cited and studied impacts are a negative impact on sexual satisfaction and fear or vulnerability. Other effects which have been noted are depression, loss of trust, nightmares, phobic reactions and loss of self-respect.[8]

The positivistic methodology used in most of these studies, coupled with the uncritical adoption of male-defined conceptions of women's sexuality, means that the majority of the studies to date are severely limited. Rather than encouraging women to discuss the range of impacts of sexual violence on them, particular effects are emphasized by the researcher and wrenched out of the context in which they occur. This context includes the specific circumstances of each woman, all the other impacts women experience and the coping options which are available to them.

All too often the impacts of sexual violence on women are described as individual psychological, and at times pathological, effects which are then deemed amenable to treatment. Phyllis Chesler's suggestion that much of the mental health profession's response to women involves pathologizing them is useful in understanding this process of medicalization.[9] Women's resistance, strength and coping strategies are transformed into an abstract pattern of negative reactions: problems to be resolved through expert intervention using, for example, 'stress inoculation, systematic desensitization and cognitive restructuring'.[10]

Coping with the consequences of sexual violence

I asked the women I interviewed what they felt the long-term impact of their experiences of rape, incest and domestic violence had been. Their responses are summarized in table 8.1. Many of the women interviewed also referred to the impact of other forms of sexual violence.

Susan Schecter conceptualizes the impact of domestic violence as a series of losses which women have to cope with.[11] This insight can be extended to all experiences of sexual violence. The losses women may experience include: loss of safety, loss of independence or autonomy, loss of control, loss of confidence and self-esteem, loss of memories, loss of status (for migrant women who leave a violent husband this may include loss of residence 'rights'), loss of trust, loss of a positive attitude to sexuality, loss of housing and property, loss of jobs, children and educational opportunities, loss of support networks including relatives and friends, loss of health and, in the most extreme cases, loss of life itself. The number of losses, how long and to what extent they influence women's lives and choices, arises out of the complex interaction between the actual assault(s), women's responses and coping options and the amount of support they get from others. It is against this background of profoundly negative consequences that positive outcomes must be placed. Within the

Table 8.1   Long-term consequences of experiences of violence[a]

Consequence	R N	R %	I N	I %	DV N	DV %	Total N	Total %
Affected attitude to men[b]	24	92	13	100	22	88	59	92
Affected attitude to sex[b]	25	96	13	100	20	80	58	91
Flashbacks[b]	22	85	11	85	17	68	50	78
Dreams/nightmares	16	62	11	85	17	68	44	69
Cues remind of abuse	13	50	11	85	18	72	42	67
Forgot/cut off to cope	15	58	12	92	12	48	39	61
Closer now to women	14	54	6	46	12	48	32	50
Vulnerability/fear	10	38	6	46	14	56	30	47
Independent/stronger	0	0	4	31	18	72	22	34
Feminist attitudes	12	46	2	15	5	20	19	30
Aware of risks for self and daughter(s)	6	23	5	38	4	16	15	23
Insecure	0	0	4	31	10	40	14	22
Breakdown linked to abuse	5	19	4	31	2	8	11	17
Has right to control own body	11	42	0	0	0	0	11	17
Negative effect on schooling	4	15	7	54	0	0	11	17
Lost custody of child(ren)	0	0	1	8	8	32	9	14
Fear of challenging men	4	15	0	0	5	20	9	14
Confusion between love/sex/affection	0	0	8	62	0	0	8	13
Can't cope with images of violence	0	0	3	23	5	20	8	13
Suicide attempt	1	4	3	23	3	12	8	13
Made vulnerable to later abuse	4	15	2	15	2	8	8	13
Vulnerable about pregnancy	1	4	2	15	2	8	5	8

[a] Data analysed separately for experiences of rape (R, N = 26), incest (I, N = 13) and domestic violence (DV, N = 25). The total column percentages are calculated on the basis of the 64 experiences of these forms of violence in the sample.
[b] Specific questions were asked about these impacts; the rest were mentioned spontaneously by women.

active process of coping with these losses, women may feel that they make positive choices and discoveries.

While the impacts of sexual violence and women's coping strategies are discussed under specific headings in the following sections, readers should bear in mind that these interacted with one another and were not separate in women's experience. Forgetting experiences of abuse is discussed first as it has implications for the sections which follow.

Forgetting and remembering

In chapter 6, the commonness of forgetting was discussed in the context of how it affected women's definitions of sexual violence. That analysis is extended here through discussion of forgetting as a coping strategy. The women speaking below describe a similar response to experiences of rape, incestuous abuse and domestic violence.

'For a long time I didn't even think about it. It hadn't happened. It didn't exist.'

'I just locked it away and never thought about it.'

'My problem is remembering for two reasons. I had an accident which has made my memory bad and my way of coping with it was to put it to the back of my mind and forget it as much as possible.'

'I've survived by thinking of the *now*, right now today, or what I'm going to be doing in five year's time. I don't look back. Then all of a sudden when things come up and you have to start looking back — that makes me feel really ill. I just want to sit and cry. I want to put myself into an institution for someone to look after me.'

'I survived through my dubious ability to push things to one side, which I suppose you could say I'm paying for now. I think women do that. They have to otherwise they just don't survive.'

In order to cope, many women bury the memory of victimization and/or attempt to suppress the feelings it evokes. The need to suppress traumatic events derives from the threat they represent to the person. But whilst forgetting may control acute distress, it does not prevent women from being affected.[12] Forgetting, therefore, complicates discussion of other impacts; it makes their identification more difficult and may affect their development over time.

There is an irony in the use of forgetting as a coping strategy since an unintended consequence is that other impacts of abuse cannot be connected to their cause, either by the woman herself or anyone she seeks help from. Many of the rape and incest survivors who had forgotten their victimization recalled emotional reactions or behaviour changes that they did not understand at the time.

'When I feel worthless now, instead of not knowing why, I know now.'

The most extreme example of this in the interviews was a woman who was sexually abused by a number of male relatives and friends. Over a ten-year period, she was hospitalized 14 times and attempted suicide a number of times. She was treated with drugs and electroconvulsive therapy. She attributed the recent improvement in her mental health to the fact that she had remembered being abused after seeing a television programme on incest. Knowing there was a cause for her distress meant that her behaviour was explicable, that she was not mad or mentally ill. The fact that in all of her treatment no one identified this cause led me to wonder how many other woman have undisclosed experiences of sexual violence at the root of mental health problems.

Whilst writing this chapter, I was involved in supporting a rape survivor who admitted herself into a psychiatric clinic as a voluntary patient. The fact that of the six other women she got to know in the clinic, four attributed their problems to rape, incest or domestic violence supported the link between women's mental health problems and sexual violence. None of these women were forgetting or minimizing, but disclosed their experiences to the hospital staff. The women's understandings were, however, dismissed or minimized by the majority of the staff and even the support they got from one another was challenged by suggestions that they should spend more time associating with male nurses and patients.

Coping through forgetting also rules out the use of other strategies which most women saw as helpful, particularly being able to talk through the experience. Talking to supportive friends was, for many women, an important factor in helping them cope. However, several women stressed that they did not remember or think about their experience until they were ready or able to work it through.

'They gave me hypnosis, drugs, when somebody was trying to get something out of me that I didn't want to give then it wouldn't come. But when I decided I was going to give it them it came.'

Glynis Breakwell sees denial, a broader term which includes forgetting, cutting off and minimizing as an attempt to cope with threat, useful as a short-term 'holding strategy', as a way of buying time out, of anaesthetizing initial pain and trauma.[13] But, whilst acute disruption to the self is controlled, the threat remains and has to be dealt with at some later point.

One of the ways that women were repeatedly reminded of their abuse was through dreams and flashbacks. Both often occurred whilst women were in the forgetting or minimizing phase, perhaps functioning as an internal reminder that there was something important the woman needed to resolve. Almost every woman who had experienced rape, incest or domestic violence had had dreams and flashbacks at some point and over half still experienced flashbacks.

'I can get that walking down the street, I can get that any instant, any time. Any little thing I do and I can be back in that situation I was in as a child.'

There appeared to be at least two forms of flashbacks. The most common was triggered by something specific that reminded women of the assault: a name, a place, a man who looked like their abuser, a kind of movement, or representations of violence.

'Certain things remind me of it, if I see a person with a moustache like that.'

'There are things that bring it back . . . I can't watch extremely violent things, I just want to turn off because the thoughts will start and I just don't want to know. That's the way I cope by suppressing it.'

This type of flashback could be momentary, making it possible for women to retrieve buried memories or alternatively to dismiss the thought from their minds. When women were not suppressing the abuse there were times when flashbacks were frequent and seldom amenable to control. Most women found them extremely distressing. The other form of flashback did not seem to be triggered by anything in particular. It occurred only when women were aware of their experience of abuse and seemed to be associated with remembering aspects of it that had been suppressed.

Remembering, acknowledging and working through experiences of sexual violence is a crucial process if women are to be able to deal positively with their past. It is extremely painful and draining and requires considerable personal strength and determination, as this description by an incest survivor illustrates.

'That's when really weird things started happening, like my dad appearing in bed next to me. I used to walk around the house and all of a sudden just see him standing there. I realized there was something wrong but I still didn't connect it with this incest in any way. One day I was speaking to this woman I know and I said to her that I felt terrible but I didn't really know why, that my dad was appearing and she just listened to me. Up until then, I had never really spoken about myself. I had always disassociated myself from myself and been able to talk without feeling or emotion . . . All of a sudden I just said "My dad used to interfere with me". I don't even know where it came from, why I said it. She said "That's what all this is about". She asked me what he used to do and I told her . . . I suppose from that moment on, although I can say it was the most painful — even more painful than all that I'd already been through — that was the most progressive conversation in my life. Because everything up to that point had been dictated by men. I just felt I was here to be abused even though I knew that wasn't right I couldn't connect it . . . I just started working it out — literally went back (nobody told me how to do it) — I just thought I had to look on it as a mathematical problem. If the total was wrong, and my total was, then I had to go back and completely add it up again and pick out the bits where it had gone wrong. I went into it so much that I literally relieved whole scenes, all the emotions started coming out . . . pouring and pouring out. That big emotional bit went on for about four or five months, I didn't go out anywhere, I didn't want to. I just literally stayed here, read books, cried and thought . . . At that initial point I didn't feel it was wrong but somewhere in me I knew that I had to know it was wrong and that's when I started hating. I don't hate anymore, that's all gone, but at the time it was terrible, as I'd never felt like that ever. I suppose that's why I started associating things with the devil. It was a real sort of psycho job. I thought I was going mad at one stage. I think the most important thing of all was when I realized that my dad was inside me, like he was part of me. He'd made me what I was being like and acting like. I went round for so long feeling in despair like there was a voice inside me that couldn't come out. I know it sounds a bit weird but that's how I thought at the time. I can remember lying on the bed one day and thinking, imagining myself throwing up, throwing him up and being sick. At the back of my throat I felt a scale or something. And I can remember it my mind pulling it out, as I pulled it out like a whole structure of me came out, what you'd expect a skeleton to look like came out. I pulled it out threw it on the floor and said the Lord's Prayer — it's terrible to think you're even doing things like that, really shows what frame of mind I was in. And yet when I did that and thought that's my dad and he's gone, that choking feeling went the minute I did that.'

Eleven women had had what they described as breakdowns

during this period of remembering and coming to terms with their past. Over half of them felt, in retrospect, that this had been positive; it was part of understanding themselves and being able to make changes in their lives.

'This breakdown for me was like a rebirth. It was when I put all the pieces back in the right places.'

In the immediate period following experiences of sexual violence, forgetting or cutting off was an important aspect of coping for many women. It is, however, also the case that remembering and working through the past was a crucial aspect of coping. Forgetting can only be a temporary palliative; if it is prolonged, women themselves, and others, may interpret the impact of abuse on their behaviour and feelings as faults or failure in themselves. Forgetting may be positive, even necessary, in the short term, yet it can have negative long-term implications.

It is not clear how far women's need or desire to forget or cut off is a semi-automatic psychological self-protective mechanism, as Glynis Breakwell suggests, or whether and how far it is a consequence of the lack of understanding and social support for women and girls experiencing sexual violence. If there is no one to talk to, one cannot talk. If one fears being blamed, there is a strong incentive to forget rather then risk this response. Feminist services have long recognized the importance for abused women and girls of access to supportive listening and sharing of common experience. It is only when this sort of support is widely available and accessible to all women and girls that we will be able to assess whether forgetting is an automatic defence mechanism or a socially conditioned coping strategy.

Loss of security and safety

Karen Horney, in her attempt to overcome the limitations of Freud's instinct theory, suggested that the two basic human needs are safety and security.[14] Both are fundamentally under-mined by sexual victimization, making vulnerability and fear issues all abused women and girls have to contend with. Whilst vulnerability and fear have been central concerns in research on the aftermath of rape, the focus has tended to be on stranger assaults. The added complexity of these issues for women who are assaulted by men they know, men who are members of their household or social network, has not been acknowledged. Many women's security and safety continued to be threatened after they left abusive men. Almost 70 per cent of the women who had left violent husbands or lovers were harassed after they left: three were raped, two coerced into having sex, two badly assaulted, five threatened with violence and two blackmailed after they had separated.

'He harassed me a lot, and he entered my name in pornography magazines, all sorts of diabolical things to put pressure on me.'

'He would never sign any papers. He was still quite violent to me. He'd drive at me in the car things like that, and he still *wanted sex*! When I finally got my flat several years later, he still used to come and say "Come on, how about it"!'

Of the women who were not subsequently harassed, over half achieved this by ensuring their abuser did not know where they were. Research in the USA suggests that many women who end relationships because of violence are assaulted after separation.[15] It is the persistence of many abusive men that results in women having to give up housing, jobs, friendships and even contact with relatives in order to protect themselves. During my involvement with the local refuge, I have seen many women return to an abusive man following continued harassment and repeated attempts to leave. They feel this is a rational decision having realistically assessed their options. Given the minimal or non-existence protection calling the police or taking legal proceedings resulted in and the man's refusal to leave them alone, they felt they would never be free of him. It is an indictment of both the law and policing priorities that abused women decide that living with the violence is preferable to the only other alternative – living in fear of being found every minute of every day. There are many women who do not return, but who continue to live in fear. Some are driven to desperate measures such as moving many miles away, changing their names and cutting off all contact with their previous life and identity. This is the price some women have to pay for safety.

'I'd gone and hired a bloke to shoot him — I just wanted him out of my life, I couldn't take anymore. I just wanted to get away from him and to know that I was free (sighs). It may sound really ridiculous. At the time I thought it was the only way I could ever get away from him.'

The desperation this woman recalls is also evident in *The Burning Bed*, an account of how Francine Hughes was driven to kill her abusive husband.[16] She repeatedly tried to leave, encountered hostility and disbelief from social agencies, a failure to act despite evidence by the police, denial by her husband's relatives and fear of involvement from her mother and friends. Her children were taken by her husband when one attempt at separation seemed likely to succeed. The escalation of the abuse coupled with the systematic failure of anyone to provide her with support or safety resulted in Francine burning the house in which her violent husband was sleeping. In the subsequent court case, the evidence of her systematic abuse was accepted as mitigating circumstances and she was found not guilty of murder.

Women who were sexually abused by male relatives came into contact with their abuser if they attended family gatherings. For women who were abused by their fathers, yet had not told their mothers, problems arose as it was difficult to justify repeated failures to visit. If their mother still lived with the man who had abused them (not all did), they often had to choose between telling their mother, having limited contact with her or engaging in painful pretence.

'It was horrible — he'd sit there as if nothing had happened. Once we were watching TV and there was some news report about child abuse. He went on and on about how men like that ought to be put away for life — I couldn't believe it! I felt really sick and just left the room.'

Three women's fathers made further sexual approaches at family functions long after the abuse had 'stopped' and the women had left home.

Several women who were raped or sexually assaulted by men they knew came into contact with them socially despite trying to prevent this. One rapist deliberately came to the bar where the woman worked in order to see her reaction. Many women changed their friendship groups and places they went out to in order to avoid meeting certain men. Women who are sexually harassed at work or by friends or acquaintances in social situations invariably came into contact with them on subsequent occasions. One of the consequences of abuse by known men is that it is often difficult for women to avoid any future contact with their abuser. Not only do they have to cope with the impact of violence, but also with the physical presence of the man who violated them.

Each incident of sexual violence had an impact on women's perceptions of the more general threat of sexual violence. Women's responses varied according to how threatened they felt and how they chose to respond. Some women responded by limiting their behaviour; some women chose to 'refuse the threat'. This latter response is not a denial of the reality of sexual violence but a refusal to be restricted by it. Many women came to see their individual experience as part of a wider reality. A group of US researchers, in discussing the impact of rape, make several points that can be extended to other forms of sexual violence:

The victim cannot find solace in returning to her everyday routine, for in her mind she is merely placing herself in continuing peril. [Rape] is no longer the isolated incident that can be avoided by locking the door at night, but rather a real danger built into every facet of her life . . . Since her feelings of vulnerability stem from her being a female, unlike victims of accidents or illness, the [rape] victim can do nothing to lesson or erase the perceived source of her vulnerability.[17]

The impact may be greater when the abuse takes place in a location previously thought of as 'safe'.

'It was horrible in terms of what had been done to me, but it was also that it was on my territory, which was even worse. There was no way I could go home without walking past there forever after. That made me very nervous for quite a long while. To begin with I'd be nervous in lots of situations, like when I got on the bus I'd be terrified that he'd be sitting there, or that his face would be on the tube. From then I did start to become nervous about walking about at night, something I'd not really felt before, and I've never lost that.'

'I think my attitudes have changed permanently — I will never feel safe walking down the street by myself ever again. I will never feel safe in a situation where I'm alone with a man I don't know very well, I will never trust men totally again. Also I will never be able to cope with harassment as well as I could before. But then that's another thing, maybe my getting angry is coping with it in a different way. I'm just learning a lot about myself at the moment and how to adapt that experience into my life.'

For many women, the accumulation of experiences of sexual violence results in a realization that no place is totally safe. The threat of violence becomes a backdrop for everyday life. Learning that friends have also been abused can reinforce women's sense of vulnerability, as may press reporting.

'The accumulation of all these incidents made me frightened *all the time* — and angry. I couldn't walk down the street normally. I walked down the street scared and angry.'

Sandra McNeill has illustrated how far-reaching the impact of the threat and reality of sexual violence is.[18] It is not just that women have to make choices about where they go, when they go and now they go. Being aware of the potential of sexual violence means that women have to spend time watching, checking, being wary in a range of contexts. As the woman above illustrates, it is not even possible to walk down the road thinking one's own thoughts. Women have to find ways of managing the threat of sexual violence. We choose from a range of coping strategies, each of which involves an assessment of risks and costs. The reality of sexual violence requires frequent reassessments of our choices and, therefore, our behaviour.

One group of US researchers has undertaken a series of studies on fear and vulnerability following rape and maintain that the desire to avoid further sexual violence can increase anxiety and fear and cause phobic reactions.[19] They move from this observation to recommending, and indeed using, desensitizing therapy within the six months after rape. They, like a number of those studying fear of crime, justify treating women's fear as an 'over-reaction' through an assessment of the low risk for women of being raped a second time. The prevalence of forced sex which is neither officially recorded nor defined at the time of the assault by women as rape, is ignored and the possibility that women's fear may be connected to a variety of actual, and possible future, experiences of sexual violence is not explored.[20]

Whilst sexual violence remains such a common experience and whilst women feel that they can expect little protection from others, be they passers-by or the police, a sense of vulnerability is a realistic response. It is one of the many costs of this reality that some women are affected so strongly that they 'choose' to limit their lives in dramatic ways.

For mothers, awareness of vulnerability extended to their children. Many had discussed protection strategies with their daughters. The incest survivors who had children felt they were constantly watching male relatives and friends, particularly husbands.

'I certainly watch how my husband treats my daughter like a hawk.'

This is a very different picture from that presented in some of the recent literature (see chapter 3) which suggests that mothers who have been sexually abused tend to have relationships with abusive men and passively accept abuse of their children. The incest survivors I talked to were determined that the same thing should not happen to their children. Mothers who had been battered attempted to bring up their male children to respect women and to be committed to not using violence.

'I talk to them about the violence, which they knew was going on, although it was kept from them. I talk to them about what it was like to live in fear like that.'

Increased awareness of the reality of sexual violence had other consequences for women. Many women commented on how it affected their response to the content of films, books, television programmes and pornography. They objected to the portrayal of violence against women as 'entertainment' and resented the way such representations triggered painful memories.

'I tend to avoid going to films now because of that, it always brings things back.'

'It's just sensitized me more and more to violence, to almost a ridiculous point where I can't — as soon as violence comes up in a book it makes me feel *physically sick*. I can make myself read it, but I really do have to *make myself*. If it comes up on the television — and it's there all the time — I find it very difficult to watch.'

Discussions of media depictions of violence in general, and violence to women in particular, tend to focus on whether they produce, reinforce or legitimate similar behaviour. The negative impact of most representation of sexual violence on those who have been abused has been totally ignored by both official investigations and a number of feminist authors.

Vulnerability to future victimization

A number of recent research projects have suggested that one of the long-term effects of sexual abuse, and particularly incest, is that it makes women vulnerable to further sexual violence.[21] Diana Russell's study is the only project with a large random sample of women which enabled comparison of multiple victimization between women with expriences of incest and women without.[22] She found that 68 per cent of incest survivors had also experienced a rape or attempted rape compared to 38 per cent of women who were not incestuously abused. She offers a number of possible explanations for the difference. First, it is possible that women with experiences of incest were more honest during the interview. Second, she repeats a suggestion made by David Finkelhor that abusive men may pick up on certain women's vulnerability.[23] Third, she suggests that incest may function as a socialization process into the role of a victim. Finally, she notes that men who later abuse women may know of the previous abuse. A further explanation related to the context in which later assaults occur has been proposed by two women researchers.[24] They note that any young women who runs away from home and/ or abuses drugs or alcohol is vulnerable to sexual exploitation and that some young women use drugs and alcohol as coping strategies in response to sexual abuse confounds the impact of the abuse itself.

The number of incest survivors interviewed in this project is not large compared with Russell's but it should be noted that there were not large differences between the incest group and other groups in relation to multiple experiences of sexual violence. However, several of Russell's explanations applied to repeat victimizations more generally. In chapter 6, I raised the possibility that incest and rape survivors may be more likely to define subsequent sexual experiences as abusive. Whilst this is not quite the same as Russell's 'honesty', it does suggest that women's prior experience and understandings may affect their response to questions about sexual violence, particularly rape. A number of women (not just incest survivors) felt that repeat victimizations were connected to vulnerability from a previous assault which men in partnerships then took advantage of. A number of instances of men using knowledge of past abuse as justification for their abusive behaviour were recorded in the interviews. This pattern emerged in every case of multiple experiences of domestic violence and in three cases where incest survivors were abused by male partners.

'I felt that when he was being violent to me it was because I had told him. I had allowed him to know that I had been abused. They think because you've been abused it's ok to do it. They should be abhorred by it!'

Distrust of men

Most of the women interviewed who had experienced incest, rape or domestic violence felt that totally to trust a man or men made them vulnerable. That women's distrust of men might be a rational and self-protective response is seldom considered by other researchers, this comment being typical: 'many of the women still retained negative, distorted attitudes to males.'[25] Researchers feel justified in making such statements because they isolate particular assaults from the continuum of abusive male behaviour discussed in chapters 4 and 5. Suggesting that women's attitudes are 'distorted' presupposes that there is a way to distinguish a relatively small number of abusive men from a non-abusive majority. Women's experience tells them otherwise.

The impact of victimization on women's trust was the outcome of a range of factors: who they were abused by, the context of the abuse, how women explained the man's behaviour and what the reaction of others was to disclosure. For example, if women defined their abusers as individual 'sick' men, or saw abusive men in terms of particular 'types', they were more likely to continue to trust some men. Alternatively, believing that any man could be abusive meant women were unlikely to trust any man. If women felt that their mother, and/or other women, had failed to support or understand them, trust in women was also undermined. On the other hand, if women's relatives or friends were supportive then trust in women increased.

Over 90 per cent of the women with experiences of rape, incest or domestic violence felt that their attitudes to men had been affected by the assaults. By far the most common response was distrust of all men or certain groups of men. Of the three women who did not feel their attitudes had been affected, two felt that their experience merely confirmed what they already knew.

'I think it has a long-term effect on you and I don't think I'll ever trust, not really trust completely, another man, because you're trying so hard not to let it happen again.'

'I think my attitude to men changed an awful lot. I'm very aware of . . . . . . the power they can have over you . . . I still feel very, very wary.'

'I think it's a sort of healthy distance. I don't trust men until they prove themselves.'

'I can't say I've got an attitude of good will to all men, because that's what I used to have.'

The distrust women described was based on a desire to prevent further abuse. Bitter experience had taught them that even limiting interaction with men to those they felt they could trust had not ensured safety. A number of women described conflicts in current heterosexual relationships which centred on their refusal to trust totally another man again. In several cases, the conflict arose out of the woman's refusal to marry.

'Deep down I know I can't get married again. I'm *scared*, just *can't go through* all that again — being *dominated*.'

Women were acutely aware that they were not able totally to control their interactions with men. Decisions such as not to marry again were attempts to retain as much control as possible. Some women's reactions were stronger than distrust.

'I hated men for years afterwards, I wouldn't go near them. I don't think even now I can relate to them properly. I'm still quite terrified of blokes.'

'They have to work very hard to prove themselves to me as being people. I hate men but I don't mind people.'

'I do feel completely angry with men and it affects my marriage. Neil has only got to do something which puts him in the same class as all other men and I really go at him.'

The seven women who said that there was only one man they trusted were all referring to their current partner. As the last quotation above illustrates, this trust also had its limits.

Many women expressed regret at feeling so distrustful of men but, given that the majority had been abused by men they knew and had trusted, they felt their caution both justified and necessary. This realization was often reinforced by subsequent interactions with men.

'It just seems as though that's all they want. It's all they think about — sex. I know four or five men who would take me out for meals and things, but I know what it would be at the end of it — a screw. That's all I can name it, because it wouldn't be anything else.'

One of the factors that lessened women's distrust of men was if they had been able to tell a man about their experiences of abuse and his reaction was supportive. This was, however, the exception rather than the rule. Many more men reacted with anger, and with revenge fantasies. A not inconsiderable number betrayed the trust women had placed in them and used their knowledge of the woman's past to justify their own abusive behaviour. This response always strongly reinforced the woman's distrust.

'I've always had this thing about feeling close and being able to communicate with someone. I think that's one of the things that affects me most in relationships to men, has made me most wary and sceptical of them . . . that's a sort of verbal violence. I felt totally betrayed, things I'd actually confided and then in fact him using that.'

'One particular time, to torment me, he bit me in exactly the same place . . . . . . It was like I went back to the very same moment. I can remember crying, screaming and begging him not to do it and he said "You must have enjoyed it because you knew the bloke's name"!'

'I think he used it against me . . . . . . he's the only one that's ever been violent to me and I think he used that knowing the effect it would have on me . . . . . . I won't tell anyone again!'

These betrayals of trust were extreme examples of problems many women encountered when they told others, particularly although not exclusively men, about their past. Many women felt that they were treated as victims and that attitudes towards them changed. Responses of horror, anger, pity, disbelief or blame upset many women.

'It's the *degrading* (angrily) was people talk to you, the way people . . . . . . just *assume* that you must have *encouraged* it some way.'

The most common feeling about talking to women friends about experiences of sexual violence was that they were supportive and helpful. Often, the other woman had had similar experiences and this increased their identification and trust of one another.

Sexuality

In chapter 5, I argued that all forms of male violence contain a sexual aspect. It is, therefore, not surprising that experiences of violence affect women's feelings about sex. Table 8.2 summarizes how women felt rape, incest and domestic violence had affected their attitudes to sexuality. Whilst the impact on survivors of domestic violence was not as strong as on survivors of incest and

Table 8.2 Impact of sexual violence on women's attitudes to sex

	R		I		DV		Total	
	N	%	N	%	N	%	N	%
Hard to relax during sex	11	42	7	54	4	16	22	34
Determined to avoid coercive sex	13	50	–	–	8	32	21	33
Chose a period of celibacy	11	42	6	46	3	12	20	31
Sex became linked to being used	7	27	4	31	2	8	13	20
Sex triggered memories of abuse	3	12	4	31	–	–	9	14
Expected coercion	2	8	4	31	–	–	6	9
Used sex as revenge	3	12	–	–	–	–	3	5

rape, over half of the domestic violence survivors recalled some form of negative impact.

A small number of women came to expect sexual coercion. All felt if they refused sex the man would respond violently. This group of women recalled a number of incidents of pressurized or coercive sex following their prior abuse.

'I don't see any sense in saying no, I wanted to, but I couldn't see the point . . . . . . I just felt worthless.'

'I think I associate violence with it [saying no to sex]. I think that was probably the rape.'

For a larger number of women, sex became linked to being used and/or it triggered memories of abuse. Women in this group were much more likely to choose a period of celibacy immediately after the assaults and/or whilst they were remembering and working through their past. This reaction was also common following experiences of sexual harassment, sexual assault and flashing.

'If I had any sexual feelings I felt dirty again.'

'I think that's what affected me most. I hate being touched by any man.'

'There were things that I didn't want him to do, because all of a sudden that reminded me.'

'I find that disgusting [fellatio] because their dad used to force me into doing it and it used to make me want to be *sick*.'

'I didn't think I would ever be able to enjoy sex again. I didn't want anything to do with sex.'

'I thought I'd be frigid forever because sex was associated with fear and *detest and loathing*.'

Previous investigators have noted that women's feelings about sex are often affected following rape; most suggest that heterosexual sex becomes associated with the assault and women may re-experience the emotions they felt at the time.[26] Whilst there was considerable evidence in the interviews of this process in relation to a number of forms of sexual violence, the effects on sexuality must also be understood in relation to how women coped with abuse at the time. For instance, coping during the assaults by cutting off had long-term implications for some women.

'Well it's made me feel that I don't get sexual feelings very much. I seem to have sort of switched it off.'

'The kind of abuse he practiced was in some way pleasurable. I didn't like it because he was doing it. The sensation of having your back rubbed, having someone rub your breasts isn't unpleasant. So I think what happened (sigh) was that I learnt to block out feeling, especially in my breasts. I can remember feeling at times that what he was doing was pleasant, and I didn't want to feel that. I hated it in my mind and I wanted to hate it in my body as well, so I had to learn to control that.'

The second quotation, from an incest survivor, illustrates the effort that is required to control one's reactions and feelings during abuse. By exerting this mental control women attempted to limit the impact of abuse (see chapter 7). It was clear that women could not simply 'switch back on' physiological sexual responses, despite feelings of attraction and relative safety. One woman felt that it still affected her even though her sexual relationships were now with other women.

Many of the incest survivors I interviewed mentioned that they had experienced difficulty distinguishing between love, sex and affection. Whilst incestuous abusve involves a confusion of these areas, this was amplified if women had forgotten their abuse for long periods of time. Their confusion was reinforced by their abuse affecting them, particularly in relationships with men, yet having no conscious memory of it. All of the incest survivors who had spent time working through their past felt that one of the positive outcomes had been understanding, and to varying extents resolving, this confusion.

'I think what I know is that I know what I don't want. I still don't really know what I want — who ever does? But I can separate the feelings of sex, love and affection.'

Some women recalled a period of 'promiscuity' following experiences of sexual violence. For a few, this occurred immediately after the abuse. For the majority, it followed a period of celibacy. All saw this as either an attempt to keep control in relationships with men by not getting emotionally involved or as a time when they were using sex to get some sort of revenge. Maggie Scarf suggests that promiscuity, for women, is often a way of expressing anger with men.[27] By making themselves available only sexually, women withdraw the emotional servicing and commitment that men expect in heterosexual relationships.

'I suppose it was a revenge thing, that I discovered the power of my body and it was getting my own back on the entire male sex for one action.'

'I found the fact that I could make these boys come by virtue of doing nothing for them — that I could remain totally unaffected made me feel very good.'

'With certain men I know I have a power sexually with them. I know that through sleeping with them it made them (sigh) more vulnerable so that in fact I could have power over them . . . . . . I'm aware of using that as a sort of — not a weapon, but as a way of getting to the man so that I can *control* the situation.'

This was not a pattern of behaviour that any of the women interviewed maintained for a long period of time. Most recognized fairly quickly that, whilst they protected themselves from harm or assuaged some of the anger they felt, it was also an alienating and in some ways negative experience.

'It sounds horrible but I felt I was getting one over on them because of all the times I feel I've been *screwed* and been used. It's stupid because they don't even know, they are so insensitive I'm sure they don't even sense a difference in me.'

'I thought that I could prove to him and to everybody that nobody could hurt me. But I don't think I got what I wanted out of it . . . I didn't get hurt but I did get totally detached from my sexuality.'

'It's an immediate reaction, or even a long-term reaction after things that have happened, but I don't think its a solution.'

Whatever the particular response or choices made by women, all were linked to their need to control sex. At the time the interviews were done, almost every woman was determined to refuse or reject coercion in sexual relationships and to be in control of her sexual choices. For many this was the end-result of a complex process of change, the basis of which was, for women wanting heterosexual relationships, a belief that they should be able to say no to sex without negative consequences. At the time we met, the choices women had made about their sexuality varied and were the product of many factors in their lives, one of which was experiences of sexual violence. Over 50 per cent were involved in heterosexual relationships, the others were either in lesbian relationships, had chosen to be celibate for the near future or just happened not to be involved with anyone at that time.

Loss of custody and control over fertility

In the introduction to this chapter I noted that the impact of sexual violence is not limited to women's feelings and behaviour. Assaults can result in or precipitate other events with which women also have to cope. Losing control over fertility and losing custody of children when leaving a violent man are two examples of this types of consequence.

Four women who were raped (one by her mother's boyfriend, the others by acquaintances) conceived. The decision to have an abortion taken by two women, a miscarriage for the third, and being forced to have her baby adopted for the fourth were still extremely painful for the women to talk about. This group, understandably, made up the majority of those who felt vulnerable about pregnancy.

'I still get upset sometimes when I see little kids. I went through real traumas and I still do occasionally. I've still got the fear in the back of my mind that if I ever get pregnant I'll be punished for . . . I don't see it as a wrong thing, but at the same time I think someone is going to punish me for it.'

The conflicts which still troubled the two women who had abortions were connected to their reactions at the time they discovered they were pregnant. Both chose to have abortions because they could not separate the potential child from the circumstances of its conception. Both also recalled feeling guilty about their inability to make this separation.

'If the baby had looked like the bloke that raped me I could have killed it because of what I felt for him. I didn't want any part of him, but on the other hand it was my baby, it was growing inside of me . . . After the abortion I used to wake up at night screaming "I want my baby back." '

There were suggestions in several of the women's discussions of domestic violence that abusive men had attempted to make women pregnant without their consent. Forced pregnancy has received minimal attention by social researchers and merits further study. I have also noticed the reverse of this pattern in working with battered women. Some abusive men, rather than tempering their violence when women are pregnant, deliberately direct it at the womb area. A not inconsiderable number of women attribute miscarriages to abuse during pregnancy and several women have told me that their babies were born with extensive bruising. In chapter 5, I argued that domestic violence was always directed towards controlling women; the control some men seek to exert extends to women's fertility.

Eight of the women who had been battered lost custody of one or all of their children when they left the violent man. If the five women who did not have children and the two women who returned to live with their husbands on the condition that the violence stopped are excluded from the numbers, then almost half of the women who had childen when they left an abusive relationship lost custody of one or more of them. This was an unexpected finding. It has not been discussed in previous research, perhaps because the majority of studies have drawn samples from women resident in refuges. Refuges make specific arrangements for children and support women in any disputes over custody. None of the women who lost custody had contacted a refuge.

Some women fled the house without their children during a violent episode in which they feared for their lives. If they decided not to return they were both unable to regain occupancy of the marital home and became ineligible for priority rehousing by the local authority as there were no dependent children in immediate need of accommodation. When court hearings took place, they seldom had adequate accommodation for themselves and their children and had already been separated from them for a considerable length of time. Custody was, therefore, awarded to the father despite his abusive behaviour. Other women were coerced by the man, through threats of continued harassment, to leave one or more of the children in his custody. In only one case had any of these men been previously committed to childcare.

'This was the irony of it, he had the children and was fighting for custody. When we went to court, I had to make all the arrangements for childcare. We weren't talking about him looking after them.'

'I used to sit there and sob my heart out thinking that it was *through him* that I had got to split my kids up, because he *wouldn't let me have all my kids*. He was determined that he wasn't going to let me have all of them, and he *knew* that was breaking me up inside. And he's not a good father.'

'He'd threatened to come and break and windows, phone me every hour, that if I got custody he'd shoot me . . . I don't know if he'd have shot me but I think he would have definitely harassed me and made my life a complete misery . . . It's quite impossible to describe what its like — it's a real physical loss like a bereavement, like losing part of you. I'll *never, ever* get over it and I'll never ever forgive him. Dan should be here with me and the other children . . . I really know I couldn't do anything else, I *had to get out* and the only way was to leave Dan behind. That was the price I had to pay.'

'He knows what he's done to me, he's taken my children away, my home away . . . He knows he can't touch me physically but mentally I can't take it. I wish I didn't have contact with him, but I have to because of the children.'

Each of these women felt that this was the most difficult aspect of her experience to come to terms with. Repeated conflicts over access or just seeing the child or children were a continual reminder of the costs of self-protection.

Further research is urgently needed to assess the number of women who lose custody when trying to end violent relationships. If the incidence is anywhere near that found in this project, it has enormous implications for social policy in this area. *Research should also address whether abusive men who gain custody actually want to bring up their children or whether they use custody as a way of maintaining control over women.*

Self-blame

It is the internalization of the generally held view that women are
responsible for men's violence (see chapter 2) that results in self-
blame. Blaming oneself is inextricably linked to ideas about
provocation and/or suggestions that it is relatively easy to prevent
or limit abuse. Some of the women interviewed had never blamed
themselves; with those who had, a number of common themes
emerged.

Domestic violence and incest usually involve repeated abuse by
a member of the household and both provide abusive men with
repeated opportunities to deflect responsibility for their violence
onto women and girls.

'Oh yes, according to him it was always my fault.'

'When I was "under the spell" as it were, I thought it was — I had done
it. He used to say "you want this" . . . . . . that was drummed into me.'

The assertion that women were responsible was particularly
strong where men were able to used evidence of women's
previous abuse to justify their violence.

'My second husband latched on to that and used it, and I do see it as
using it because I obviously told him all about it. Then, when things
started happening between us, it was all on me you know — "It must be
you, you must bring this out in men".'

Men's repeated insistence that the women or girl was complicit
in or responsible for the violence had an impact on women's
perceptions and understandings. In order to reject the man's
interpretation, women invariably questioned their own behaviour
before they felt able to assert, sometimes only to themselves, that
the violence was his responsibility.

'Well yeah, I should have kept my mouth shut when he was arguing
with me. But on the other hand *why* should I have done? Who's got the
right to say you're not allowed to talk, you're not allowed to put your
point of view, you're not allowed to argue.'

Several of the women who were either beaten up by their
partners or subjected to repeated forced sex felt responsible in so
far as they were not able to prevent the repetition of the abuse.

'I was terrified — *absolutely terrified* — and yet I felt as if I deserved it because I *wasn't strong enough* to do anything about it. Although I knew it was him that was wrong I *despised myself* for not being the kind of woman who could stand up to him.'

'I did think it was my fault, that I was so pathetic that this happened to me.'

This process of reviewing one's own behaviour, in terms of provocation, 'risk-taking' and avoiding assault, was also evident where women were assaulted by men they did not know. In the case of stranger rape, this often amounted to being in the wrong place at the wrong time.

'Everyone tells me I had a right to be in a station by myself because I am a person and I have a right to be where I want to be. But something inside me says — well you asked for it by being there, you put yourself in that situation and you knew there was a risk (although I didn't, I wasn't really aware there was a risk). I still feel if I hadn't gone out that night then it wouldn't have happened.'

That women feel they are responsible simply by 'being there' demonstrates the power of the ideology that women are responsible for men's violence. That an assault happens at all becomes sufficient reason for women to feel that they might be at fault.

'I felt it was partially my fault just for *being there* I suppose (ironic laugh).'

'Well I felt all the time I was provoking him just by *being there*.'

These women were discussing incest and domestic violence. The woman talking below reflects on this issue in the context of a rape which happened when she was walking alone in the countryside.

'If I have behaved differently, with more caution *because* men do rape women, then it would not have happened. So I was responsible only within the framework of male violence being a known phenomenon. I could have avoided it but this doesn't mean I *should* have avoided it, and certainly not that women in general should avoid behaving in that way. They should be absolutely free to decide what they do about unacceptable risks — it's men who are responsible for those risks being there.'

This is a slightly different concept of 'being there'. Here it is the reality of men's violence which is 'there', a reality within which women have to exist and make choices about 'unacceptable risks'. It is precisely this reality that women are aware of when they question their own behaviour. They are acutely aware of both the ways in which women are held responsible for men's violence and the unacceptable, but all too real, risks. Self-blame involves engaging in an examination of the circumstances of an assault in order to discover if it could have been prevented. This process is not just a reaction to woman-blaming, but is also a part of women's reconstruction of personal safety following sexual violence. Through examining their own behaviour, women hope to discover what they could have done differently *in order to avoid future victimization.*

This complexity of self-blame for women has seldom been explored in the literature. It was further illustrated in the interviews by the fact that, whilst women may have held themselves responsible in some way, this did not diminish how responsible they thought the man was for his violence. Whilst courts and general public attitudes link women's supposed 'provocation' to decreased responsibility for the man (see chapter 3), abused women do not. They make a clear distinction between the cause of the violence (which is men's responsibility) and why they were victimized on a specific occasion.

At the same time as enabling women to work through their feelings of vulnerability, self-blame also had negative consequences for women's sense of self. An important aspect of coping was dealing with these feelings. For some women, the passage of time made them less self-critical. For other women, placing all the responsibility for an assault on the abusive man was an important change. At the time of the interviews, very few women still blamed themselves and only four women in the whole sample felt women ever 'provoked' sexual violence. A number expressed anger at the years they had blamed themselves and at the concept of 'provocation' itself.

'It's difficult for me to stay rational when I hear that now. But part of me sits back and says "Yeah, well it's part of the whole process of just making sure men don't get blamed for it." '

Loss of self-respect

A number of the immediate reactions to sexual violence related to self-respect (see chapter 7). Feelings of shame, guilt, having been violated and self-blame all negatively affected women's sense of self. This threat to a positive sense of self was strongest where women were abused by men they had trusted, where there were aspects of the context of the assaults that women felt others would see as 'provocation', and/or where the abusive man had engaged in repeated verbal criticism.

'I found it very difficult to keep any self-respect. I felt very, very low, my self-esteem had been really destroyed. I also felt it was my fault. I felt that I'd got myself into a really awful situation . . . I just *couldn't understand* how I'd made myself so completely vulnerable. That I'd sort of "asked for it" by just having contact with him and not breaking if off sooner.'

'I've not really gone into the whole sort of verbal abuse, constant "you're stupid, you're thick, you can't do this, you can do that". Everything I did was hopeless. I think I have a much less destructive view of myself since I left. One gets to define oneself in the terms of the other person — it wouldn't have made any different other people telling me — I had to prove that I could do it and I have.'

Systematic verbal abuse and undermining of confidence was a common feature of domestic violence and father–daughter incest, resulting in many survivors of these forms of violence saying that one long-term impact on them was insecurity. These same women, however, also made up the majority of those who said that in coping with the abuse and its aftermath they had become stronger and more independent.

The impact of victimization on women's self-respect and self-image can be seen as the cumulative outcome of all the other impacts and the coping strategies women used or that were available to them. If women had few internal and external resources to draw on, reconstructing a positive sense of self was extremely difficult. It is in these situations that women may experience short-or long-term mental health problems. Whilst all the women I interviewed who had had 'breakdowns' had managed to use that period to work through their internal confusion and pain, I have no doubt that are many women who have not yet been able to do this.

Realistic responses or pathological effects?

In this chapter I have illustrated the range of potential consequences of sexual violence. Women's testimony made clear that many of the consequences of sexual violence involve significant losses, loss of trust and loss of safety being the most common. Other losses which occurred during abuse or immediately afterwards, such as losing a job, friendship networks or custody of children, had long-term implications.

Whatever the particular impact of an experience of sexual violence was, women used a variety of coping strategies to come to terms with the experience and its consequences. Glynis Breakwell's analysis of coping strategies includes important insights which can be applied to the aftermath of sexual violence. She defines coping strategies as 'any thought or action which succeeds in eliminating or ameliorating threat to the self . . . whether it is consciously recognized as intentional or not'.[28] Whilst stressing that coping strategies are interactive, Breakwell develops a complex typology by distinguishing between form and intent. Coping may be limited to reassessments of the self (no longer blaming onself), may involve an individual moving to a safer situation (leaving an abusive man), or a more fundamental shift in one's social context (limiting interactions with all men). She also notes that individual coping may become a route to forms of collective action, a point I will take up in chapter 9.

Breakwell suggests that there are always phases in coping. Initially, the threat to self may be perceived as so potentially devastating that the individual engages in denial (forgetting, cutting off, minimizing). At some point, however, the threat to the self has to be resolved (remembering and working through). There may be phases in coping which have some short-term benefit but which have long-term negative implications (forgetting, using sex as revenge). The continued use of a particular strategy may become a trap closing off other potentially helpful options. She also recognizes that individuals may stop coping (suicide attempts, breakdowns).

Coping strategies should not be conceptualized as mutually exclusive alternatives nor is it a simple matter to calculate an optimal combination. The best available combination may not be the best possible. For example many women were aware that being able to talk to someone or seeking help would be helpful. Disclosure of victimization, however, makes women vulnerable. If they choose to seek help or discuss their experience and they encounter hostility, disbelief or judgemental attitudes this is likely to push them back into coping through either denial or silence.

Access to resources and networks of support places limits on each individuals' options. The work of three groups of American women researchers on the aftermath of rape emphasizes the importance of resources which either widen or lessen women's coping options.[29] Older women, poor women, women who had experienced a major life stress before the assault and women with little social support had more difficulty in coping. They had fewer internal and/or external resources to draw on. Libby Ruch and Susan Chandler found that, in the USA, ethnicity influenced coping; the immediate impact of rape was more intense for Asian and Hawaiian women. They suggest this may be connected to different cultural attitudes to sexuality and rape which result in greater shame and less access to support within community networks. How race and ethnicity affects women's experience and their coping options has received limited attention in research and is a crucial area for further study, particularly in the UK.

Breakwell also stresses that coping strategies have to be assessed in terms of their usefulness to the individual, not in relation to value-laden assumptions about 'normality' and 'health'. Here she expands on a point made by two American men but not generally recognized in research on the impact of sexual violence: 'an important caution to victimization researchers is not to interpret all reactions to victimization as pathological'.[30]

Women's coping strategies are directed towards both controlling the impact of sexual violence and protecting themselves from further abuse. Distrust of men and conflicts about heterosexuality are not 'dysfunctional' reactions but part of women's active and adaptive attempts to cope with the reality of sexual violence. They can only be defined as 'dysfunctional' if men's interests are the starting point for analysis. Whilst so much of women's experience of heterosexual sex is neither pleasurable nor freely chosen, it is in women's interests to refuse to enter, or stay in, heterosexual relationships in which they feel pressured or coerced. Whilst sexual violence is so prevalent and the vast majority of men so unwilling to change their attitudes and behaviour, it is in women's interests to insist that trust will not be given automatically – it has to be earned. It is the reality of men's violence which creates the necessity of women's distrust.

9

'I'll challenge it now wherever I see it': from individual survival to collective resistance

I will do this work until I wake up and there is no more violence in the lives of women in the world.

S. McCawley, *Grassroots Survivors On the Move with the Movement*

Battered women are survivors in a struggle for our lives. We are not helpless, not weak. We are courageously strong women. We are women who never stop hoping, fighting or dreaming for our sanity. We are soldiers in a shadow war. This is a war that has not been officially declared you see – but whether we want it or not we are in a war and we are all vulnerable. Have you counted the casualties recently? Can we survive without losing our spirits and souls?

M. Zavala, *My Story, Our Story*

At the 1986 National Coalition Against Domestic Violence Conference in St Louis the three keynote speeches were given by survivors. The excerpts above are from the speeches of Sojourner McCawley and Maria Zavala, both now tireless activists working to end violence in the lives of women and children. The first keynote address was given by Judy Carne, an English Hollywood actress, who was ostracized by her community when she publicly named Burt Reynolds as an abuser. Each of their accounts illustrated the complexity of women's experience: the range of abuse they experienced; the different points at which they defined the abuse as violence; how their options and choices were circumscribed by an ideology which encourages women to feel responsible for men's violence; the failure of social agencies to support abused women and act in their interests; the drift into depression and/or negative coping strategies; and the enormous strength and determination it takes to become a survivor. This chapter explores the routes the women I interviewed took to their individual survival, and how this might be extended to collective resistance.

Kathleen Barry devotes a chapter in *Female Sexual Slavery* to discussing the concepts of victim and survivor.[1] She maintains that feminist demands that the extent and seriousness of women's victimization be recognized has had the unintended consequence of reinforcing the role and status of victim. This status is not chosen by women who have been victimized but is assigned to them by others: both those who seek to blame them and those who offer them support. The woman speaking below, who had been abused as a child but is here referring to a fight with her lover, illustrates the way in which victim status can be conferred by others.

'I felt more like a victim than I'd ever felt. I felt other people could see that I was a victim because I had a bruised eye and a scratch on my forehead and finger points on my chest. I felt men in the tube looked at me as someone who could be hit. I found that very upsetting.'

Barry's concept of 'victimism' is one of the most insightful in her analysis of sexual violence. Victimism occurs when the fact of victimization becomes, usually for others but sometimes for abused women themselves, the defining feature of an individuals identity and life experience. This 'way of seeing' results in many facets of a woman's experience being either distorted or unnoticed.

Victimism is an objectification which establishes new standards for defining experience, those standards dismiss any question of will, and deny that the woman even whilst enduring sexual violence is a living, changing, growing, interactive person . . . It denies the reality of [women's] circumstances and the very real human efforts they make to cope with those circumstances . . . Surviving is the other side of being a victim. It involves will, action, initiative. Any woman caught in sexual violence must make moment-by-moment decisions about her survival.[2]

In the previous two chapters I have drawn attention to the many and varied ways in which women engage in an active process of resistance to, and coping with, sexual violence and its consequences. Barry concludes her discussion by distinguishing between individual and effective survival; the latter requires the collective action of women in order to end sexual violence in the lives of women and girls. I will explore this same distinction but in terms of individual survival and collective resistance.

Individual survival

This section draws on women's reflections about the present and future in the context of their past: what they felt had enabled them to cope with victimization and its consequences and whether and how they had been changed by their experience. Each woman who had experienced rape, incest or domestic violence was asked what had helped her most in coping and whether or not there was anything, at any point, that would have been of more help. Talking to other women was by far the most commonly cited source of help, support and insight. Other factors which had enabled women to cope were: time, their children, a sympathetic man, work and relatives (in order of frequency mentioned). The only thing that emerged as potentially more helpful was earlier support and understanding.

Many women emphasized the importance of being able to talk through their experiences; as noted in chapter 1, some felt their participation in the research had enabled them to do this.

'It does you good to talk about it, it's no good burying it. I think that if you are talking about it and you're looking at it in relation to your life now, it does you good.'

'I would like to completely rid myself of the scars, but I don't know if that's possible. It's really a matter of being able to talk about it and recognize it for what it is without feeling terrible. As time goes by, it affects me less in that sense.'

'Doing the interview was absolutely positive. It was the first time I talked to somebody that I didn't know and in such depth. It surprised me how much I could say without cracking up. It's like another bit of saying "Yes, I'll get through it somehow." '

Whilst women stressed the importance of support from others, their own strength and determination was, in fact, the crucial factor. It was impossible to read the transcripts and not be moved by an awareness of how women had grown and changed through the process of coping. It was often only after reading their own interview transcript, however, that many women noticed this in themselves. By far the most frequent response women had to a follow-up interview question on whether they felt they had learnt anything from participating in the research was that they had become aware of their own strength in survival.

'It's certainly given me some insights and I think that my experiences — having survived them — I've gone on and become stronger because of them . . . I managed to turn a bad experience into having some profitable aspect.'

'I realized I survived because I refused to be his victim any more.'

'It's taking all these negative things and turning them into something positive.'

The majority of representations of, and research on, sexual violence focuses on women's victimization and ignores the fact that, as Barry puts it, 'the woman even whilst enduring sexual violence is a living, changing, growing, interactive person'. This neglect is also evident in the ways abused women and girls are treated by statutory agencies, voluntary bodies and even friends. The cumulative result of this blinkered vision is that vital aspects of women's experience are unrecognized, even by women themselves. It was precisely because research questions in this study attempted to tap this hidden reality that women were able to notice, and feel positive about, 'the other side of being a victim'.

The changes that women perceived in themselves at the actual time of the interviews were in certain critical ways different from the impacts discussed in chapter 8. They included: being more independent and/or stronger; blaming themselves less; having acquired a political understanding of men's violence; empathizing with other women who had been abused; and knowing that they were not alone in their experience (again in order of frequency mentioned). Table 9.1 summarizes women's responses to the question 'Do you feel you learnt anything from your experiences?'.

Women talked about many of these changes positively despite the connections with the negative consequences of sexual violence discussed in chapter 8. The understandings and choices women had arrived at were the result of having coped with these impacts.

Table 9.1   What women learnt from their experiences of sexual violence[a]

	R		I		DV		Total	
	N	%	N	%	N	%	N	%
Decreased trust of men	7	27	4	31	6	24	17	27
Wider role for women	7	27	4	31	6	24	17	27
Knows what does/does not want	6	24	2	15	8	32	16	25
Aware of political aspects	8	31	3	23	3	12	14	22
More empathy for other women	4	15	2	15	5	20	11	17
Awareness for own daughters	3	12	3	23	4	16	10	16
Knows who she is	5	19	2	15	2	8	9	14
Sees reality of rape/violence	3	12	0	0	4	16	7	11
Hatred of men	2	8	0	0	2	8	4	6
Right to control own body	4	15	0	0	0	0	4	6
Increased awareness of risks	2	8	0	0	0	0	2	3

[a] Data analysed for experiences of rape (N = 26), incest (N = 13) and domestic violence (N = 25). The total column percentages are calculated on the basis of the 64 experiences of these forms of violence in the sample.

Vulnerability

I asked every woman whether she felt rape and/or domestic violence could happen to her in the future. Very few women felt that they could say no with total certainty; most felt it was as likely to happen to her as to any woman. Every woman felt that rape, incest or domestic violence could happen to any woman or girl. These responses demonstrate that the women interviewed felt that they, and other women, were at risk because they were women. However, many had reflected on their own experiences and decided that in a similar situation they would now act differently. The first two women are talking about domestic violence, the third incest, the fourth rape by an acquaintance, and the fifth a relationship in which she was coerced into having sex on many occasions.

'If I could go back to it now, I think the first thing I would do is to stand up for myself, which is what I would advise anyone else to do. When I did do it, as I say, I was amazed at the response — I wish I'd done it before.'

'I can say now, because in a sense I know I wouldn't get into that situation — or if I did inadvertently I'd know how to get out of it because *I'd just leave* (determined) and I know I could survive. But looking back to then, escape seemed impossible.'

'The fear has gone from me. There is no need for me to have to put up with something I don't like anymore.'

'Well, I wouldn't get myself into that position with a man again. If I did, I think I'd be able to *really fight* back so that I would leave some mark on the man — a real mark on the man.'

'I don't like to think that it will happen again but I wouldn't like to say for definite it won't. But I'm not frightened anymore.'

Having already survived life-threatening assaults, many women had developed a strong belief in their ability to survive which in turn affected their determination to fight back.[3] Women who saw their previous vulnerability as the result of lack of knowledge or naive trust felt that being aware of the possibility of sexual violence was itself a form of protection.

A minority of the women interviewed either resisted discussing vulnerability or felt as powerless as they had done in the past. The first group were women who had recalled relatively few incidents and who had constructed their personal safety through not thinking about sexual violence as a reality or possibility in their lives. The second group consisted of two women whose experiences of domestic violence had resulted in them feeling unable to cope with male aggression in any form.

Most women articulated a concern to protect themselves from victimization, whilst at the same time, being aware that they could not create a totally safe environment. Like the women in the Wandsworth survey,[4] they looked to themselves to construct personal safety. Very few felt that the police, the courts, their local community or male partners could be relied upon for protection.

Sexual relationships and relationships with men

The two most common impacts discussed in chapter 8 were changes in women's attitudes to sexual relationships and to men. Women were also asked to discuss their attitudes and feelings at the time of the interview. Table 9.2 illustrates that, whilst sexual relationships were still problematic for many women, some areas of change were also evident.

Of the eleven women who were currently celibate, almost half

Table 9.2 Women's attitudes to sexual relationships at the time of the first interview[a]

	R		I		DV		Total	
	N	%	N	%	N	%	N	%
Still wary/confused/ ambivalent	12	46	7	54	0	0	19	30
Positive within present relationship	8	31	0	0	8	32	16	25
Still struggling with the past	7	27	0	0	5	20	12	19
Chosen period of celibacy	2	8	1	8	8	32	11	17
Has to be in her control/her choice	8	31	2	15	0	0	10	16
Generally positive	2	8	4	31	4	16	10	16

[a] Calculated on the same basis as table 9.1.

felt this choice was directly connected to their experiences of victimization. For the others, whilst their experiences of abuse had some influence, the decision also reflected feelings about sexual relationships prior to and following the abuse. Each woman saw this decision as a way of taking control; choosing celibacy both removed the possibility of pressurized sex and provided time and space in which to consider whether, with whom and in what circumstances she wanted sexual relationships.

For women currently in heterosexual relationships, positive change was always discussed in relation to becoming more determined to and/or confident about saying no to sex. For women, being able to refuse sex (or particular sexual practices) without negative consequences is the basis on which a consensual heterosexual relationship becomes possible. Like celibacy, it involves taking control over one's sexual choices; unlike celibacy it also requires change in, and/or the co-operation of, others. As with other shifts in gender relations, it was women who made and negotiated these changes. There were no examples in the interviews of men who had independently changed their sexual practice, although many women recounted examples of the reverse – men resisting change. Women who felt both that they had changed and that this had been accepted and responded to positively by a male partner were a minority of those currently in heterosexual relationships.

'I think my attitude to sex has changed a great deal. It's much nicer, lovely to be able to say no and to have no taken. Yes, that's been the nicest bit, learning to say no. It just *changes you completely*, it gives you *so much more confidence.*'

'Within my marriage it's something that is very deep. I don't love him, and I can't have sex with him because I don't love him. I'd start feeling better and then feel he was using me. It comes down to I won't because no one is going to take my control away from me.'

'It's been a process of finding out what I want and being able to take control in a sexual relationship and not being frightened of saying no.'

Of the women interviewed who had experienced rape, incest or domestic violence, 90 per cent felt that their relationships with men had been, and continued to be, affected by their experience. The distrust of men discussed in chapter 8 had not diminished over time; only one woman said that she liked men. The question about women's current attitudes to men did not refer to sexual violence, nor did it follow explicit questions on violence. Yet it was here that many more women expressed generalized anger with men. I suspect that at this point in the interview women were placing their experiences of particular forms of sexual violence within the context of relationships with men throughout their lives; a further illustration of the usefulness of the concept of a continuum.

'It just opened my eyes to so much of what happens between men and women. I suppose to the fact that I never really had any pleasure out of sex, the double standards . . . . . . in the long term it's had very dramatic effects.'

'Well I hate them. (laughs) It's no good me saying I don't, because I think I can get on individually with a man and then they turn out to be utter shits. It's just *consistently* one after another. I really mean it. John is the only man I can spend any amount of time with to talk to.' (bitter and angry)

'If another man was ever violent to me I would drop him immediately. I am also very, very wary of chauvinistic tendencies in men. That would cause me to end a relationship very quickly.'

There is an interesting irony in men's use of violence which is particularly apparent when men abuse women lovers. Whilst in the short term men may achieve their goal, be it sexual access or controlling the woman's behaviour, in the long term overt violence increases the possibility that the woman will resist the coercion and withdraw from the relationship. Withdrawal ranges from leaving a particular man to distrusting most and, in some cases, all men. This range of distancing and the underlying reasons for it are discussed by Marilyn Frye in an essay on separatism.[5] She extends an analysis of political separatism to the variety and complexity of ways in which women separate from men in order to achieve autonomy and safety.

Strength and independence

Women's survival often required drawing on inner strengths that many were unaware they possessed. One woman used the phrase 'what doesn't kill you makes you stronger' to describe this process. She, like many of the women interviewed, only recognized her own strength in retrospect. Whenever this recognition occurred, even if it was not until the first research interview, it changed both the way the woman saw herself and other women.

'I [The interview] made me go back through the emotions, how I felt then and how I feel about it now. In some ways it strengthened me an awful lot, bringing it *all* back like that, because I usually just bring up little bits . . . . . . I think I realized I have got this strength to get over hurdles along the way. It's taken five years and it has been constant work on it, but not quite as positive as that before.'

Whilst the women speaking below had experienced different forms of sexual violence, they all felt that the abuse had totally undermined their self-confidence. Their survival required re-building, or sometimes developing for the first time, a belief in themselves as competent individuals.

'I'm independent — that's one thing. Well, I always was fairly, but it's made me really independent. I've learnt by my experiences — it makes you quite strong really. I want to make something of my life, which I have done. I don't want that awful man to have the last laugh on me. You know you can feel so depressed and wish you weren't here, but who's going to have the last laugh then — they are!'

'For nearly eight years I was a stay-at-home housewife with very few interests outside the family, apart perhaps from my job. Now I'm much more independent with interests of my own . . . . . . I feel that I could cope with just about any crisis on earth having gone through that.'

'I've got a lot of confidence back — he'd taken from me. I see life now not as existence from day to day, I see a future, whereas I didn't see one before. I'm me, I belong to me, I don't belong to anyone.'

'I'm a person. I can choose not only sexually whether I want to take part, I can have my own opinions, choice of clothes, choice of everything — I can be myself.'

This acknowledgement of personal strength and determination was also reflected in women's responses to a question on where, what or from whom they currently got the most strength. By far the most common and definite response was from within themselves.

'I get strength from other women, but mainly from the knowledge that I did actually *leave*. That gives me a great amount of strength — I am living on my own, I have organized this house, I am looking after the children.'

'How we are as strong as we are given what we've been through is amazing.'

Relationships with other women

The changes in women's feelings about, and relationships with, men were mirrored by changes in female friendships. The process of coping and survival produced a marked increase in trust between, and identification with, other women.

'I feel much closer to women now — I can *understand* them so much better, because I know how they think, how they felt towards things. I'm just *totally different* from how I was.'

'It has made my relationships with women stronger . . . . . . The elusive male/female relationship I'm searching for, I don't know whether I will attain it. And, yet, with women I attain a very, very close relationship, in that I trust them implicitly. I can talk to them about my innermost feelings and problems. I enjoy their company. I just feel much more that they won't let me down, whereas in the back of my mind I constantly expect that a man will let me down.'

'My general pattern of growth through to being a feminist has obviously — I basically love women as a sex now and I see so many strengths and warmths and such tremendous courage in such awful situations. My determination is to bloody well get somewhere in my life in whatever roles I see as important. I still get very low and think what's the point, but it's become such a part of me that I can't go back on it.'

'It opened my mind to so much of what happens between men and women. It's made me want to live with women, question my sexuality and probably means I won't ever "settle down" and get married.'

Within this consistent pattern of coming to value female friendships there were also variations. For some women it was primarily a change in attitude; for others it reflected being able for the first time to make their own friendships and priorities. The extent of change within women's daily lives also varied. Women who were living alone or with their children were more likely to see their female friends as the most important adults in their lives than were those who lived with men. For women who had chosen to live with other women and/or define themselves as lesbians, relationships with other women were central to their lives. The importance of female friends to the majority of the women interviewed, both as the major source of support when coping with the aftermath of sexual violence and in their daily lives, adds contemporary data to feminist historical studies of the significance of female friendships in women's lives.[6]

The future

Each interview ended with a series of questions about the future and every woman was also asked what she felt was her greatest problem and what she felt most positive about. Twelve women felt their problems connected back to their victimization; other women's problems were more diverse and included money, work, coping as a single parent, conflicts within their current relationship, loneliness, poor health and finding a purpose or goal in life. Some of these issues also related directly or indirectly to prior victimization. Whilst there were impacts of sexual violence which many women still spent time and energy coping with, when asked what they felt positive about most stressed that they now knew they would cope and continue to make positive changes in their lives. By the time of the interviews, no woman's life was dominated by painful memories, fear, and a sense of powerlessness. Their individual survival had involved coping with these issues. In coping, they had became committed to personal independence, aware of their own and other women's strength and determined to resist male sexual aggression.

'I'm just a totally different person. I won't accept that again and if I ever come across anything like that again, I'll shout about it, I'll do things about it, I won't accept it.'

Collective resistance

In *From Margin to Centre*, bell hooks is critical of a tendency in (white) feminism; for women to identify (bond) with one another around common victimization rather than around their strength and ability to act. She further suggests that women who identify themselves as victims are "accepting" their lot in life without visible question, without organized protest, without collective anger or rage'.[7] Whilst the fact that women's resistance and protest is not publicly visible does not mean that women accept victimization or do not question 'their lot in life', the fundamental point of bell hooks' analysis is that ending sexual violence in the lives of women and girls and achieving women's liberation requires collective action — a movement from individual survival to collective resistance.

It has been the contention of a number of political theorists that an oppositional political consciousness and organized resistance can develop out of oppressive social relations and conditions. The precise way in which this process occurs has seldom been specified but it involves at least three stages of understanding and action. Individuals must see that the cause of their personal experiences is oppressive social relations. This understanding must be accompanied by a belief that social change is both necessary and possible. Individuals must then come together in some form of collective organization which is directed towards achieving the necessary change. Each of these stages is relatively independent of the others and the movement from first to second and second to third is by no means automatic.

In the interviews, aspects of personal politicization were evident in women's questioning of men's power and in their commitment to personal independence. There were also other indicators of a wider political perspective emerging out of their experience; 14 women explicitly attributed an awareness of the political aspects of sexual violence to their experience of victimization and their subsequent understanding of it. Women's attributions of the cause of the forms of violence they had

Table 9.3 Why rape, domestic violence and incest occur

	R		I		DV		Cl		Total[a]	
	N	%	N	%	N	%	N	%	N	%
Men's attitudes to women	5	50	7	70	6	60	8	53	26	58
Men's attitudes to sex	4	40	6	60	1	10	6	40	17	38
Male dominance	5	50	1	10	3	30	2	13	11	24
Relationships based on power	3	30	0	0	2	20	4	27	9	20
Men are allowed to be violent	2	20	3	30	1	10	1	17	7	16
Stress	0	0	0	0	2	20	3	20	5	11
Women seen by men as property	0	0	1	10	3	30	0	0	4	9
Violent individuals	0	0	1	10	1	10	2	13	4	9
Alcohol	0	0	0	0	1	10	1	7	2	4

[a] Women gave more than one answer. Percentages calculated on number of women in subgroup R, I and DV = 10, Cl = 15, Total = 45.

experienced, as recorded in table 9.3, offer further evidence of politicization. Every woman was also asked what she felt caused sexual violence in general. The most common responses were: men's attitudes to women, men treating women and children as property, and relationships being based on power.

Whilst the majority of the women I interviewed did not define themselves as feminists, their causal explanations draw on an experiential understanding of men's dominance and women's subordination. In one sense, this is not surprising. Feminist theoretical perspectives take women's experience as their starting point. None the less, it is still important to note how few women drew on the dominant 'common-sense' individual/psychological explanations of sexual violence (such as stress, violent individuals, alcohol). The first stage of the transition from individual survival to collective resistance had, therefore, occurred. Most of the women interviewed saw their personal experiences as being caused by oppressive social relations.

'I think I had hated him in particular because he was the one that raped me. He seemed to be the one who screwed me up when I was young. But he's just one of millions now, it could have been any man. So I don't like

Table 9.4   How can sexual violence be prevented?

	R		I		DV		C1		C2		Total[a]	
	N	%	N	%	N	%	N	%	N	%	N	%
Change men	9	90	4	40	2	20	5	33	5	33	25	42
Change whole society/ family structure	4	40	2	20	4	40	6	40	9	60	24	40
Make women stronger	2	20	0	0	4	40	4	27	6	40	16	27
Educate women and children	1	10	2	20	4	40	2	13	4	27	13	22
Punish men	3	30	1	10	1	10	0	0	1	7	6	10
Earlier intervention	0	0	0	0	2	20	1	7	2	13	5	8

[a] More than one answer possible. Percentages calculated on the same basis as table 9.3.

him or hate him any more than any other man — I feel indifferent to him as an individual, I see all men as being possibly him now.'

'Because I've been through all that, I just fight everything as I see it. I think my way of dealing with it is partly trying to come to terms with me and trying to get over it but also by putting my energy into dealing with men in general, trying to question everything. Because it's part of the whole way in which men function, it's nothing by itself, it's part of that whole thing.'

The connection between feminist theory and women's experiential understanding was also evident in how women felt sexual violence could be prevented (see table 9.4). Some women focused only on change that would enhance the individual survival of women and girls (making women and girls stronger, education, and earlier intervention). For many more, however, their causal attributions were reflected in the solutions proposed: namely, fundamental changes in gender relations. It is important to note here that, whilst few women saw punishing abusive men as an effective means of preventing or ending sexual violence, most felt that abusive men should, in fact, be punished.

Most of the women interviewed, therefore, believed fundamental changes in gender relations were necessary if sexual violence was to be prevented. Some of their responses and comments also pointed to ways in which that change might be achieved. However, many women were acutely aware of the enormity of the changes they were suggesting and all had experience of individual men's resistance to fairly minimal demands for changes in their attitudes and behaviour.

'Well I know what needs to change — it's the way men see and relate to women — but how you make that happen I just don't know.'

'Men are like that because they are allowed to be . . . stopping it involves things like the breakdown of the nuclear family and marriage — this idea that a man's home is his castle that he can rule the roost and no one can question it. Apart from that total revolution.' (laughs)

This woman was one of the few who explicitly articulated the extent of change necessary — 'total revolution'. She was also one of the few who pointed to the connections between sexual violence and other aspects of male dominance and women's subordination. For many of the other women, these interconnections, and the necessity of wholesale transformation, lurked between the lines of their comments. Lacking both a coherent vision of an egalitarian society in which sexual violence no longer occurred and a clear sense of the extent of changes that would make this a possibility, most women focused on ensuring their own safety and integrity.

Whilst there was a clear connection between women's experiential understanding of sexual violence and feminist analysis, a minority of the women identified with feminism and a smaller number still called themselves feminists. Thus, the third stage of transition had not occurred. Very few of the women were involved in collective action to achieve social change.

The relevance of feminism

The reasons why feminism was not perceived by the majority of the women interviewed as providing either a framework which validated their understanding of sexual violence, or access to support and ways of working to end sexual violence, are complex. Undoubtedly, stereotypical representations of feminism and feminists were an important factor. The most common questions raised after the interviews were finished were 'What is feminism?' and 'Was I a "typical" feminist?' Many of the women had had no direct access to, or contact with, feminism and most had limited knowledge of feminist services for abused women and campaigns around sexual violence: many, for example, were shocked to discover that marital rape was not a crime in UK law. Where women were aware of refuges or rape crisis lines, there were a range of factors which accounted for the fact that they had not used these services. Predominant was a notion of comparative 'need', that their need was not as great as other women's.

The one factor which resulted in explicit sympathy for, but not necessarily partipation in, the women's movement was some form of direct contact with feminism or feminists. This contact ranged from reading feminist literature, taking a women's studies course, living in a Women's Aid refuge through to having a feminist neighbour.

'Part of me was always independent, part of me always believed in feminism and that kind of thing, but it was all bottled up. I knew I was different, I could see I was more independent, didn't want to settle down and be married. Since I've been to the refuge, I've glimpsed that way of life. I know I'm not weird and that there are millions of other women out there the same as me.'

'The feminist door in my head has been opened since I've been here [university]. Its so hard to put into words because my whole way of being has changed in the last two years. It's like all these windows in my head have been opened and I can see — I mean a lot of these things I had thought about and it makes me so angry that for all those years I've felt guilty and responsible for all these things that happened.'

'I was wary of her at first — I remember thinking "what's someone like that doing in a council flat". But one day she asked to use the phone for an emergency, we got talking and I found out that she'd had the same things happen to her as me . . . I had these ideas about "women's libbers" — I never thought I'd have one as my best friend!' (laughs)

The importance of personal and relevant contact with feminism was also evident in the experience of three incest survivors who, after their interviews, joined a local self-help group run by Rape Crisis or contacted the Incest Survivors Campaign. They made a point of contacting me long after the interviews to tell me that they now saw themselves as feminists.

Reflecting on the disjunction between many women's experiential analysis of sexual violence and their perceptions of feminism raises a crucial question. Are there ways of organizing for feminists which would facilitate the kind of personal and relevant direct contact to which a number of the women interviewed attributed their identification with feminism? Looking at the same question from a slightly different vantage point, are there ways of organizing which, by reflecting the range of women's experiences and ways of coping with sexual violence, would involve more women in working collectively to support abused women and children whether or not they define themselves as feminists?

Implications for feminism

I have already noted the commitment of the women I interviewed to their individual survival and to female friendships. In some cases, this resulted in a supportive network within which women friends were able to talk through past and current male violence. Several women explicitly stated that they wanted to do more than this, but they were either uneasy about joining existing groups in their home towns or felt that they did not have the time or energy that such involvement required. Two working-class women I interviewed had become informal community activists, picking up many instances of past and current victimization and offering support and advice to women within and beyond their friendship groups. They both used me as a resource, for practical information they did not have (for example, on the law) and as support in talking through their feelings and conflicts.

Women who have worked in refuges and/or on crisis lines know that they provide support for a minority of women who have experienced or are currently experiencing sexual violence. As far as the UK is concerned, this is partly the result of minimal funding for such projects. In 1987, there were only two twenty-four hour Rape Crisis Lines and both had major financial crises during the year. Evidence from the interviews, however, suggests that some women may not even consider contacting these services because they define their own needs as falling short of a 'crisis'. Whilst it is crucial that crisis lines and refuges both have secure funding and are accessible to all women, feminists also need to think about other ways of supporting and involving women.

At the 1986 National Coalition Against Domestic Violence (NCADV) Conference there were a number of examples of innovative projects which were attempting to meet the needs of more women by both extending the types of services offered and being based in local communities. The Park Slope Safe Homes

Project in New York includes a phone line, a network of safe homes, a small refuge and the production of a bi-lingual newsletter, *Wives' Tales: a newsletter about ending violence against women in the home.* The newsletter reflects both a feminist analysis of men's violence and the differences between women in the community it serves.

Sojourner McCawley (quoted at the beginning of this chapter) works in the East Harlem Victim's Intervention Project (VIP). This organization begins from a recognition that institutional racism means that certain options, such as using the Criminal Justice System, are not accessible to many Black and Hispanic women. Their alternative strategy is to attempt to make the community accountable for, and responsive to, sexual violence. Rather than set up a refuge with a confidential address, the addresses where violence has occurred are publicized. An information campaign and a crisis phone line are backed up by a team of women 'safety watchers'. When a report of abuse is received, safety watchers go to the home, remain till the violence has stopped and encourage the abusive man to leave. They also encourage neighbours to intervene if violence occurs subsequently. VIP hopes that this strategy, coupled with their education work, will result in an opposition to domestic violence and a willingness to act in abused women's interests emerging within the local community.

These are just two examples of projects which combine a range of services with education and campaigning work and which focus attention on the needs of women within a particular community. Whilst development projects like these in the USA tend to be funded and, therefore, have paid workers, they either emerged out of the kind of feminist services that already exist in many countries or drew on existing community based organizations or informal networks. They represent a possible way of tapping the potential support and energy of women within their own communites and a form of feminist organizing that is applicable cross-culturally. For example, where feminist services already exist, there are always women who have used them, benefited from them and want to do something themselves. They may well live in areas where local provision is minimal, for example, in small towns or rural areas. Feminist organizing in this context could involve enabling and encouraging women to organize local networks, connecting networks with one another and providing back-up support. These networks could include a combination of crisis support and self-help groups in which women can talk through past experiences.

Whilst these forms of organizing are primarily directed at broadening the ways in which women can achieve individual survival, they do so by enabling and encouraging women to act collectively in challenging sexual violence in their communities. This dual vision and purpose – a world free of male violence alongside a commitment to ensure safety for all abused women and children in the here and now – was the central theme at the 1986 NCADV conference. Community networks based on this philosophy could make feminism a vital and living politics within local communities.

The importance of direct action as a resistance strategy was also a major theme at the NCADV conference. Susan McGee, and many other speakers, argued that direct action was a necessary part of any movement for social change. Her definition of direct action included traditional forms such as lobbying, marches, petitions and vigils, as well as door-too-door campaigning, sit-ins, confrontations of institutions and individual abusive men, and illegal acts such as spray painting and civil disobedience. In encouraging members of the Coalition to use direct action, Susan McGee highlighted the many functions it serves. It makes women's resistance to sexual violence public. It may decrease the isolation of individual survivors. It is directed towards making institutions and/or individuals accountable. Finally, it offers a positive outlet for the anger and frustration that work around sexual violence generates.

The Duluth Women's Action Group combines community networking with direct action. All the women in the group identify as survivors of sexual violence and their session at the NCADV conference charted their individual and collective journey 'from crisis through hope and possibility to social action'. A local informal network developed into a supportive women's group, which in turn became a group committed to regular public direct action as 'a way of resisting'. The transformation of the group accompanied the transformation in the members. Women recalled 'the despair of the oppressed' – feelings of hopelessness, self-blame, negative coping strategies – being overtaken by the possibility of change when someone showed they cared, when they were able to name and talk about sexual violence, when they placed responsibility for the abuse on the abusive man and when they recognized and validated actions they took whilst being abused which were based on hope and self-respect. The movement from support to action was the result of expressing anger, having the support of a community of survivors and analysing why sexual violence happens. These women had moved from individual survival to collective resistance within their community women's group.

Beyond specialization?

The analysis of sexual violence as a continuum raises a further question about feminist services for abused women and children. Should we continue to develop services which focus on specific forms of sexual violence – refuges for battered women, rape crisis lines – or should we develop services based on women's needs? What women who have been abused need does not simplistically follow from the particular form of violence that they have experienced. Women who have experienced different forms of sexual violence may need to talk anonymously, may need a support group of other survivors, may need advice and infor-mation, may need the safety and on-going support a refuge provides.

It is, in fact, already the case in practice that some feminist services already address a range of forms of sexual violence. Rape Crisis Lines counsel women who were abused as children, women who have been sexually harassed and, sometimes, women who are being abused by their partner. Women living in refuges may have been raped by the abusive man. They may have also been sexually abused as a child or have discovered that one or more of their children has been sexually abused. This work in practice is not, however, well known to many women and does not amount to an integrated system of support services based on women's needs.

This research project has led me to question our specializations and to suggest that feminist activists begin to discuss ways in which our services could be more integrated, at least at a local level. Integration, in this model, does not mean that autonomous groups should merge with one another, but simply that their services should be available to any women or girl who has experienced sexual violence. For example, crisis lines would offer supportive listening, discussion of options and referrals for any woman with past or current experience(s) of any form of sexual violence. Self-help groups which provide on-going contact with, and support from, other survivors could be organized both across forms of sexual violence and to address the specific needs and experiences of individual women. Refuges would provide safety for any woman and children who are or feel at risk in their own homes and/or support for women who feel overwhelmed in crisis.

This move away from specification to a broader focus on sexual violence would also facilitate the emergence of local coalitions of grass-roots campaigning, education and direct action. Co-operation across local groups would also make the emergence of the community networks discussed earlier more likely and might also result in other new projects based on unmet needs. One area of unmet need which is recognized by many women's organizations in the UK is specialist care for women who are currently in acute distress as the result of victimization. Women in this group may be rape survivors, incest survivors or survivors of domestic violence. There are currently few alternatives to psychiatric care where the cause of women's distress is often not recognized let alone addressed in treatment.

Some women's organizations have begun to move in this direction and a number of local initiatives also suggest that change and reassessment is taking place. In 1981, the Women's Aid Federation, England (WAFE) extended refuge provision to women and children where the children had been sexually abused by a member of the household. It would be a further step to offer refuge to women who have been sexually assaulted in or near to their home and who do not, therefore, feel safe there. For WAFE to implement fully these policies would require a large increase in refuge places. The number of refuge places in the UK is still nowhere near the minimum recommended provision (one place per 10,000 of the population) in the 1975 *Report* of the Select Committee on Violence in Marriage.[8]

The theme for the 1987 Scottish Women's Liberation Conference was 'Working Against Violence Against Women'. Women working in groups or as individuals were encouraged to 'celebrate past achievements, make links with each other and look to the future'. A number of the programmed workshops reflected many of the issues and possibilities raised in this section: how to organize in rural areas; how to combine crisis support with strategies aimed at stopping sexual violence including direct action; how links can be forged between feminist groups and individuals working in this area; and evaluating the effectiveness of feminist services like refuges and self-help groups.

In Norwich, links have been established between a number of feminist groups over the past two years. Sexual violence has been placed on the public agenda through the establishment of an official Working Group on Violence Against Women attached to the City Council Equal Opportunities Committee. This group provides a forum in which women from feminist organizations meet with representatives from statutory bodies. By pooling energies and resources and working with the city council, changes have been achieved in police practice in relation to sexual assault and domestic violence, a leaflet, 'No One Deserves to be Abused', has been widely distributed, the local press reporting of sexual violence has been monitored and an open advice session staffed by women from the local refuge and rape crisis groups has begun. A further outcome of working together is a consultancy group which planned and facilitated a training day on sexual violence for a range of professionals and voluntary groups.[9]

In suggesting that, as feminists, we review the ways we work on the issue of sexual violence, I am not only questioning whether our services reflect the diversity of experiences amongst women and their diverse needs but I am also arguing that more attention and energy be directed towards collective resistance. It was never the intention of those of us who chose to work in this area in the 1970s that our work become limited to 'band aid' solutions: as Maria Zavala puts it, 'a MASH unit, patching up the wounded and sending them back to front line'. By concentrating solely on the individual survival of abused women and children, whether through our own projects or campaigning for changes in law and professional practice, we run the danger of losing sight of our ultimate aim: ending sexual violence. No matter how effective our services and support networks, no matter how much change in policy and practice is achieved, without a mass movement of women committed to resisting sexual violence in all its forms there will continue to be casualties in the 'shadow war' and women's and girls' lives will continue to be circumscribed by the reality of sexual violence.

Notes

Chapter 1 'Sharing a particular pain': researching sexual violence

1 See, for example, R. Morgan (ed.), *Sisterhood is Global*, (Middlesex, Penguin, 1984), and *Manushi*, an Indian feminist journal.
2 See, for example, J. Hanmer and S. Saunders, *Well-Founded Fear* (London, Hutchinson, 1984); C. MacKinnon, 'Violence against women – a perspective', *Aegis*, 33 (1982), pp. 51–7; D. Russell, *Sexual Exploitation* (Beverley Hills, Sage, 1984).
3 See, D. Spender (ed.), *Men's Studies Modified: The Impact of Feminism on the Academic Disciplines* (Oxford, Pergamon Press, 1981).
4 S. Laws, *The Social Meanings of Menstruation: A Feminist Investigation*, PhD Thesis, Warwick University, 1986.
5 Ibid., p. 58.
6 L. Stanley and S. Wise, *Breaking Out: Feminist Consciousness and Feminist Research* (London, Routledge and Kegan Paul, 1983).
7 H. Eisenstein, *Contemporary Feminist Thought* (London, Unwin paperbacks, 1984).
8 bell hooks, *From Margin to Centre* (Boston, South End Press, 1984).
9 H. Becker, 'Whose side are we on?', *Social Problems*, 14 (1967) pp. 239–47.
10 A. McRobbie, 'The politics of feminist research: between talk and action', *Feminist Review*, 12 (1982), p. 52.
11 Stanley and Wise, *Breaking Out*, p. 18.
12 S. Scott, 'Qualitative methods and feminist research', unpublished paper (1983).
13 H. Roberts, 'Women and their doctors: power and powerlessness in the research process', in *Doing Feminist Research* (London, Routledge and Kegan Paul, 1981), ed. H. Roberts, p. 16.
14 See, for example, E. Fee, 'A feminist critique of scientific objectivity', *Science For the People*, 14 (1982), pp. 5–32; S. Harding, *The Science Question and Feminism* (Milton Keynes, Open University Press, 1986).
15 B. Du Bois, 'Passionate scholarship: notes on values, knowing and method in feminist social science', in *Theories of Women's Studies* (London, Routledge and Kegan Paul 1983), ed. G. Bowles and R. Duelli Klein, p. 113.

16 Stanley and Wise, *Breaking Out*.
17 See ibid., and L. Stanley, 'Experiences of sexism and what these can tell us about women's oppression and women's liberation', *Studies in Sexual Politics* 1 (1984), University of Manchester.
18 S. Acker, K. Barry and J. Esseveld, 'Objectivity and truth: problems in doing feminist research', *Women's Studies International Forum*, 6 (4) (1983), pp. 423–35.
19 Ibid., p. 428.
20 Ibid., p. 429.
21 See, for example, H. Barker, 'Recapturing sisterhood: a critical look at "process" in feminist organizing and community work', *Critical Social Policy*, 16 (1986), pp. 80–90; F. Poland, *Breaking the Rules*, Studies in Sexual Politics 4 (1985), University of Manchester.
22 A good example is the work of Gail Omvedt. See, for example, *We will Smash this Prison* (London, Zed Press, 1980).
23 P. Rock, 'Research as it is written, research as it is done', unpublished paper (1983); Stanley and Wise, *Breaking Out*.
24 C. Bell and H. Newby (eds), *Doing Sociological Research* (London, Allen and Unwin, 1977); C. Bell and H. Roberts (eds), *Social Researching: Politics, Problems and Practice* (London, Routledge and Kegan Paul, 1986).
25 See, for example, P. Bart, *Avoiding Rape*, final report to NIMH, Washington DC (1980); L. Bowker, *Beating Wife Beating* (Lexington, Lexington Books, 1983).
26 Bart, *Avoiding Rape*.
27 See, for example, P. Fairbrother, 'Experience and trust in sociological work', *Sociology*, 11 (1977), pp. 359–68; S. Reinharz, *On Becoming a Social Scientist* (New York, Josey-Bass, 1979).
28 Irene Freize found that 34% of her random control group had also experienced domestic violence: I. Frieze, 'Perceptions of battered wives', in *New Approaches to Social Problems*, ed. I. H. Frieze, D. Ban-Tal and J. S. Carroll (New York, Josey Bass, 1978).
29 A. Oakley, 'Interviewing women: a contradiction in terms', in *Doing Feminist Research*, ed. Roberts.
30 Reinharz, *On Becoming a Social Scientist*.
31 S. Reinharz, 'Experiential analysis: a contribution to feminist research', in *Theories of Women's Studies* (London, Routledge and Kegan Paul, 1983), ed. G. Bowles and R. Duelli Klein.
32 L. Kelly, 'Some thoughts on feminist experience of feminist research', in *Studies in Sexual Politics* 2 (1984), University of Manchester.
33 Hanmer and Saunders, *Well-Founded Fear*.

Chapter 2   A central issue: sexual violence and feminist theory

1 See, for example, A. Clark, *Women's Silence Men's Violence: Sexual Assault in England 1770–1845* (London, Pandora Press, 1987); L. Du Bois and L. Gordon, 'Seeking ecstasy on the battlefield: danger and pleasure in nineteenth century feminist thought', *Feminist Studies*, 9 (1)

(1983), pp. 7–25; S. Jeffreys, *The Spinster and Her Enemies: Feminism and Sexuality 1880–1930* (London, Pandora Press, 1985).

2 S. Brownmiller, *Against Our Will: Men Women and Rape* (New York, Simon and Schuster, 1975); S. Griffin, 'Rape: the all American crime', *Ramparts*, 10 (3) (1971), pp. 26–35; K. Millett, *Sexual Politics*, (London, Abacus, 1972).

3 See, for example, M. Barrett, *Women's Oppression Today* (London, Verso, 1980).

4 L. Kelly, *Women's Experiences of Sexual Violence*, PhD Thesis, Essex University (1985); S. Walby, *Patriarchy at Work* (Cambridge, Polity Press, 1987).

5 Walby, ibid., p. 30.

6 A. Rich, *Of Woman Born* (London, Virago, 1977), p. 57.

7 D. Gittins, *The Family in Question* (London, Macmillan, 1985).

8 J. Hearn and W. Parkin, *'Sex' at 'Work': The Power and Paradox of Organisation Sexuality* (Brighton, Wheatsheaf Books 1987); B. Weinbaum, *Pictures of Patriarchy* (Boston, South End Press, 1983).

9 See also, J. Hanmer, 'Male violence and the social control of women', in *Power and the State*, ed. G. Littlejohn, B. Smart, J. Wakeford and N. Yuval-Davies (London, Croom Helm, 1978).

10 M. Frye, *The Politics of Reality* (New York, Crossing Press, 1983).

11 H. Arendt, *On Violence* (New York, Harcourt, Brace and World, 1970); A. Gramsci, *Selections From Political Writings 1921–1926* (London, Lawrence and Wishart, 1971).

12 L. Bienen, 'Rape 111 – national developments in rape reform legislation', *Women's Rights Law Reporter*, 6 (3) (1980) pp. 170–213; Brownmiller, *Against Our Will*; R. and R. Dobash, *Violence Against Wives: A Case Against the Patriarchy* (New York, Free Press, 1979).

13 See, R. Morgan (ed.), *Sisterhood is Global* (Middlesex, Penguin, 1985); J. Seager and A. Olson, *Women in the World: An International Atlas* (London, Pan, 1986).

14 E. Stanko, *Intimate Intrusions: Women's Experience of Male Violence* (London, Routledge and Kegan Paul, 1985).

15 J. Hanmer and S. Saunders, *Well-Founded Fear* (London, Hutchinsons, 1984); J. Radford, 'Policing male violence – policing women', in *Women, Violence and Social Control* (London, Macmillan, 1987), ed. J. Hanmer and M. Maynard.

16 Brownmiller, *Against Our Will*, p. 404.

17 P. Reeves Sanday, 'The socio-cultural context of rape: a cross-cultural study', *Journal of Social Issues*, 37 (4) (1981) pp. 5–27; L. and H. Schwendinger, *Rape and Inquality* (Beverley Hills, Sage, 1983).

18 A. Edwards, 'Male violence in feminist theory: an analysis of the changing conceptions of sex/gender violence and male dominance', in *Women, Violence and Social Control* (London, Macmillan, 1987), ed. J. Hanmer and M. Maynard.

19 See, for example, Z. Eisenstein, *Capitalist Patriarchy and the Case for Socialist Feminism* (New York, Monthly Review Press, 1979); J. Mitchell, *Women's Estate* (Middlesex, Penguin, 1971); S. Rowbotham, *Women's Consciousness, Man's World* (Middlesex, Penguin, 1973).

242   *Notes*

20 K. Young and O. Harris, 'The subordination of women in cross-cultural perspective', in *Papers on Patriarchy* (Brighton Women's Publishing Collective, 1978).
21 A. Jagger, *Feminist Politics and Human Nature* (Brighton, Harvester Press, 1983).
22 L. Leghorn and K. Parker, *Women's Worth: Sexual Economics and the World of Women* (London, Routledge and Kegan Paul, 1981).
23 See, for example, S. Lukes, *Power: a Radical View* (London, Macmillan 1974); D. Wrong, *Power: It's Forms, Bases and Uses* (Oxford, Basil Blackwell, 1979).
24 S. Bartky, 'Female masochism and the politics of personal transformation', *Women's Studies International Forum*, 7 (5) (1984), pp. 323–34.
25 See, for example, R. and R. Dobash, *Violence Against Wives*; C. MacKinnon, *The Sexual Harassment of Working Women* (New Haven, Yale University Press 1979); E. Ward, *Father–Daughter Rape* (London, Women's Press, 1984).
26 N. Henley and J. Freeman, 'The sexual politics of interpersonal behaviour' in *Women: A Feminist Perspective* (Palo Alton, Mayfield, 1979), ed. J. Freeman.
27 H. Lips, *Women, Men and the Psychology of Power* (New Jersey, Prentice Hall, 1981).
28 S. MacIntyre, unpublished manuscript (1986); C. Ramazanoglu, 'Sex and violence in academic life or you can keep a good woman down'. In *Women, Violence and Social Control*, ed. Hanmer and Maynard.
29 Lukes, *Power: A Radical View*.
30 E. Janeway, *Powers of the Weak* (New York, Alfred A. Knopf, 1980).
31 See, R. Tong, *Women, Sex and the Law* (New Jersey, Rowan and Allenchild, 1984).
32 S. Wise and L. Stanley, *Georgie Porgie: Sexual Harassment in Everyday Life* (London, Pandora Press, 1987).
33 Hearn and Parkin, '*Sex*' at '*Work*', pp. 59–61.
34 C. MacKinnon, 'Feminism, Marxism, method and the state: an agenda for theory', *Signs* 7 (3) (1982), p. 526.
35 See Bartky, 'Female masochism'; MacKinnon, 'Feminism, Marxism'.
36 R. Hall, *Ask Any Woman* (Bristol, Falling Wall Press, 1984), p. 48.
37 Gittins, *Family in Question*.
38 A. Rich, 'Compulsory heterosexuality and lesbian existence', *Signs*, 5 (4) (1980), pp. 631–60.
39 D. Scully and J. Marolla, 'Convicted rapists' vocabularies of motive: excuses and justifications', unpublished mimeograph (1984), p. 27.
40 L. Lederer (ed.), *Take Back the Night: Women on Pornography* (New York, William Morrow, 1980).
41 For how this influences the processing of rape complaints see, S. Chandler and M. Tomey, 'The decisions and processing of the rape victim through the criminal justice system', *California Sociologist*, 4 (2) (1983), pp. 156–69.
42 N. Hartsock, *Money, Sex and Power: Towards a Feminist Historical Materialism* (London, Longman, 1983), p. 7.

43 See, for example, C. Vance (ed.), *Pleasure and Danger: Exploring Female Sexuality* (London, Routledge and Kegan Paul, 1984).

44 See Clark, *Women's Silence Men's Violence*, for the influence of this perspective in the number of references to women's 'right' to pleasure.

45 E. Stanko, 'Typical violence, normal precaution: men, women and interpersonal violence in England, Wales, Scotland and the USA', in *Women, Violence and Social Control*, ed. Hanmer and Maynard.

46 M. Cliff, 'Sister/outsider: some thoughts on Simone Weil', in *Between Women* (Boston, Beacon Press, 1984), ed. S. Ruddick, p. 318.

47 Brownmiller, Against Our Will, M. Daly, *Gyn/Ecology: The Mataethics of Radical Feminism* (London, Women's Press 1979); S. Griffin, *Rape: the Power of Consciousness* (New York, Harper and Row, 1979).

48 K. Barry, *Female Sexual Slavery* (New Jersey, Prentice Hall, 1979) p. 139.

49 Ibid., p. 165.

50 Radford, 'Policing male violence'.

51 MacKinnon, 'Feminism, Marxism'.

52 S. Pfohl, *Images of Deviance and Social Control: A Sociological History* (New York, McGraw Hill, 1985), p.3.

53 Ibid., p. 376.

54 M. Pagelow, 'Blaming the victim – parallels in crimes against women: rape and battering', paper at the Society for the Study of Social Problems, September, 1977, San Francisco, p. 2.

55 L. Holmstrom and A. Burgess, *The Victims of Rape: Institutional Reaction* (New York, Wiley and Co., 1978).

56 G. Chambers and A. Millar, *Investigating Sexual Assault*, Edinburgh, HMSO, 1983; K. Holmes, 'Justice for whom? Rape victims assess the legal-judicial system', *Free Inquiry in Creative Sociology*, 8 (2) (1980), pp. 126–30; T. W. McCahill, S. Meyer and L. Fischman, *The Aftermath of Rape* (Lexington, Lexington Books, 1979).

57 V. Binney, G. Harkell and J. Nixon, *Leaving Violent Men* (Leeds, NWAF, 1981); R. and R. Dobash, *Violence Against Wives*; T. Faragher, 'The police response to violence against women' in J. Pahl, *Private Violence and Public Policy* ed. J. Pahl (London, Routledge and Kegan Paul, 1985); M. Homer, A. Leonard and P. Taylor, *Private Violence: Public Shame* (Middlesborough, CRAWC, 1984).

58 F. Wassoff, 'Legal protection from wifebeating: the processing of domestic assaults by Scottish prosecutors and criminal courts', *International Journal of the Sociology of Law*, 10, (1982), pp. 107–204.

59 For US model see, H. Giaretto, 'A comprehensive child sexual abuse treatment programme', *Child Abuse and Neglect*, 6 (3) (1982), pp. 262–78. For UK support see, BAPSCAN, *Child Sexual Abuse* (Northampton, BAPSCAN 1981); CIBA Foundation, *Child Sexual Abuse Within the Family* (London, Tavistock, 1984).

60 A. T. Laszlo and T. McKean, 'Court diversion: an alternative for spousal abuse cases', in *Battered Women: Issues of Public Policy*, Washington DC (1978), US Commission on Civil Rights; L. Lerman, 'Criminal prosecution of wife beaters', *Response*, 4 (3) (1981), pp. 1–19;

L. Wermuth, 'Domestic violence reforms: policing the private', *Berkley Journal of Sociology*, 27 (1982), pp. 27–49.

61 S. Edwards, 'Provoking her own demise': From common assault to homicide', in *Women, Violence and Social Control*, ed. Hanmer and Maynard; J. Radford, 'Marriage licence or licence to kill? Woman-slaughter in the criminal justice system', *Feminist Review*, 11 (1982) pp. 88–100; L. Radford, 'Legalising woman abuse', in *Women, Violence and Social Control*, ed. Hanmer and Maynard.

62 Incest Survivors Campaign, personal communication.

63 See, for example, M. Maynard, 'Response of social workers to battered women', in *Private Violence and Public Policy*, ed. J. Pahl; S. Sgroi, 'Kids with clap': gonorrhoea as an indicator of child sexual assault', *Victimology*, 2 (1977), pp. 251–67.

64 C. A. Dietz and J. L. Craft, 'Family dynamics of incest: a new perspective', *Social Casework* (December, 1980), pp. 602–9; M. Borkowski, M. Murch and V. Walker, *Marital Violence: the Community Response* (London, Tavistock, 1983).

65 See, for example, K. Donato and L. Bowker, 'Understanding the help-seeking behaviour of battered women: a comparison of traditional social service agencies and women's groups', *International Journal of Women's Studies*, 7 (1984), pp. 99–109.

66 M. Hirsch, *Women and Violence* (New York, Van Nostrand Reinhold, 1981).

67 H. Scott, *Working Your Way to the Bottom: The Feminization of Poverty* (London, Panodra Press, 1985).

68 K. Barry, 'Social etiology of crimes against women', *Victimology*, 10 (1–4) (1985), p. 164.

69 Wise and Stanley, *Georgie Peorgie*.

70 D. Klein, 'Violence against women: some considerations regarding its causes and its elimination', *Crime and Delinquency*, 27 (1) (1981), pp. 64–80.

71 S. Ardener, 'Sexual insult and female militancy', in *Perceiving Women* (New York, Halstead, 1975), ed. S. Ardener; Leghorn and Parker, *Women's Worth*.

72 Bartky, 'Female Masochism'.

73 See, for example, R. Coward, 'Sexual violence and sexuality', *Feminist Review*, 11, (1982), pp. 9–22; Lederer, *Take Back the Night*.

74 L. Kelly, 'Feminist v. feminist', *Trouble and Strife*, 7 (1985), pp. 3–9.

75 A. Dworkin, *Pornography: Men Possessing Women* (London, Women's Press, 1981); R. Morgan, 'Theory and practice: pornography and rape', in *Going Too Far* (New York, Vintage Books, 1978).

76 E. Wilson, *What Is to be Done About Violence Against Women* (Middlesex, Penguin, 1983).

77 Frye, *Politics of Reality*, pp. 2–3. Frye also acknowledge bell hooks' point that since specific groups of women have fewer choices than others, the 'barriers and forces' they are caught between leave even less room to move.

Chapter 3   The knowledge explosion: an overview of previous research

1 The National Center For the Prevention and Control of Rape, Washington DC; The National Clearinghouse on Domestic Violence, Washington DC.

2 See, for example, *Rape and its Victims: A Report For Citizens, Health Facilities and Criminal Justice Agencies*, US Department of Justice (1975); *Battered Women: Issues of Public Policy*, US Commission on Civil Rights (1978); *Sexual Abuse of Children: Selected Readings*, US Department of Health and Human Services (1980).

3 For example the Family Violence Research Laboratory, Durham, New Hamphire.

4 R. Gelles, 'Applying research on family violence to clinical practice', *Journal of Marriage and the Family*, 44 (1) (1982), pp. 9–20.

5 Copies of these tables appear in the appendices of my PhD thesis, *Women's Experiences of Sexual Violence*, Essex University.

6 See, for example, P. Gebhard, H. Gagnon, W. Pomeroy and C. Christenson, *Sex Offenders: An Analysis of Types* (New York, Harper and Row, 1965), K. Soothill, A. Jack and T. Gibbons, 'Rape: A 20 year cohort study', *Medicine, Science and the Law*, 16 (1) (1976), pp. 62–7.

7 See, for example, G. Fisher and E. Rivlin, 'Psychological needs of rapists', *British Journal of Criminology*, 11 (1971), pp. 182–5.

8 For an overt example see, T. Garrett and R. Wright, 'Wives of rapists and incest offenders', *Journal of Sex Research*, 11 (2) (1975), pp. 149–57.

9 G. Abel, D. Barlow, E. Blanchard and D. Guild, 'The components of rapists sexual arousal', *Archives of General Psychiatry*, 34 (1977), pp. 895–903; H. Barbaree, W. Marshall and R. Lamther, 'Deviant sexual arousal in rapists', *Behaviour Research and Therapy*, 17 (1979), pp. 215–22.

10 R. Semmel Albin, 'Psychological studies of rape', *Signs*, 3 (1977), pp. 423–35.

11 J. Rabkin, 'Epidemiology of forcible rape', *American Journal of Orthospychiatry*, 49 (4) (1979), pp. 634–47.

12 G. Abel, J. Becker and L. Skinner, 'Aggressive behaviour and sex', *Psychiatric Clinics of North America*, 3 (1980), pp. 133–51.

13 D. Smithyman, *The Undetected Rapist*, PhD thesis, Claremont Graduate School (1978).

14 N. Malamuth, 'Rape proclivity in males', *Journal of Social Issues*, 37 (4) (1981), pp. 138–57; N. Malamuth and J. Check, 'Sexual arousal to rape and consenting depictions: the importance of the woman's arousal', *Journal of Abnormal Psychology*, 89 (6) (1980), pp. 763–6; N. Malamuth and J. Check, 'Sexual arousal to rape depictions: individual differences', *Journal of Abnormal Psychology*, 92 (1) (1983) pp. 55–67; N. Malamuth and S. Haber, 'Testing hypotheses regarding rape: exposure to sexual violence, sex differences and the "normality" of rape', *Journal of Research into Personality*, 14 (1980), pp. 121–37.

15 D. Scully and J. Marolla, 'Convicted rapists' vocabulary of motive: excuses and justifications', unpublished mimeograph, (1984), p. 4.

16 A. Groth, R. Longo and J. McFadin, 'Undetected recidivism among rapists and child molesters', *Crime and Delinquency*, 28 (3) (1982), pp. 450–8.

17 Even using this limited definition, Soothill et al., 'A 20 year study', found the recidivism rate increased when the time period of the study was extended.

18 M. Amir, *Patterns in Forcible Rape* (Chicago, University of Chicago, 1971).

19 M. Wolfgang, *Patterns in Criminal Homicide* (Philadelphia, University of Pennsylvania Press, 1950).

20 L. Curtis, 'Victim precipitation and violent crime', *Social Problems*, 21 (4) (1975), pp. 594–605.

21 P. Bart, 'Rape doesn't end with a kiss', *Viva* (1975), pp. 40–2 and 101–7; A. Burgess and L. Holmstrom, *Rape: Victims of Crisis*, (Bowie, Robert J. Brady, 1974); D. Russell, *The Politics of Rape: The Victims Perspective* (New York, Stein and Day, 1975).

22 D. Russell, *Sexual Exploitation* (Beverley Hills, Sage, 1984).

23 A. Burgess and L. Holmstrom, *Rape, Crisis and Recovery*, (Bowie, Robert J. Brady, 1979).

24 S. Sutherland and D. Scherl, 'Patterns of response among victims of rape', *American Journal of Orthopsychiatry*, 40 (1970), pp. 503–11.

25 D. Kilpatrick and P. Resnick, 'The aftermath of rape: recent empirical findings', *American Journal of Orthopsychiatry*, 49 (4) (1979), pp. 650–69. L. Veronen and D. Kilpatrick, 'Rape a precursor of change', unpublished mimeography (1979); J. Williams and K. Holmes, *The Second Assault: Rape and Public Attitudes* (Westport, Greenwood Press, 1981).

26 A. Kreutner, D. Kilpatrick, C. Best and L. Veronen, 'The adolescent rape victim', in *Adolescent Obstetrics and Gyneacology* (Chicago, Yearbook Medical Publishers, 1978).

27 Williams and Holmes, *The Second Assault*.

28 L. Davis, 'Rape and the older woman', in *Rape and Sexual Assault: Management and Intervention* (Germantown, Aspen, 1980), ed. C. Warner; A. Groth, 'The older rape victim and her assailant', *Journal of Geriatic Psychology*, 11 (2) (1978), pp. 203–15.

29 R. Hall, *Ask Any Woman: A London Rape Inquiry* (Bristol, Falling Wall Press 1985); L. Ruch and S. Chandler, 'Ethnicity and rape impact: the response of women from different ethnic backgrounds to rape and rape crisis treatment services in Hawaii', *Social Process in Hawaii*, 27 (1979), pp. 52–67; Williams and Holmes, *The Second Assault*.

30 R. Gundlach, 'Sexual molestation and rape reported by homosexual and heterosexual women', *Journal of Homosexuality*, 2 (4) (1977), pp. 367–84.

31 P. Bart, *Avoiding Rape: A Study of Victims and Avoiders*, final project report, NIMH, Washington DC (1980); E. Ellis, B. Atkeson and K. Calhoun, 'An examination of differences between multiple and single incident victims of sexual assault', *Journal of Abnormal Psychology*, 91

(3) (1982), pp. 321–4; J. Miller, 'Recidivism among sexual assault victims', *American Journal of Psychiatry*, 135 (1978), pp. 1103–4; D. Russell, 'The prevalence and incidence of forcible rape and attempted rape of females', *Victimology*, 7 (1) (1982), pp. 81–93.

32 P. Bart and P. O'Brien, 'Stopping rape: effective avoidance strategies', *Signs*, 10 (1984), pp. 83–101, J. McIntyre, *Victims Response to Rape: Alternative Outcomes*, final project report, NIMH, Washington DC (1980).

33 P. Belcastro, 'A comparison of latent sexual behaviour patterns between raped and never-raped females', *Victimology*, 7 (1–4) (1982), pp. 224–30; J. Orlando and M. Koss, 'The effect of sexual victimization on sexual satisfaction: a study of the negative association hypothesis', *Journal of Abnormal Psychology*, 92 (1) (1983), pp. 104–6.

34 P. Di Vasto, A. Kaufman, R. Jackson, L. Ballen and P. Selfmode, 'Caring for rape victims: its impact on providers', *Journal of Community Health*, 5 (3), (1984), pp. 204–8; D. Kilpatrick and A. Amick, 'Intrafamilial and extrafamilial sexual assault: results of a random community study', paper at the Second International Conference for Family Violence Researchers, August, University of New Hampshire (1984).

35 Hall, *Ask Any Woman*.

36 Russell, 'Prevalence and incidence'.

37 A. Johnson, 'On the prevelance of rape in the United States', *Signs*, 6 (1) (1980), pp. 136–46; C. Nelson, 'Victims of rape: who are they?', in C. Warner, *Rape and Sexual Assault: Management and Intervention*, ed. Warner.

38 See, for example, S. Fulmo and C. DeLara, 'Rape victims and attributed responsibility: a defensive attribution approach', *Victimology*, 1 (4) (1976), pp. 551–63; J. Krulewitz and J. Nash, 'Effects of rape victims resistance, assault outcome, and sex of the observer on attributions about rape', *Journal of Personality*, 47 (4) (1979), pp. 557–74; L. Schultz and S. De Savage, 'Rape and rape attitudes on a college campus', in *Rape Victimology* (Springfield, Charles C. Thomas, 1975), ed. L. Schultz; C. Seligman, 'Rape and physical attractiveness, assigning responsibility to the victim', *Journal of Personality*, 45 (4) (1977), pp. 554–63.

39 M. Burt and R. Semmel Albin, 'Rape myths, rape definitions and probability of conviction', *Journal of Applied Social Psychology*, 11 (3) (1981), pp. 212–30; H. Field, 'Attitudes towards rape: a comparative analysis of police, rapists, crisis counsellors and citizens', *Journal of Personality and Social Psychology*, 36 (1978), pp. 156–79.

40 K. Weis and S. Borges, 'Victimology and rape: the case of the legitimate victim', *Issues in Criminology*, 8 (1973), pp. 71–115.

41 S. Chandler and M. Tomey, 'The decisions and processing of the rape victim through the criminal justice system', *California Sociologist*, 4 (2) (1983), pp. 156–69; G. LaFree, 'The effect of sexual assault by race on official reactions to rape', *American Sociological Review*, 45 (5) (1980), pp. 842–54; T. McCahill, S. Meyer and L. Fischman, *The Aftermath of Rape* (Lexington, Lexington Books, 1979).

42 G. Chambers and A. Millar, *Investigating Sexual Assault* (Edinburgh, HMSO, 1983).
43 V. McNickle Rose and S. Randall, 'Where have all the rapists gone?', in *Violent Crime: Historical and Contemporary Issues* (Beverley Hills, Sage, 1978), ed. J. Incavdi and S. Pottieger.
44 S. Feldman Summers and C. Ashworth, 'Factors related to reporting rape', *Journal of Social Issues*, 37 (4) (1981), pp. 53–70.
45 Hall, *Ask Any Woman*.
46 W. Loh, 'The impact of common law and reform rape statutes on prosecution: an empirical study', *Washington Law Review*, 55 (1980), pp. 543–652; J. Marsh and N. Caplan, *Law Reform in the Prevention and Treatment of Rape*, final project report (NIMH, Washington DC, 1980).
47 See note 32.
48 L. Bowker, 'Marital rape: a distinct syndrome?', *Social Casework*, 64 (6) (1983), pp. 347–52; I. Freize, 'Investigating the causes and consequences of marital rape', *Signs*, 8 (3), (1983), pp. 532–53; B. Lewis, 'Wife abuse and marital rape in a clinical population', paper at the Second International Conference for Family Violence Researchers, (August, 1984) University of New Hampshire; N. Shields and C. Hanneke, 'Battered wives' reactions to marital rape', in *The Dark Side of Families* (Beverley Hills, Sage, 1983), ed. D. Finkelhor, R. Gelles, G. Hotaling and M. Straus.
49 J. Doran, 'Conflict and violence in intimate relationships: focus on marital rape', paper at the American Sociological Association Annual Conference, New York (1980); D. Finkelhor and K. Yllo, *Licence to Rape: Sexual Abuse of Wives* (New York, Holt Rhinerhart, 1985); Hall, *Ask Any Woman*; D. Russell, *Rape in Marriage* (New York, Macmillan, 1982).
50 E. Kanin, 'Male aggression in dating–courtship relationships', *American Journal of Sociology*, 63 (1957), pp. 197–204; E. Kanin and S. Parcell, 'Sexual aggression: a second look at the offended female', *Archives of Sexual Behaviour*, 6 (1) (1977), pp. 67–76.
51 R. Giarusso, P. Johnson, J. Goodchilds and G. Zellman, 'Adolescents cues and signals: sex and sexual assault', unpublished mimeograph (1979); M. Koss, K. Leonard, D. Beezley and C. Oros, 'Male sexual aggression: a discriminant analysis of psychological dimensions', unpublished mimeography (1982); M. Koss and C. Oros, 'Sexual experiences survey: a research instrument investigating sexual aggression and victimization', *Journal of Consulting and Clinical Psychology*, 50 (1982), pp. 455–7.
52 J. Collins, J. Kennedy and R. Francis, 'Insights into a dating partners' expectations of how behaviour should ensue during the courtship process', *Journal of Marriage and the Family* (May, 1976), pp. 373–8; D. Knox and K. Wilson, 'Dating behaviour of university students', *Family Relations*, 30 (2) (1981), pp. 255–58; L. Peplau, Z. Rubin and C. Hill, 'Sexual intimacy in dating relationships', *Journal of Social Issues*, 33 (2), pp. 86–109.
53 M. De Young, *The Sexual Victimization of Children* (Jefferson,

McFarland 1982); A. Groth, 'Sexual trauma in the life histories of rapists and child molesters', *Victimology*, 4 (1) (1979), pp. 10–16; R. Langevin, *Sexual Strands: Understanding and Treating Sexual Anomalies in Men* (Hillside, Erlbaum Associates, 1983).

54 G. Abel, J. Becker, W. Murphy and B. Flanagan, 'Identifying dangerous child molesters', in *Violent Behaviour* (New York, Brunner/ Mazel 1981), ed. C. Stuart; K. Freund and R. Langevin, 'Bisexuality in homosexual pedophilia', *Archives in Sexual Behaviour*, 5 (1976), pp. 415–23; V. Quinsey, C. Steinman, S. Bergerson and T. Holmes, 'Penile circumference, skin conduction and rating responses of child molesters and "normals" to sexual and non-sexual visual stimuli', *Behaviour Therapy*, 6 (1975), pp. 213–19.

55 D. Laws and D. O'Neil, 'Variations on masturbatory conditioning', paper at the Second National Conference on the Treatment and Evaluation of Sexual Aggressives (June, 1979) New York.

56 G. Abel, 'The treatment of sexual aggressors', *Crime, Justice and Behaviour*, 5 (1978), pp. 291–3.

57 W. Whitman and V. Quinsey, 'Heterosocial skill training for institutionalized rapists and child molesters', *Canadian Journal of Behavioural Science*, 13 (1981), pp. 81–97.

58 R. Kelley, 'Behavioural re-orientation of pedophiles: can it be done?', *Clinical Psychology Review*, 2 (1982), pp. 387–408.

59 F. Berlin and C. Meinecke, 'Treatment of sex offenders with antiandrogenic medication: conceptualization, review of treatment modalities and preliminary findings', in *Sexual Aggression: Current Perspectives on Treatment*, volume II (New York, Van Nostrand Reinhold, 1982).

60 P. Rossman, *Sexual Experience Between Men and Boys*, (Hounslow, Maurice Temple Smith, 1985).

61 R. Snowdon, 'Working with incest offenders: excuses, excuses, excuses', *Aegis*, 35 (1982), pp. 56–63.

62 W. Marshall and M. Christie, 'Pedophilia and aggression', *Crime, Justice and Behaviour*, 8 (2) (1981), pp. 145–58.

63 For psychoanalytic case studies see, L. Gordon, 'Incest as revenge against the preoedipal mother', *Psychoanalytic Review*, 42 (1955), pp. 284–292; M. Rachovsky and A. Rachovsky, 'On consumated incest', *International Journal of Psychoanalysis*, 31 (1950), pp. 42–7; J. Tompkins, 'Penis envy and incest: a case report', *Psychoanalytic Review*, 27 (1940), pp. 319–25. For cultural milieu perspective see, for example, S. Kubo, 'Researchers and studies on incest in Japan', *Hiroshima Journal of Medical Science*, 8 (1959), pp. 291–305; S. Reimer, 'A research note on incest', *American Journal of Sociology*, 45 (1940), pp. 554–65; T. Sondon, 'Incest crimes in Sweden and their causes', *Acta Psychiatrica et Neurologica*, 11 (1936), pp. 379–401.

64 L. Bender and A. Blau, 'The reaction of children to sexual relationships with adults', *American Journal of Orthospychiatry*, 7 (1937), pp. 500–18; L. Bender and A. Grudgett, 'A follow-up report on children who had atypical sexual experiences', *American Journal of Orthopsychiatry*, 22 (1952), pp. 825–37.

65 J. Weiss, E. Rodgers, M. Darwin and C. Dutton, 'A study of girl sex victims', *Psychiatric Quarterly*, 29 (1) (1955), pp. 71–115.
66 See, for example, T. Gibbons, 'Incest and sexual abuse of children', in *Perspectives on Rape and Sexual Assault* (London, Harper and Row 1984) ed. J. Hopkins; E. Pizzey and J. Shapiro, 'Sexual abuse within the family', paper at the Second International Conference for Family Violence Researchers, (August, 1984) University of New Hampshire.
67 Bender and Grudgett, 'Children who had atypical sexual experiences'; A. Kinsey, W. Pomeroy, C. Martin and P. Gebhard, *Sexual Behaviour in the Human Female* (Philadelphia, Saunders, 1955); N. Lucianowicz, 'Paternal incest', *British Journal of Psychiatry*, 120 (1972), pp. 301–13; A. Yorukoglu and J. Kemph, 'Children not severely damaged by incest', *Journal of American Academy of Child Psychiatry*, 8 (1969), pp. 606–10.
68 D. West, 'The victims contribution to sexual offences', in *Perspectives on Rape and Sexual Assault*, (London, Harper and Row, 1984), ed. J. Hopkins, p. 10.
69 K. Dolan, 'Evaluation of outcomes for reported cases of child sexual abuse in Tarrant and Travis counties, Texas', final project report (NIMH, Washington DC, 1984).
70 I. Kaufman, A. Peck and C. Taguri, 'The family constellation and overt incestuous relationships between father and daughter', *American Journal of Orthopsychiatry*, 24 (1954), pp. 266–77.
71 N. Lustig, J. Dresser, S. Spellman and T. Murray, 'Incest – a family group survival pattern', *Archives of General Psychiatry*, 14 (1966), pp. 31–40.
72 M. De Young, *Sexual Victimization of Children*, p. 9.
73 J. Herman, *Father–Daughter Incest* (Cambridge, Harvard University Press, 1981).
74 D. Finkelhor, *Child Sexual Abuse: New Theory and Research*, (New York, Free Press, 1984).
75 N. Greenburg, 'The epidemiology of childhood sexual abuse', *Pediatric Annals*, 8 (5) (1979), p. 28.
76 See, for example, H. Maisch, *Incest* (New York, Stein and Day (1972); Y. Tormes, *Child Victims of Incest* (Colorardo, American Humane Association 1968); K. Weinburg, *Incest Behaviour* (New York, Citadel, 1955).
77 B. Cormier, M. Kennedy and J. Sangowicz, 'Psychodynamics of father–daughter incest', *Canadian Psychiatric Association Journal*, 7 (5) (1962), pp. 203–17.
78 H. Cavellin, 'Incestuous fathers', *American Journal of Psychiatry*, (122) (1966), pp. 1132–8.
79 Kaufman et al., 'Family constellation', p. 276; Reimer, 'Research note on incest'.
80 E. Ward, *Father–Daughter Rape* (London, Women's Press, 1984).
81 Pizzey and Shapiro, 'Sexual abuse within the family', pp. 4–5.
82 See, for example, A. Marrarino and J. Cohen, 'A clinical–demographic study of sexually abused children', paper at the Second International

Conference for Family Violence Researchers (August, 1984) University of New Hampshire.

83 Dolan, 'Evaluation of outcomes'; *Off Our Backs*, news items (May, 1985).

84 D. Finkelhor and G. Hotaling, 'Sexual abuse in the national incidence study of child abuse and neglect: an appraisal', paper at the Second International Conference for Family Violence Researchers, (August, 1984) University of New Hampshire.

85 H. Giaretto, 'Humanistic treatment of father–daughter incest', in *Child Abuse and Neglect*, Cambridge, Ballinger, 1976) ed. R. Helfer and H. Kempe; H. Giaretto, 'A comprehensive child sexual abuse treatment programme', *Child Abuse and Neglect*, 6 (3) (1982), pp. 263–78.

86 BAPSCAN, *Child Sexual Abuse* (Northampton, BAPSCAN, 1981); CIBA Foundation, *Child Sexual Abuse Within the Family* (London, Tavistock, 1984).

87 J. Conte, 'Progress in treating sexual abuse of children', *Social Work*, 29 (3) (1984); pp. 258–63.

88 L. Kelly, 'Incest', *RRF Newsletter*, 9 (1982), pp. 9–16.

89 G. Molnar and P. Cameron, 'Incest syndromes', *Canadian Psychiatric Association Journal*, 20 (5) (1975), pp. 373–7; P. Phelan and B. Joyce, 'CASTP program model: clients treatment and family growth' (Palo Alto, Scripps Centre, 1980).

90 J. Gagnon, 'Female child victims of sex offences', *Social Problems*, 13 (1965), pp. 176–92.

91 Herman, *Father–Daughter Incest*, p. 17.

92 D. Finkelhor, *Sexually Victimized Children* (New York, Free Press, 1979).

93 Finkelhor, *Child Sexual Abuse: New Theory an Practice*.

94 See, for example, B. Brandt and V. Tiza, 'The sexually misused child', *American Journal of Orthopsychiatry*, 47 (1977), pp. 80–90; R. Davies, 'Incest some neuropsychiatric findings', *International Journal of Psychiatry in Medicine*, 9 (2) (1979), pp. 117–21; E. Sarafino, 'An estimate of nationwide incidence of sexual offences against children', *Child Welfare*, 58 (1979), pp. 127–34.

95 Finkelhor, *Sexually Victimized Children*; G. Fritz, K. Stoll and N. Wagner, 'A comparison of men and women who were sexually molested as children', *Journal of Sex and Marital Therapy*, 7 (1981), pp. 54–9; M. Fromuth, 'The long-term psychological impact of childhood sexual abuse', PhD thesis, Auburn University, USA (1983); A. Seidner and K. Calhoun, 'Childhood sexual abuse: factors related to differential adult adjustment', paper at the Second International Conference for Family Violence Researchers (August, 1984) University of New Hampshire.

96 Finkelhor, *Child Sexual Abuse: New Theory and Practice*; C. Kercher and M. McShane, 'The prevalance of child sexual abuse: victimization in an adult sample of Texas residents', unpublished mimeograph (1983); D. Kilpatrick and A. Amick, 'Intrafamilial and extrafamilial sexual assault: results of a random community study', paper at the Second International Conference for Family Violence Researchers

(August, 1984) University of New Hampshire; D. Russell, 'The incidence and prevelance of intrafamilial and extrafamilial sexual abuse of female children', *Child Abuse and Neglect*, 7 (1983), pp. 133–46.

97 T. Baker, 'Readers survey on sexual abuse', *19 Magazine*, (September, 1983), pp. 34–6 and 48–52; Hall, *Ask Any Woman*.

98 D. West (ed.), *Sexual Victimisation*, (Aldershot, Gower, 1986).

99 A. Ronstrom, 'Sexuella overgrepp po barn I Serverige', paper at Radda Barnens Nordiska Seminarium om Barnmisshandel, (Jallberg, Sweden, 1983).

100 L. Pierce and R. Pierce, 'Race as a factor in childhood sexual abuse', paper at the Second International Conference for Family Violence Researchers (August, 1984), University of New Hampshire.

101 K. McFarlane and J. Bulkley, 'Treating child sexual abuse: an overview of current treatment programmes', in *Social Work and Child Sexual Abuse* (New York, Haworth, 1982), ed. J. Conte and D. Shore.

102 J. Conte, 'Progress in treating sexual abuse of children', *Social Work*, 29 (3) (1984), pp. 259–63.

103 Finkelhor, *Child Sexual Abuse: New Theory and Practice*.

104 C. Dietz and J. Craft, 'Family dynamics of incest: a new perspective', *Social Casework* (December, 1980), pp. 602–9; J. La Barbara, J. Martin and J. Dozier, 'Child psychiatrists view of father–daughter incest', *Child Abuse and Neglect*, 4 (3) (1980), pp. 147–52.

105 R. Galdston, 'Current thinking on sexual abuse of children', *Medical Aspects of Human Sexuality*, 12 (1978), pp. 44, 45 and 47.

106 Finkelhor, *Child Sexual Abuse: New Theory and Practice*.

107 Ibid.

108 J. Conte, 'Research on the prevention of sexual abuse of children', paper at the Second International Conference for Family Violence Researchers (August, 1984) University of New Hampshire; J. Conte, 'Prevention programmes: our visions and missed steps', panel contribution at the National Coalition Against Sexual Assault Conference (July, 1986) Chicago.

109 C. Plummer, 'Preventing sexual abuse', paper at the Second International Conference for Family Violence Researchers (August, 1984) University of New Hampshire; J. Ray, 'Evaluation of the child sexual abuse prevention project', paper at the Second International Conference for Family Violence Researchers (August, 1984) University of New Hampshire.

110 S. McClintock, *Crimes of Violence* (London, Macmillan, 1963); H. Voss and J. Hepburn, 'Patterns of criminal homicide', *Journal of Criminal Law, Criminology and Police Science*, 59 (1968), pp. 499–508; M. Wolfgang, 'Husband–Wife homicides', *Journal of Social Therapy*, 2 (1956), pp. 263–71.

111 R. Chester and J. Streater, 'Cruelty in English divorce: some empirical findings', *Journal of Marriage and the Family*, 34 (1972), pp. 706–10; G. Levinger, 'Sources of marital disatisfaction', *American Journal of Orthopsychiatry*, 36 (5) (1966), pp. 803–7; J. O'Brien, 'Violence in divorce-prone families', *Journal of Marriage and the Family*, 33 (4) (1971), pp. 692–9.

112 M. Faulk, 'Men who assault their wives', *Medicine, Science and the Law*, 114 (3) (1974), pp. 180–3; L. Schultz, 'The wife assaulter', *Journal of Social Therapy*, 6 (2) (1960), pp. 103–11.

113 K. Coleman, 'Conjugal violence: what 33 men report', *Journal of Marriage and Family Therapy*, 6 (1980), pp. 207–13; D. Dutton and J. Browning, 'Power struggles and intimacy anxieties as causative factors of wife assault', paper at the Second International Conference for Family Violence Researchers (August, 1984) University of New Hampshire; J. Edelson and M. Brygger, 'Gender differences in reporting battering incidents', paper at the Second International Conference for Family Violence Researchers (August, 1984) University of New Hampshire. E. Gondolf, 'Men who batter: how they stop their abuse', paper at the Second International Conference for Family Violence Researchers (August, 1984) University of New Hampshire.

114 M. Johnson, 'Correlates of early violence experiences among men who are abusive to female mates', paper at the Second International Conference for Family Violence Researchers (August, 1984), University of New Hampshire.

115 See, for example, M. Eddy and T. Myers, 'Helping men who batter: a profile of progress in the US', paper at the Second International Conference for Family Violence Researchers (August, 1984), University of New Hampshire.

116 See, for example, R. Reynolds and E. Siegle, 'A study of casework with sadomasochistic marriage partners', *Social Casework*, 40 (1959), pp. 545–551; J. Snell, 'The wife beater's wife: a study in family interaction', *Archives of General Psychiatry*, 11 (2) (1964), pp. 107–12.

117 W. Goode, 'Force and violence in the family', *Journal of Marriage and the Family*, 33 (1971), p. 624.

118 B. Grey-Little and N. Banks, 'Power and satisfaction in marriage: a review and critique', *Psychological Bulletins*, 93 (5) (1983), pp. 513–38; C. Safilios-Rothschild, 'The study of family power structure: a review 1960–1969', *Journal of Marriage and the Family*, 32 (1970), pp. 539–52.

119 E. Pizzey, *Scream Quietly or the Neighbours Will Hear*, (Middlesex, Penguin, 1974).

120 See, for example, J. Gayford, 'Wife battering – a preliminary survey of 100 cases', *British Medical Journal*, 1 (1975), pp. 194–7; M. Roy, 'Current survey of 150 cases', in *Battered Women* (New York, Van Nostrand Reinhold, 1977), ed. M. Roy.

121 R. and R. Dobash, *Violence Against Wives: A Case Against the Patriarchy* (New York, Free Press 1979); R and R. Dobash, 'The context specific approach', in *The Dark Side of Families*, ed. Finkelhor; R. and R. Dobash and C. Cavanagh, 'The professions construct the problems of women: medical and social work responses to battered wives', paper at the Society for the Study of Social problems (August, 1982), San Francisco.

122 L. Walker, *The Battered Woman* (New York, Van Nostrand Reinhold, 1979).

123 L. Walker, *The Battered Woman Syndrome* (New York, Springer, 1984).

124 M. Pagelow, *Woman Battering* (Beverley Hills, Sage, 1981).

125 K. Ferraro, 'Physical and emotional battering', *California Sociologist*, 2 (2) (1979), p. 147.

126 E. Hilberman and K. Munson, 'Sixty battered women', *Victimology*, 2 (3–4) (1977), pp. 460–70; R. Post, A. Willet, R. Franks, R. House and S. Back, 'A preliminary report on the prevelance of domestic violence among psychiatric inpatients', *American Journal of Psychiatry* 137 (8) (1980), pp. 974–5.

127 A. Flitcraft, 'Battered women: an emergency room epidemiology with a description of a clinical syndrome and critique of present therapeutics', thesis, Yale Medical School (1977).

128 M. Straus, 'Measuring intrafamily conflict and violence (the Conflict Tactics Scale)', *Journal of Marriage and the Family*, 41 (1979), pp. 75–88.

129 M. Straus, R. Gelles and S. Steinmetz, *Behind Closed Doors* (New York, Anchor Books, 1980).

130 M. Schulman, 'A survey of spousal abuse against women in Kentucky', US Department of Justice (1979); R. Teske and M. Parker, *Spouse abuse in Texas: a study of women's attitudes and experiences*, (Huntsville, Survey Research Department, 1983).

131 S. Steinmetz, 'The battered husband syndrome', *Victimology*, 2 (3–4) (1978), pp. 499–507.

132 Dobash and Dobash, 'The context specific approach'; E. Pleck, J. Pleck, M. Grosman and P. Bart, 'The battered data syndrome – a reply to Steinmetz', *Victimology*, 2 (3–4) (1978), pp. 380–3; S. Schecter, *Women and Male Violence: The Visions and Struggles of the Battered Women's Movement*, (Boston, South End Press, 1982).

133 K. Ferraro and J. Johnson, 'The meanings of courtship violence', paper at the Second International Conference for Family Violence Researchers (August, 1984), University of New Hampshire; J. Makepeace, 'The severity of courtship violence: injuries and individual precautionary measures', paper at the Second International Conference for Family Violence Researchers (August, 1984), University of New Hampshire.

134 K. Yllo and M. Straus, 'Interpersonal violence among married and cohabiting couples', *Family Relations*, 30 (3) (1981), p. 343.

135 M. Straus, 'Conflicts Tactics Scale revision paper', unpublished paper (1986).

136 M. Bograd, 'Methodological approaches to domestic violence: a theoretical and empirical comparison', paper at the Second International Conference for Family Violence Researchers (August, 1984), University of New Hampshire, p. 8.

137 T. Benson and K. Barbri, 'Premarital violence on campus', paper at the US Society for the Study of Social Problems (April, 1984), San Francisco; R. Cate, J. Henton, J. Koval, F. Christopher and S. Lloyd, 'Premarital abuse: a social psychological perspective', *Journal of Family Issues*, 3 (1) (1982), pp. 9–90; C. Comins, 'Courtship violence: a recent study and its implications for future research', paper at the Second International Conference for Family Violence Researchers, (August, 1984), University of New Hampshire; J. Makepeace, 'Courtship

violence among college students', *Family Relations*, 30 (1) (1981), pp. 97–102; J. Murphy, 'Date abuse and forced intercourse among college students', paper at the Second International Conference for Family Violence Researchers (August, 1984), University of New Hampshire; M. Riege Larner and J. Thompson, 'Abuse and aggression in courting couples', *Deviant Behaviour* 3 (1982), pp. 229–44.

138 Larner and Thompson, ibid., p. 241.

139 D. Martin, *Battered Wives* (San Francisco, Glide, 1976).

140 M. Bard and J. Zacker, 'The prevention of family violence: dilemmas of community intervention', *Journal of Marriage and the Family*, 33 (4) (1971), pp. 677–82.

141 L. Sherman and R. Berk, 'The specific deterrant effects of arrest for domestic violence', *American Sociological Review*, 49 (2) (1984), pp. 261–72.

142 L. Lerman, 'Criminal prosecution of wife beaters', *Response*, 4 (3) (1981), pp. 1–19.

143 A. Laszlo and T. McKean, 'Court diversion: an alternative for spousal abuse cases', in *Battered Women: Issues of Public Policy* (Washington DC, US Commission of Human Rights (1978); F. Wassoff, 'Legal protection from wife beating: the processing of domestic assaults by Scottish prosecutors and criminal courts', *International Journal of the Sociology of Law*, 10 (1982) pp. 107–204.

144 V. Binney, G. Harkel and J. Nixon, *Leaving Violent Men*, (Leeds, NWAF, 1983); M. Homer, A. Leanard and M. Taylor, *Private Violence: Public Shame* (Middlesborough, CRAWC, 1984).

145 See, for example, M. Maynard, 'Response of social workers to battered women', in *Private Violence and Public Policy* (London, Routledge and Kegan Paul, 1985), ed. J. Pahl.

146 M. Borkowski, M. Murch and V. Walker, *Marital Violence: The Community Response* (London, Tavistock, 1983).

147 E. Stark and A. Flitcraft, 'Social knowledge, social policy and the abuse of women: the case against patriarchal benevolence', in *The Dark Side of Families* ed. Finkelhor et al., p. 332.

148 C. Cavanagh, *Battered Women and Social Control*, MA thesis, Stirling University (1978).

149 See, for example, Binney, Harkell and Nixon, *Leaving Violent Men*; K. Donato and L. Bowker, 'Understanding the help-seeking behaviour of battered women: a comparison of traditional social service agencies and women's groups', *International Journal of Women's Studies*. 7 (1984), pp. 99–109.

150 E. Cohn and D. Sugarman, 'Marital abuse: abusing the one you love', *Victimology*, 5 (2–4) (1980) pp. 203–12; E. Cohn and D. Sugarman, 'Spousal abuse: an attributional approach', paper at the Second International Conference for Family Violence Researchers (August, 1984), University of New Hampshire; A. Sedlak, 'Violence between intimate partners: calling it 'battering' and allocating blame', paper at the Second International Conference for Family Violence Researchers (August, 1984), University of New Hampshire.

151 Borkowski, Murch and Walker, *Marital Violence*.

152 L. Bowker, *Beating Wife Beating* (Lexington, Lexington Books, 1983); Cavanagh, *Battered Women and Social Control*; P. Smith, 'Breaking silence', unpublished manuscript (1984).
153 P. Schwartz, 'The scientific study of rape', in *Methodology and Sex Research* (Washington DC, NIMH, 1980), p. 154.
154 F. Heidersohn, *Women and Crime* (London, Macmillan, 1985).

Chapter 4 'It's happened to so many women': sexual violence as a continuum (1)

1 See, for example, L. Clark and D. Lewis, *Rape: The Price of Coercive Sexuality* (Toronto, Women's Press, 1979); J. Williams and K. Holmes, *The Second Assault: Rape and Public Attitudes* (Westport, Greenwoord Press, 1981).
2 L. Gilbert and P. Webster, *Bound by Love*, (Boston, Beacon Press, 1982), p. 114.
3 J. Marolla and D. Scully, 'Rape and psychiatric vocabularies of motive' in *Gender and Disordered Behaviour* (New York, Brunner/Mazel, 1979), ed. E. S. Goldberg and N. Franks.
4 J. Herman, *Father–Daughter Incest* (Cambridge, Harvard University Press, 1981), p. 110.
5 Several feminist researchers have also applied this form of analysis to sexual harassment and domestic violence.
6 M. Koss and K. Leonard, 'Sexually aggressive men', in *Pornography and Sexual Aggression*, (New York, Academic Press, 1984) ed. N. Malamuth and E. Donnerstein.
7 E. Stanko, *Intimate Intrusions: Women's Experience of Male Violence* (London, Routledge and Kegan Paul, 1985), p. 10.
8 M. Leidig, 'Violence against women: a feminist psychological analysis', in *Female Psychology* (New York, St Martins Press, 1981), ed. S. Cox.
9 See also, Stanko, *Intimate Intrusions*.
10 See, for example, J. Hanmer and S. Saunders, *Well-Founded Fear* (London, Hutchinson, 1984); J. McDermott, 'Women and crime prevention', *Social Policy* (Summer, 1982), pp. 48–50.
11 Gilbert and Webster, *Bound by Love*; Leidig, 'Violence against women'.
12 R. Hall, *Ask Any Woman* (Bristol, Falling Wall Press, 1985); E. Herold, D. Mantle and O. Zenitis, 'A study of sexual offences against females', *Adolescence*, 14 (1976), pp. 65–72; D. Russell, *Sexual Exploitation* (Beverley Hills, Sage, 1984).
13 Hanmer and Saunders, *Well-Founded Fear*; J. Radford, 'Policing male violence – policing women', *Women, Violence and Social Control* (London, MacMillan, 1987), ed. J. Hanmer and M. Maynard.
14 See, for example, S. Brownmiller, *Against Our Will: Men, Women and Rape* (New York, Simon and Schuster 1975); S. Griffin, 'Rape: the all American crime', *Ramparts*, 10 (3) (1971), pp. 26–35; D. Poggi,. 'The city: off limits to women', *Liberation* (July/August, 1974), pp. 10–13.
15 Hall, *Ask Any Woman*.
16 Radford, 'Policing male violence'.

17 E. Stanko, 'Safekeeping: women's negotiations of male violence', lecture in the Women In Context series (March, 1987), University of East Anglia.

18 C. Jones, 'Sexual tyranny: male violence in a mixed secondary school', in *Just a Bunch of Girls* (Milton Keynes, Open University Press, 1985), ed. G. Weiner; P. Mahony, *Schools for the Boys? Co-education Reassessed* (London, Hutchinson, 1985).

19 L. Bienen, 'Rape 111 – national developments in rape reform legislation', *Women's Rights Law Reporter*, 6 (3) (1980), pp. 170–213.

20 *Spare Rib* magazine, news item (July, 1984).

21 C. Safran, 'Survey on sexual harassment', *Redbook Magazine* (November 1976), pp. 216–20.

22 Merit Systems Protection Boards, 'Sexual harassment in the federal workplace – is it a problem?', unpublished mimeograph (1981).

23 NALGO, 'Sexual harassment at work', unpublished mimeograph (1981); C. Cooper and M. Davidson, *High Pressure: Working Lives of Women Managers* (London, Fontana, 1982).

24 Hall, *Ask Any Woman.*

25 See also, P. Bart, 'Women of the right: trading safty for rules and love', *New Women's Times Feminist Review*, (November-December, 1983), pp. 1–2 and 9–11.

26 Hall, *Ask Any Woman.*

27 L. Stanley and S. Wise, 'Experiences of sexism and what these can tell us about women's oppression and women's liberation', in *Studies in Sexual Politics 1* (University of Manchester, 1984).

28 Study by Pease, article in *The Daily Telegraph*, 20 June 1985.

29 Herold et al., 'A study of sexual offences against females'.

30 M. Straus, R. Gelles and S. Steinmetz, *Behind Closed Doors* (New York, Anchor Books, 1980).

31 M. Schulman, *A Survey of Spousal Abuse Against Women in Kentucky* (Washington DC, US Department of Justice, 1979).

32 J. Makepeace, 'Courtship violence amongst college students', *Family Relations*, 30 (1) (1981), pp. 97–102; M. Riege Larner and J. Thompson, 'Abuse and aggression in courting couples', *Deviant Behaviour*, 3 (1982), pp. 229–44.

33 R. Kinsey, J. Lea and J. Young, *Loosing the Fight Against Crime*, (Oxford, Basil Blackwell, 1986).

34 R. and R. Dobash, *Violence Against Wives: A Case Against the Patriachy* (New York, Free Press, 1979).

35 J. Gagnon, 'Female child victims of sex offences', *Social Problems*, 13 (1965), pp. 176–92; J. Landis, 'Experiences of 500 children with adult sexual deviation', *Psychiatric Quarterly*, 30 (1956), pp. 91–101.

36 D. Finkelhor, *Sexually Victimized Children* (New York, Free Press, 1979).

37 Hall, *Ask Any Women.* T. Baker, 'Readers survey on sexual abuse',*19 Magazine* (September, 1983), pp. 34–6 and 48–52.

38 D. Russell, 'The prevalence and incidence of forcible rape and attempted rape of females', *Victimology*, 7 (1–4), (1983), pp. 81–93.

39 D. Cox and B. McMahon, 'Incidence of male exhibitionism in the US as

reported by victimized college students', *International Journal of Law and Psychiatry*, 1 (1970) pp. 453–5; N. Gitterson, S. Eacott and B. Mehta, 'Victims of indecent exposure', *British Journal of Psychiatry*, 132 (1975), pp. 61–6; J. Rhoads and E. Borges, 'The incidence of exhibitionism in Guatamala and the USA', *British Journal of Psychiatry*, 139 (1981), pp. 242–4.

40 S. McNeil, 'Flashing – its effect on women', in *Women, Violence and Social Control*, ed. Hanmer and Maynard.

41 Hall, *Ask Any Woman*; Russell, Incidence and prevalence' pp. 133–46.

42 Russell, *Sexual Exploitation*.

43 *Australian Womens' Weekly* (June, 1980).

44 Finkelhor, *Sexually Victimized Children*.

45 Hall, *Ask Any Woman*.

46 See, D. Finkelhor, 'Risk factors in the sexual victimization of children', *Child Abuse and Neglect*, 4 (1980), pp. 265–73; Russell, *Sexual Exploitation*.

47 See, for example, E. Ellis, B. Atkeson, K. Calhoun, 'An examination of differences between multiple and single incident (1982), pp. 521–4; victims of sexual assault', *Journal of Abnormal Psychology*, 91 (3) (1982), pp. 321–4; J. Miller, 'Recidivism among sexual assault victims', *American Journal of Psychiatry*, 135 (1978), pp. 1103–4.

48 See, S. Katz and M. Mazur, *Understanding the Rape Victim: A Synthesis of Research Findings* (New York, John Wiley, 1979).

49 Russell, *Sexual Exploitation*.

50 G. La Free, 'The effect of sexual assault by race on official reactions to rape', *American Sociological Review*, 45 (5) (1980), pp. 842–54.

Chapter 5   'It's everywhere': sexual violence as a continuum (2)

1 K. Schepple and P. Bart, 'Through women's eyes: defining danger in the wake of sexual assault', *Journal of Social Issues*, 39 (2) (1983), p. 44.

2 J. Hanmer and S. Saunders, *Well-Founded Fear* (London, Hutchinson, 1984).

3 S. McNeill, 'Flashing – its effects on women', in *Women, Violence and Social Control* (London, MacMillan, 1987), ed. J. Hanmer and M. Maynard.

4 See, for example, S. Levine and J. Koenig, *Why Men Rape: Interviews With Convicted Rapists* (Toronto, MacMillan, 1980).

5 The British Samaritans introduced a special service in the early 1980s, 'Call Rita', for men wanting to make obscene phone calls. It was not successful so women volunteers are still asked to listen to such male callers as part of their work.

6 J. Hearn and W. Parkin, *'Sex' and 'Work': The Power and Paradox of Organisation Sexuality* (Brighton, Wheatsheaf Books, 1987).

7 L. Farley, *Sexual Shakedown* (London, Melbourne House, 1978).

8 S. Lees, *Learning to Loose* (London, Hutchinson, 1987).

9 Hearn and Parkin, *'Sex' at 'Work'*.

10 See, for example, L. Clark and D. Lewis, *Rape: The Price of Coercive*

Sexuality (Toronto, Womens Press, 1977); A. Dworkin, *Right-Wing Women: The Politics of Domesticated Females* (London, Women's Press, 1983); C. MacKinnon, 'Violence against women – a perspective', *Aegis*, 33 (1982), pp. 51–7.

11 P. Bart, 'Women of the right: trading for safety, rules and love', *The New Women's Times Feminist Review* (November-December, 1983), pp. 1–2 and 9–11.

12 Lees, *Learning to Loose*: P. Willis, *Learning to Labour: How Working-Class Kids Get Working-Class Jobs* (Farnborough, Saxon House, 1977).

13 Willis, ibid., p. 67.

14 J. Herman, *Father–Daughter Incest* (Cambridge, Harvard University Press, 1981).

15 See, G. Ni Carthy, *Talking It Out* (Boston, Seal Press, 1984) for a discussion of the range of controls and emotional abuse that men use in intimate relationships.

16 See also, R. and R. Dobash, *Violence Against Wives: A Case Against the Patriarchy* (New York, Free Press 1979); M. Pagelow, *Woman Battering* (Beverley Hills, Sage, 1981).

17 P. Smith, 'Breaking Silence', unpublished manuscript (1984).

18 C. Lynch, 'Safe Streets', unpublished manuscript (1980).

19 See also, I. Freize, 'Perceptions of battered wives', in *New Approaches to Social Problems* (San Francisco, Josey Bass, 1978), ed. I. Freize, D. Ban-Tal and J. Carroll.

20 D. Finkelhor, *Sexually Victimized Children* (New York, Free Press, 1979); J. Herman and L. Hirshman, 'Father–daughter incest', *Signs*, 2 (4) (1977), pp. 735–56; M. Pagelow, 'Blaming the victim – parallels in crimes against women: rape and battering', paper at the Society for the Study of Social Problems, (April, 1977) Chicago.

21 D. Russell suggests that marital rape is often a determining factor in women leaving relationships, D. Russell, *Rape In Marriage* (New York, Macmillan, 1982).

22 See, for example, D. Finkelhor, *Child Sexual Abuse: New Theory and Research* (New York, Free Press, 1984); M. De Young, *The Sexual Victimization of Children* (Jefferson, McFarland, 1982).

23 N. Bryson, 'Two narritives of rape in the visual arts: Lucretia and the Sabine women', in ed. S. Tomaselli and R. Porter; *Rape* (Oxford, Basil Blackwell, 1986); plus review article by S. Kappeler, forthcoming in the *Journal of Art History*.

24 A. Burgess and L. Holmstrom, *Rape: Victims of Crisis* (Bowie, Robert J. Brady, 1974); Clark and Lewis, *Rape: The Price of Coercive Sexuality*.

25 P. Foa, 'What's wrong with rape', in *Philosophy and Women* (Belmont, Wadsworth 1978) ed. S. Bishop and M. Weinzweig; M. Plaza, 'Our damages and their compensations: Rape – the will not to know of Michel Foucault', *Feminist Studies*, 1 (3) (1981), pp. 25–36.

26 MacKinnon, 'Violence against women – a perspective', p. 52.

27 Herman and Hirshman, 'Father–daughter incest'.

Chapter 6 'I'm not sure what to call it but . . .': defining sexual violence

1 D. Smith, 'Women's perspective as a radical critique of sociology', *Sociological Quarterly*, 44 (1974), pp. 7–13.

2 See, for example, S. Kappeler, *The Pornography of Representation* (Cambridge, Polity Press, 1986); D. Spender, *Man-Made Language* (London, Routledge and Kegan Paul, 1980).

3 See chap. 9 of, S. Schecter, *Women and Male Violence: The Visions and Struggles of the Battered Women's Movement* (London, Pluto Press, 1982).

4 D. Finkelhor and K. Yllo, *Licence to Rape: Sexual Abuse of Wives* (New York, Holt Rinehart 1985); D. Russell, *Rape in Marriage* (New York, Macmillan, 1982).

5 C. MacKinnon, *The Sexual Harassment of Working Women* (New Haven, Yale University Press, 1979), pp. 27–8.

6 D. Russell, *Rape in Marriage*, pp. 39–40.

7 F. Rush, 'The Freudian Cover-up' *Trouble and Strife*, 4 (1984), pp. 29–37.

8 See also, S. E. Taylor, J. V. Wood, R. R. Lichtman, 'It could be worse: selective evaluation as a response to victimization', *Journal of Social Issues*, 39 (2) (1983), pp. 19–40.

9 Thanks to Michelle Stanworth for this insight.

10 J. Radford, 'Policing male violence – policing women', in *Women, Violence and Social Control*, (London, Macmillan, 1987), ed. J. Hanmer and M. Maynard; L. Kelly and J. Radford, ' "Nothing really happened": Can the law ever reflect women's experience of sexual violence?', lecture in Women in Context series (March, 1987), University of East Anglia.

11 S. McNeill, 'Flashing: its effects on women', in *Women, Violence and Social Control*, ed. Hanmer and Maynard.

12 K. Ferraro and J. Johnson, 'How women experience battering: the process of victimization', *Social Problems*, 30 (3) (1983), pp. 325–39.

13 G. Zellman, J. Goodchilds, P. Johnson and R. Giarusso, 'Teenagers application of the label "rape" to non-consensual sex between acquaintances', paper at the American Psychological Association (August, 1981), Los Angeles, pp. 7–8.

14 C. Wright Mills, 'Situated actions and vocabularies of motive', *American Sociological Review*, 5 (1940), pp. 904–13; G. M. Sykes and D. Matza, 'Techniques of neutralization: a theory of delinquency', *American Sociological Review*, 22 (1957), pp. 664–70.

15 The Domestic Violence Act (1976); the Housing [Homeless Persons Acts] (1977).

Chapter 7 Victims or survivors?: resistance, coping and survival

1 See, for example, C. Moraga and G. Anzaldua (eds), *This Bridge Called my Back* (Watertown, Persephone Press, 1981); bell hooks, *From Margin to Centre* (Boston, South End Press, 1984); G. Hull, *All the Women are*

White, All the Men are Black, But Some of us Are Brave: Black Women's Studies (New York, The Feminist Press, 1981).

2 See, V. Gerhardt, 'Coping and social action', *Sociology of Health and Illness*, 1 (2) (1979), pp. 212–30; L. Pearlin and C. Schooler, 'The structure of coping', *Journal of Health and Social Behaviour*, 19 (1978), pp. 2–21.

3 J. McGrath (ed.), *Social and Psychological Factors in Stress* (New York, Holt, Reinhart and Winston, 1970).

4 L. Kelly, 'Effects or survival strategies?: the long-term consequences of experiences of sexual violence', paper at the Second International Conference for Family Violence Researchers (August, 1984), University of New Hampshire.

5 Gerhardt, 'Coping and social action'.

6 J. Hanmer and S. Saunders, *Well-Founded Fear* (London, Hutchinson, 1984).

7 On rape, A. Burgess and L. Holmstrom, *Rape: Victims of Crisis* (Bowie, Robert J. Brady, 1974); D. Kilpatrick and P. Resnick, 'The aftermath of rape – recent empirical findings', *American Journal of Orthopsychiatry*, 49 (4) (1979), pp. 658–69; K. Schepple and P. Bart, 'Through women's eyes: defining danger in the wake of sexual assault', *Journal of Social Issues*, 39 (2) (1983), pp. 63–80. On domestic violence, R. and R. Dobash, *Violence Against Wives* (New York, Free Press, 1979); M. Pagelow, *Woman Battering* (Beverley Hills, Sage, 1981).

8 L. Gilbert and P. Webster, *Bound by Love* (Boston, Beacon Press, 1982).

9 Ibid., p. x.

10 Ibid., p. vii.

11 Ibid., p. xviii.

12 Ibid., p. xvii.

13 Ibid., p. xxii.

14 P. Bart and P. O'Brien, 'Stopping rape: effective avoidance strategies', *Signs*, 10 (1984), pp. 83–101.

15 A. Burgess and L. Holmstrom, 'The coping behaviour of the rape victim', *American Journal of Psychiatry*, 133 (4) (1976), pp. 413–18.

16 J. Chapman and M. Gates (eds), *The Victimization of Women*, (Beverley Hills, Sage, 1978), p. 13.

17 Bart and O'Brien, 'Stopping rape'.

18 K. Barry, 'The social etiology of crimes against women', *Victimology*, 10 (1–4) (1985) pp. 164–73; N. Roberts, *The Front Line* (London, Grafton, 1986).

19 J. Herman and L. Hirschman, 'Father–daughter incest', *Signs*, 2 (4) (1977), pp. 735–56.

20 J. Goodwin, M. Simms and R. Bergman, 'Hysterical seizures: sequel to incest', *American Journal of Orthopsychiatry*, 49 (4) (1979), pp. 690–703. M. Gross, 'Incestuous rape: cause for hysterical seizures in four adolescent girls', *American Journal of Orthopsychiatry*, 49 (4) (1979), pp. 704–8.

21 K. Barry, *Female Sexual Slavery* (San Francisco, Prentice-Hall, 1979).

22 J. James and J. Meyerling, 'Early sexual experience as a factor in prostitution', *Archives of Sexual Behaviour*, 7 (1) (1979), pp. 31–42; M.

Silbert and A. Pines, 'Early sexual exploitation as an influence in prostitution', *Social Work*, 28 (4) (1983), pp. 285–9.

23 T. Mills, 'The assault on the self: stages in coping with battering husbands', *Qualitative Sociology*, 8 (2) (1985), pp. 103–23.

24 A. Browne, *When Battered Women Kill* (New York, Free Press, 1987).

25 Dobashes, *Violence Against Wives*; M. Borkowski, M. Murch and V. Walker, *Marital Violence: The Community Response* (London, Tavistock, 1983).

26 Pagelow, *Woman Battering*.

27 L. Walker, *The Battered Woman Syndrome* (New York, Springer, 1984).

28 C. Cavanagh, *Battered Women and Social Control*, MA thesis (1978), University of Stirling.

29 See also, K. Donato and L. Bowker 'Understanding the help-seeking behaviour of battered women: a comparison of traditional social service agencies and women's groups', *International Journal of Women's Studies*, 7 (1984) pp. 99–109; V. Binney, G. Harkel and J. Nixon, *Leaving Violent Men* (Leeds, NWAF 1981); M. Homer, A. Leonard and P. Taylor, *Private Violence: Public Shame* (Middlesborough, CRAWC, 1984).

30 P. Smith, *Breaking Silence*, unpublished manuscript (1984).

31 See note 2.

32 Lynne Segal, *Is The Future Female: Troubled Thoughts on Contemporary Feminism* (London, Virago, 1987), p. 36.

Chapter 8   'It leaves a mark': coping with the consequences of sexual violence

1 P. Bart, 'Rape as a paradigm of sexism in society: victimization and its discontents', *Women's Studies International Quarterly*, 11 (3) (1979), pp. 347–57.

2 See, for example, E. Ellis, B. Atkeson, and K. Calhoun, 'An assessment of long-term reaction to rape', *Journal of Abnormal Psychology*, 90 (3) (1981), pp. 263–6; S. Feldman Summers, P. Gordon and J. Meagher, 'The impact of rape on sexual satisfacton', *Journal of Abnormal Psychology*, 81 (1979), pp. 101–5; D. Kilpatrick, P. Resnick and L. Veronen, 'Effects of a rape experience: a longitudinal study', *Journal of Social Issues*, 37 (4) (1981) pp. 105–22; R. Silver, C. Boon and M. Stones, 'Searching for meaning in misfortune: making sense of incest', *Journal of Social Issues*, 39 (2) (1983), pp. 81–102.

3 J. Becker, L. Skinner, G. Abel and E. Treacy, 'Incidence and types of sexual dysfunctions in rape and incest victims', *Journal of Sex and Marital Therapy*, 8 (1) (1982), pp. 65–74; C. Courtois, 'The incest experience and its aftermath', *Victimology*, 4 (4) (1979), pp. 337–47; Ellis et al., 'Assessment of long-term reaction'; P. Gordy, 'Group work that supports adult victims of childhood incest', *Social Casework*, 64 (5) (1983), pp. 300–8; K. Meiselman, *Incest: A Psychological Study of Causes and Effects with Treatment Recommendations* (San Francisco, Josey Bass, 1978); J. Norris and S. Feldman Summers, 'Factors related to the psychological impact of rape on the victim', *Journal of Abnormal*

Psychology, 90 (6) (1981), pp. 562–7; J. Orlando and M. Koss, 'The effect of sexual victimization on sexual satisfaction: a study of the negative association hypothesis', *Journal of Abnormal Psychology*, 92 (1) (1983), pp. 104–6; P. Peretti and D. Banks, 'Negative psychological effects on the incestuous daughter of sexual relations with her father', *Paninerva Medica*, 22 (1) (1980), pp. 27–30.

4 M. De Young, *The Sexual Victimization of Children* (Jefferson, McFarland, 1982).

5 'Lesbian survivors of incest', *Off Our Backs* (October, 1982).

6 See notes 2 and 3 and also, De Young, *Sexual Victimization*; D. Finkelhor, *Sexually Victimized Children* (New York, Free Press, 1979); J. Herman, *Father–Daughter Incest* (Cambridge, Harvard University Press, 1980); M. Silbert and A. Pines, 'Early sexual exploitation as an influence in prostitution', *Social Work*, 28 (4) (1983), pp. 285–9; M. Tsai and N. Wagner, 'Therapy groups for women sexually molested as children', *Journal of Sexual Behaviour*, 7 (5) (1978), pp. 417–27.

7 A. Seidner and K. Calhoun, 'Childhood sexual abuse: factors related to differential adult adjustment', paper at the Second International Conference for Family Violence Researchers (August, 1984), University of New Hampshire.

8 See notes 2 and 3 and also, K. Calhoun, B. Atkeson and P. Resnick, 'A longitudinal examination of fear reactions in victims of rape', *Journal of Counselling Psychology*, 29 (6) (1982), pp. 655–61; M. Felice, J. Grant and B. Reynolds, 'Follow-up observations of adolescent rape victims', *Clinical Pediatrics*, 17 (4) (1978), pp. 311–15; E. Frank, S. Turner and B. Duffy Stewart, 'Depressive symptoms in rape victims', *Journal of Affective Disorders*, 1 (4) (1979), pp. 269–77; T. McCahill, S. Meyer and L. Fischman, *The Aftermath of Rape* (Lexington, Lexington Books, 1979).

9 P. Chesler, *Women and Madness* (New York, Doubleday 1972).

10 S. Girelli, P. Resnick, S. Marhoefer-Dvorak, C. Kotsis Hutter, 'Subjective distress and violence during rape: their effects on long-term fear', *Violence and Victims*, 1 (1) (1986), pp. 35–46.

11 S. Schecter, personal communication.

12 Orlando and Koss, 'Effect of sexual victimization on sexual satisfaction'.

13 G. Breakwell, *Coping With Threatened Identities* (London, Methuen, 1986).

14 K. Horney, *New Ways in Psychoanalysis* (New York, W. W. Norton, 1939).

15 M. Straus, R. Gelles and S. Steinmetz, *Behind Closed Doors* (New York, Anchor Books, 1980).

16 F. McNulty, *The Burning Bed* (New York, Bantam, 1981).

17 McCahill et al., *The Aftermath of Rape*, p. 182.

18 S. McNeil, 'Flashing – its effects on women', in *Women, Violence and Social Control*, (London, Macmillan, 1987), ed. J. Hanmer and M. Maynard.

19 D. Kilpatrick and P. Resnick, 'The aftermath of rape – recent empirical findings', *American Journal of Orthopsychiatry*, 49 (4) (1979), pp. 658–69; D. Kilpatrick, L. Veronen and P. Resnick, 'Psychological sequelae to

rape: assessment and treatment strategies', in *Behavioural Medicine: Assessment and Treatment Strategies* (New York, Plenum, 1982), ed. D. Doleys, R. Meredith and A. Ciminero.

20 J. Radford, 'Policing male violence – policing women', in *Women, Violence and Social Control*, ed. Hanmer and Maynard; E. Stanko, 'Typical violence, normal precaution: men, women and interpersonal violence in England, Wales, Scotland and the USA', in *Violence and Social Control*, ed. Hanmer and Maynard.

21 See, for example, De Young, *Sexual Victimization*; J. Miller, 'Recidivism among sexual assault victims', *Journal of Social Issues*, 39 (2) (1978), pp. 139–52; Seidner and Calhoun, 'Childhood sexual abuse'.

22 D. Russell, *Sexual Exploitation* (Beverley Hills, Sage, 1984). ,

23 D. Finkelhor, 'Risk factors in the sexual victimization of children', *Child Abuse and Neglect*, 4 (1980), pp. 265–73.

24 P. Harrison and A. Limrey, 'Female sexual abuse victims: perspectives on family dysfunction, substance abuse and psychiatric disorders', paper at the Second International Conference for Family Violence Researchers (August, 1984), University of New Hampshire.

25 Peretti and Banks, 'Negative psychological effects', p. 29.

26 Feldman Summers et al., 'Impact of rape'; Kilpatrick and Resnick, 'Aftermath of rape'.

27 M. Scarf, *Unfinished Business: Pressure Points in the Lives of Women* (London, Fontana, 1980).

28 Breakwell, *Coping with Threatened Identities*, p. 79.

29 B. Atkeson, K. Calhoun, P. Resnick and E. Ellis, 'Victims of rape: repeated assessment of depressive symptoms', *Journal of Consulting and Clinical Psychology*, 50 (1982), pp. 196–202; A. Burgess and L. Holmstrom, 'Adaptive strategies and recovery from rape', *American Journal of Psychiatry*, 136 (10) (1979), pp. 1278–82; L. Ruch and S. Chandler and R. Hater, 'Life change and rape impact', *Journal of Health and Social Behaviour*, 21 (3) (1980), pp. 240–60.

30 C. Peterson and M. Seligman, 'Learned helplessness and victimization', *Journal of Social Issues*, 39 (2) (1983), p. 104.

Chapter 9   'I'll challenge it now wherever I see it': from individual survival to collective resistance

1 K. Barry, *Female Sexual Slavery* (New Jersey, Prentice-Hall, 1979).

2 Ibid., pp. 38–9.

3 See also, P. Bart, 'A study of women who both were raped and avoided rape', *Journal of Social Issues*, 37 (4) (1981), pp. 123–37.

4 J. Radford, 'Policing male violence – policing women', in *Women, Violence and Social Control* (London, Macmillan, 1987), ed. J. Hanmer and M. Maynard.

5 M. Frye, *The Politics of Reality: Essays in Feminist Theory* (New York, The Crossing Press, 1983).

6 See, for example, Lillian Faderman, *Surpassing the Love of Men* (London, Women's Press, 1985); Janice Raymond, *A Passion for Friends: Toward a*

Philosophy of Female Affection (London, Women's Press, 1986).
7 bell hooks, *From Margin to Centre* (Boston, South End Press, 1984).
8 *Report* of the Select Committe on Violence in Marriage (London, HMSO, 1975).
9 Norwich Consultants on Sexual Violence, 'Claiming our status as experts: community organising on sexual violence', *Feminist Review*, 28, pp. 144–9.

Select bibliography

Ageton, Susan, *Sexual Assault Among Adolescents*, Lexington, Lexington Books, 1983.

Barry, Kathleen, *Female Sexual Slavery*, New Jersey, Prentice Hall, 1979.

Bart, Pauline and O'Brien, Patricia, *Stopping Rape: Successful Survival Strategies*, Oxford, Pergamon Press, 1986.

Binney, Val, Harkell, Gina and Nixon, Judy, *Leaving Violent Men*, Leeds, NWAF, 1981.

Bograd, Michelle and Yllo Kersti (eds), *Feminist Perspectives on Wife Abuse*, Beverley Hills, Sage, forthcoming.

Bowker, Lee, *Beating Wife Beating*, Lexington, Lexington Books, 1983.

Browne, Angela, *When Battered Women Kill*, New York, Free Press, 1987.

Brownmiller, Susan, *Against Our Will: Men, Women and Rape*, New York, Simon and Schuster, 1975.

Burgess, Ann (ed.), *Child Pornography and Sex Rings*, Lexington, Lexington Books, 1984.

Burgess, Ann, and Holmstrom Linda, *Rape, Crisis and Recovery*, Bowie, Robert J. Brady, 1979.

Cameron, Deborah, and Frazier, Liz, *The Lust to Kill*, Cambridge, Polity Press, 1987.

Clark, Anna, *Women's Silence Men's Violence: Sexual Assault in England 1770–1845*, London, Pandora Press, 1987.

Delacoste, Frederique, and Newman, Felice, *Fight Back: Feminist Resistance to Male Violence*, Minneapolis, Cleis Press, 1981.

Dobash, Rebecca, and Dobash, Russell, *Violence Against Wives: A Case Against the Patriarchy*, New York, Free Press, 1979.

Droisen Audrey, and Driver Emily, (eds), *Sexual Abuse of Children*, London, Macmillan, forthcoming.

Dworkin, Andrea, *Pornography: Men Possessing Women*, London, Women's Press, 1981.

Dworkin, Andrea, *Right-Wing Women: the Politics of Domesticated Females*, London, Women's Press, 1983.

Farley, Lin, *Sexual Shakedown*, New York, McGraw Hill, 1978.

Family Secrets: Child Sexual Abuse Today, Feminist Review, 28, Spring, 1988.

Finkelhor, David, *Sexually Victimized Children*, New York, Free Press, 1979.
Finkelhor, David, *Child Sexual Abuse: New Theory and Research*, New York, Free Press, 1984.
Frye, Marilyn, *The Politics of Reality*, New York, Crossing Press, 1983.
Hall, Ruth, *Ask Any Woman*, Bristol, Falling Wall Press, 1985.
Hanmer Jalna, and Saunders, Sheila, *Well-Founded Fear*, London, Hutchinson, 1984.
Hanmer Jalna, and Maynard Mary, (eds), *Women, Violence and Social Control*, London, Macmillan, 1987.
Homer, Marjorie, Leonard, Ann and Taylor, Pat, *Private Violence: Public Shame*, Middlesborough, CRAWC, 1984.
Kappeler, Susanne, *The Pornography of Representation*, Cambridge, Polity Press, 1986.
Lederer Laura, (ed.), *Take Back the Night*, New York, William Morrow, 1980.
London Rape Crisis, *Strength in Numbers*, London Rape Crisis, 1987.
MacKinnon, Catharine, *Sexual Harassment of Working Women*, New Haven, University of Yale Press, 1979.
MacKinnon, Catharine, *Feminism Unmodified*, Cambridge, Harvard University Press, 1987.
McNeill, Sandra, and Rhodes, Dusty, *Women Against Violence Against Women*, London, Onlywomen Press, 1985.
Nelson, Sarah, *Incest: Fact and Myth*, rev. edn., Edinburgh, Sramullion Press, 1987.
Pahl Jan, (ed.), *Private Violence, Public Policy*, London, Routledge and Kegan Paul, 1985.
Rich, Adrienne, *Compulsory Heterosexuality and Lesbian Existence*, London, Onlywomen Press, 1983.
Russell, Diana, *Rape in Marriage*, New York, Macmillan, 1982.
Russell, Diana, *Sexual Exploitation*, Beverley Hills, Sage, 1984.
Russell, Diana, *The Secret Trauma: Incest In the Lives of Girls and Women*, New York, Basic Books, 1986.
Schecter, Susan, *Women and Male Violence: The Visions and Struggles of the Battered Women's Movement*, London, Pluto Press, 1982.
Stanko, Elizabeth, *Intimate Intrusions: Women's Experience of Male Violence*, London, Routledge and Kegan Paul, 1985.
Tong, Rosemary, *Women, Sex and the Law*, New Jersey, Rowan and Allanchild, 1984.
Williams, Joyce, and Holmes Karen, *The Second Assault: Rape and Public Attitudes*, Westport, Greenwood Press, 1981.
Ward, Elizabeth, *Father–Daughter Rape*, London, Women's Press, 1984.
Wise, Sue, and Stanley, Liz, *Georgie Porgie: Sexual Harassment in Everyday Life*, London, Pandora Press, 1987.

Index